WALKING
DICKENSIAN
LONDON

WALKING DICKENSIAN LONDON

RICHARD JONES

NEW
HOLLAND

First published in 2004 by
New Holland Publishers (UK) Ltd
London • Cape Town • Sydney • Auckland

www.newhollandpublishers.com

Garfield House
86–88 Edgware Road
London W2 2EA
United Kingdom

80 McKenzie Street
Cape Town 8001
South Africa

14 Aquatic Drive
Frenchs Forest, NSW 2086
Australia

218 Lake Road
Northcote
Auckland
New Zealand

ISBN 1 84330 483 X

Publishing Manager: Jo Hemmings
Editor: Camilla MacWhannell
Editorial Assistant: Ruth Hamilton
Designer: Gülen Shevki
Production: Joan Woodroffe

Reproduction by Pica Digital (Pte) Ltd, Singapore
Printed and bound by Kyodo Printing Co (Singapore) Ltd

Picture Acknowledgements
Front cover: Middle Temple at dusk.
Back cover: Restoration House, Rochester
Page 2: Railway through London

CONTENTS

INTRODUCTION

Charles John Huffam Dickens was born at 13 Mile End Terrace, Portsmouth (now the Dickens Birthplace Museum) on Friday, 7th February, 1812. His father, John, was a clerk in the naval pay office, and Charles's early years were spent moving whenever and wherever his father's postings dictated. In January 1815, John was transferred to London, and the young Dickens first encountered the city with which his later life and fiction would become so indelibly linked. Two years later, the family moved to Chatham in Kent where Charles enjoyed the happiest years of his childhood. His mother taught him the rudiments of reading, and he received an education courtesy of a schoolmaster named William Giles. Charles also enjoyed long walks through the Kent countryside with his father.

Life in London

Dickens's childhood idyll ended abruptly in 1822 when John Dickens was transferred back to London and his income reduced severely. John, a man who was never able to live within his means, plunged heavily into debt. His wife, Elizabeth, attempted to alleviate the family's financial predicament by opening a school for young ladies, but that failed and, in 1824, John Dickens was arrested for debt, and incarcerated in the Marshalsea Prison. Elizabeth and the younger children went with him. However, the sensitive Charles was sent to begin work at Warren's Blacking Factory.

The young boy, who had truly believed he was destined to be a gentleman, now found himself sticking labels onto pots of boot blacking. His misery was exacerbated by the fact that his beloved elder sister, Fanny, had been enrolled at the Royal College of Music. Charles longed to resume his education, but left to his own devices, he roamed the streets of the capital, where he mixed with the low life of early 19th-century London, taking in everything he saw.

John Dickens was released from prison after 14 weeks, as his mother-in-law had died and left him a little money. But he was still not out of debt. However, in 1825, he took Charles away from the blacking factory, and despite vociferous objections from Elizabeth, who wanted their son to continue bringing in a useful weekly wage, John sent him to school at Wellington House Academy. Charles never forgave his mother.

Dickens stayed at the Academy for about two years, before his father's debts forced him back into employment, this time for Ellis and Blackmore, a firm of solicitors in London's Gray's Inn. Whilst there, he learned shorthand, and after 18 months felt confident enough to establish himself as a shorthand writer at Doctors' Commons, near St Paul's Cathedral in the City. By 1830 he had met and fallen madly in love with a banker's daughter named Maria Beadnell. A year later he began work as a reporter for his uncle's newspaper *The Mirror of Parliament*. In 1832, he applied for, and was granted, an audition at the Covent Garden Theatre, but on the day in question illness prevented him from attending. Dickens's love of the theatre and desire to perform remained with him for the rest of his life and resulted in his amateur theatricals and later his public reading tours.

Dickens's career as writer takes off

By May 1833, Maria's ardour had cooled considerably and their relationship ended. In an attempt to overcome his broken heart Dickens flung himself into his writing, and at the end of the year his first story *A Dinner at Poplar Walk* was published. By 1834 he was working for the *Morning Chronicle* newspaper and became friends with its music critic, George Hogarth. In 1835 Hogarth became editor of the *Evening Chronicle*, and he invited Dickens to contribute sketches to the paper. These would eventually appear in print as *Sketches by 'Boz'*. Dickens had also fallen in love with Hogarth's daughter, Catherine, and on 2nd April, 1836 the two were married at St Luke's Church, Chelsea. Following a honeymoon in Kent, they settled into chambers in Furnival's Inn, Holborn. By this time the first instalment of *Pickwick Papers* had appeared, despite the suicide of its originator and illustrator Robert Seymour. Hablot Browne, who for the next 20 years remained Dickens's chief illustrator, replaced Seymour, and when Dickens introduced the character of Sam Weller, *Pickwick Papers* became a publishing phenomenon. In December 1836, Dickens met John Forster, who at the time was the literary and drama editor of *The Examiner*. The two became firm friends, and Forster effectively became Dickens's agent for the rest of his life and, following the author's death, his primary biographer.

In January 1837, Charles and Catherine's first child, also named Charles, was born, and by April the family had moved to a house in Doughty Street more suited to both Dickens's growing family and reputation. Catherine's younger sister, Mary, moved in with them, and Dickens developed an intense platonic relationship with her. Then, on 6th May, 1837, Mary died suddenly at their house, leaving Dickens utterly devastated by the loss.

Over the next few years while living at Doughty Street, Dickens cemented his reputation with *Oliver Twist* (1837–38), *Nicholas Nickleby* (1838–39), and began work on *Barnaby Rudge* (1841). His family also increased with two daughters, Mary and Kate, born in 1838 and 1839. By 1839 Dickens's growing fame enabled them to move to a grander house at 1 Devonshire Terrace, Marylebone. Their fourth child, Walter, was born in 1841, and in January

1842, Charles and Catherine set off on a six-month tour of America. Such was his fame now that Dickens found himself mobbed on several occasions. Back in London he wrote *Martin Chuzzlewit* (1843–44) and, a year later, what is perhaps one of his best known works, *A Christmas Carol* (1843).

By 1855, with his family swollen to ten children, one of which, Dora, had died in infancy, Dickens was becoming restless. In February, he received a letter from Maria Beadnell, now Mrs Winter. He replied enthusiastically, pouring scorn on her assertion that she was now toothless, fat and middle aged. 'You are always the same in my remembrance' he wrote. They planned to meet at his house when his wife was 'not at home', but Dickens was shattered to find that Maria was exactly as she had described herself. His passion cooled and he, rather cruelly, portrayed her in *Little Dorrit* (1855–57) as Flora Finching, once pretty and enchanting, but now fat, diffuse and silly.

In 1856, he purchased Gad's Hill Place in Kent, a house he had first seen whilst walking with his father in the idyllic years of his childhood. In January 1857, he directed and acted in Wilkie Collins's play *The Frozen Deep* and as he researched professional actresses to play the female parts, he met the young actress Ellen Lawless Ternan who became his intimate friend and probably his lover. The following year Dickens formally separated from his wife, and viciously attacked her in an article published in several newspapers. His daughter Kate later recalled, 'My father was like a madman... He did not care a damn what happened to any of us. Nothing could surpass the misery and unhappiness of our house.' His younger sister-in-law, Georgina Hogarth, became his housekeeper, and rumours began to circulate that it was his affair with her that had caused his marital breakdown.

In August 1858, Dickens began the first of a series of reading tours that would, over the next 12 years, prove extremely profitable. By 1860 Gad's Hill became his permanent residence. Over the next ten years, as he and Ellen Ternan became more involved with each other, his personal life became more and more enigmatic. It is possible that he took a house in France for Ellen and her mother, where he visited them frequently. However, Dickens's secret life came close to exposure in 1865 when he, Ellen and her mother, were travelling back from France and their train was involved in a serious accident at Staplehurst in Kent. Although Dickens tended to the injured and dying, he refused to attend the subsequent inquest probably for fear it would make public the fact he was travelling with Ellen Ternan.

Over the next few years, Dickens undertook several private reading tours in England and America. But his health was failing and by 1870 he looked considerably older than his 58 years. Then on the 8th June, 1870, having spent the day working on what was to be his last unfinished novel *The Mystery of Edwin Drood*, he collapsed at the dinner table and died the next evening.

About the book

In the pages that follow you will find 23 walks around London and two in Kent. The walks feature places he knew and wrote about. They are not trawls through Dickens's works, and do not feature extensive quotations. Indeed, you can enjoy them without having any real knowledge of Dickens and his novels. Each walk is paced to provide an entertaining and atmospheric route and, thus, I have left out several 'Dickensian' locations that entailed a long walk. When a name appears in bold type it indicates that further information about this person or place can be found elsewhere in the book. A glance at the index will help you locate the relevant pages. The book is not just about Dickens, it is about his London, and, as such, features many of the people and places he knew; it also touches on the great changes that visited London throughout the 19th Century. I have included as many sites and anecdotes as space has allowed and apologize if you find a favourite site missing. I would welcome any suggestions for inclusion in future editions of the book.

I have found the research for this book an enjoyable and fascinating experience, and I hope that you will enjoy walking the routes as much as I have enjoyed writing them.

KEY TO MAPS

Each of the walks in the book is accompanied by a map in which the route is shown in blue. Places of interest along the walk, such as historic buildings, former sites of key Dickensian landmarks and pubs are clearly identified.

The following is a key to the symbols used on the maps.

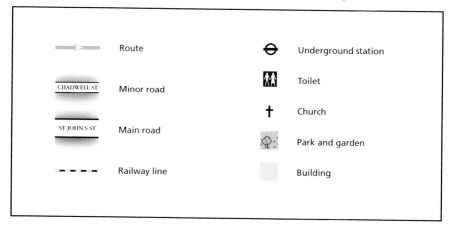

Route		⊖	Underground station
Minor road		🚻	Toilet
Main road		†	Church
Railway line			Park and garden
			Building

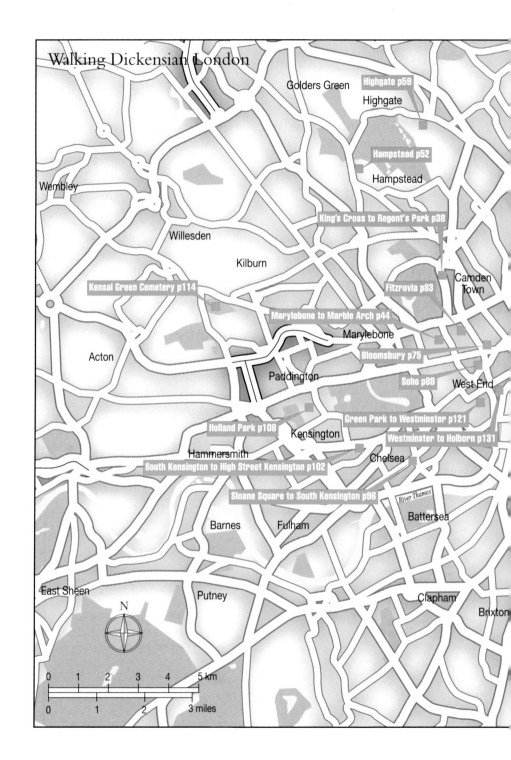

Walking Dickensian London

Golders Green

Highgate p59

Highgate

Hampstead p52

Hampstead

Wembley

King's Cross to Regent's Park p38

Willesden

Kilburn

Camden Town

Kensal Green Cemetery p114

Fitzrovia p83

Marylebone to Marble Arch p44

Marylebone

Acton

Bloomsbury p75

Paddington

Soho p88

West End

Green Park to Westminster p121

Holland Park p108

Kensington

Westminster to Holborn p131

Hammersmith

Chelsea

South Kensington to High Street Kensington p102

Sloane Square to South Kensington p96

River Thames

Battersea

Barnes

Fulham

East Sheen

Putney

Clapham

Brixton

N

0 1 2 3 4 5 km

0 1 2 3 miles

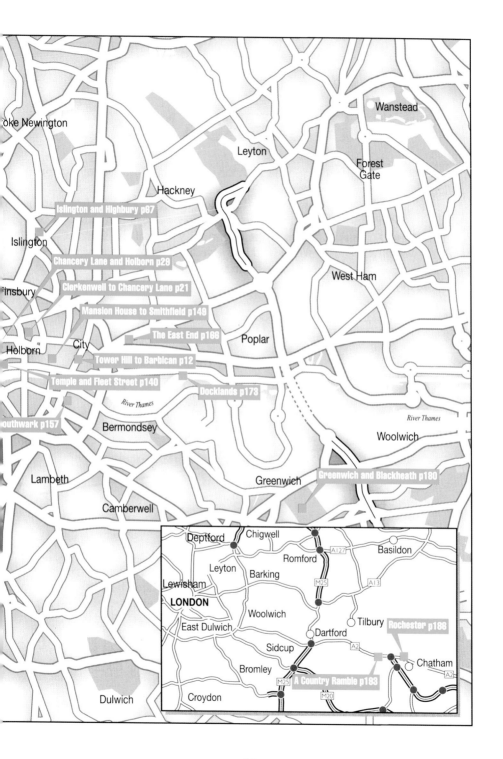

oke Newington

Wanstead

Leyton

Forest
Gate

Hackney

Islington and Highbury p67

Islington

Chancery Lane and Holborn p29

West Ham

insbury

Clerkenwell to Chancery Lane p21

Mansion House to Smithfield p149

The East End p166

City

Poplar

Holborn

Tower Hill to Barbican p12

Temple and Fleet Street p140

River Thames

Docklands p173

River Thames

outhwark p157

Bermondsey

Woolwich

Lambeth

Greenwich and Blackheath p180

Camberwell

Greenwich

Deptford

Chigwell

Romford

A127

Basildon

Leyton

Barking

Lewisham

M25

A13

LONDON

Woolwich

East Dulwich

Tilbury

Rochester p188

Dartford

Sidcup

A2

Bromley

Chatham

A2

A Country Ramble p183

M25

Croydon

M20

Dulwich

TOWER HILL TO BARBICAN

This eventful walk twists its way through the very heart of the City of London, and features many landmarks that Dickens both knew and wrote about. It takes in Lombard Street where Charles Dickens's first great love, Maria Beadnell, lived, and passes through a warren of back alleys that can only be described as 'Dickensian'. There is the opportunity to visit the Guildhall Art Gallery, where you can view the works of several artists mentioned in other walks and, as a finale, you can wander through the Victoriana displayed at the Museum of London.

Start:	Tower Hill Station (Circle and District Underground lines).
Finish:	Barbican Station (Circle, Metropolitan and Hammersmith & City Underground lines).
Length:	2 miles (3.2 km).
Duration:	2½ hours.
Best of times:	Weekends, and times when the Guildhall Art Gallery and Museum of London are open (*see* page 201).
Worst of times:	Evenings.
Refreshments:	Ship Tavern, George and Vulture restaurant (both closed at weekends) and the Museum of London café.

The Tower of London

Exit Tower Hill Underground Station, pausing to look left at the sundry buildings that collectively make up the Tower of London. Founded by William the Conqueror in the 11th century and added to by successive monarchs, the site has been a royal palace, but is best known as a place of imprisonment and execution. The names of those who have been incarcerated behind its grim, grey walls reads like a who's who of English history. It was here 'in a dreary room whose thick stone walls, shut out the hum of life and made a stillness which the records left by former prisoners with those silent witnesses seemed to deepen and intensify...' that Lord George Gordon languished in *Barnaby Rudge*. And, in *David Copperfield* (1849–50), whilst managing Clara Peggotty's

Opposite: The gruesome skulls that surmount the gate of St Olave's led Dickens to dub it the church of 'Saint Ghastly Grim'.

affairs, David varied 'the legal character of these proceedings by going to see...
the Tower of London'.

On the evening of 30th October, 1841, calamity almost overtook the ancient
fortress when the Bowyer Tower caught fire. The castle's nine hand-operated
fire engines were quickly brought into action, but proved useless since there
was only sufficient water to feed one of them. As the flames began to spread,
crowds gathered on Tower Hill to watch the conflagration. Anxious to avoid
loss of life, Major Elrington, the officer in charge, sent for the assistance of the
London Fire Engine Establishment, and gave orders that no one was to be
admitted to the Tower. But, as *Punch* scathingly reported: '... military rule
knows no exceptions, the orders given were executed to the letter by
preventing the ingress of the firemen... leaving the fire to devour at its leisure
the enormous meal that fate had prepared for it.' When the fire fighters were
finally admitted they could do little but aim their hoses on those buildings that
had not yet caught fire, leaving the rest to be consumed by the flames. The
spectators on Tower Hill watched with a horrified fascination. According to
one witness, 'It was a majestic sight, and many around us observed, "I shall not
forget this fire even on my death-bed".' The appearance of today's Tower of
London as a complex of medieval buildings is largely the result of the
restoration that followed this disaster.

St Olave's Church
Turn immediately left into Trinity Square and keep going ahead, passing Trinity
House on your right. Immediately after No 10, go right into Muscovy Street,
right again into Seething Lane, and having passed the bust of Samuel Pepys
(whose office was situated where the gardens on your right now stand), cross
to the left side and pause outside the gate of St Olave's Church. In his essay
'The City of the Absent' in *The Uncommercial Traveller*, Dickens describes this
as 'One of my best beloved churchyards... I call [it] Saint Ghastly Grim...' He
continued: 'It is a small churchyard, with a ferocious strong spiked iron gate,
like a jail. This gate is ornamented with skulls and cross-bones, larger than life,
wrought in stone; but it likewise came into the mind of Saint Ghastly Grim, that
to stick iron spikes a-top of the stone skulls, as though they were impaled,
would be a pleasant device. Therefore the skulls grin aloft horribly, thrust
through and through with iron spears...' The gate has survived the ravages of
time and pollution, and its skulls still leer down from their timeworn perch.

The scent of dead citizens
Go left into Hart Street, where a brief history of St Olave's Church is displayed
on the north wall. Continue ahead, admiring the colourful frontage of the Ship
Tavern on the left, then go right along Mark Lane, and just after the ancient

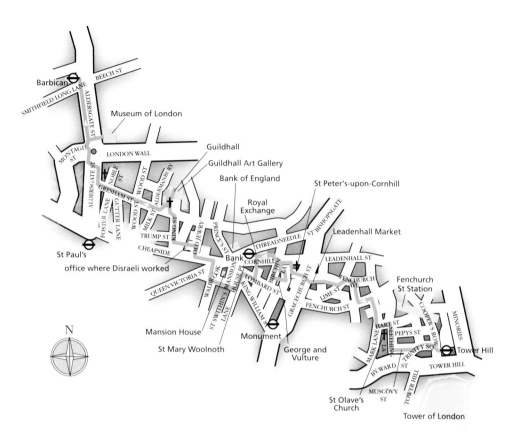

tower of All Hallows Staining (c.1320), veer left along Star Alley. Follow it as it sweeps right onto Fenchurch Street, where you turn left. Take the first right to pass through Fen Court, an unprepossessing throughway where several gravestones and table-top tombs bring to mind Dickens's comments on the area in *The Uncommercial Traveller*: 'Rot and mildew and dead citizens formed the uppermost scent...'

Leadenhall Market

Turn left onto Fenchurch Avenue, and as the gleaming modernity of the Lloyd's Building looms over you, go left along Lime Street, then right into Leadenhall Place to keep ahead into the exquisitely ornate Leadenhall Market, designed in 1881 by the architect Horace Jones. Dickens mentioned the market's predecessor in *Pickwick Papers, Dombey and Son* (1847–48), and also in *Nicholas Nickleby* when Tim Linkinwater dismisses life in the country with the observation that 'I can buy new-laid eggs in Leadenhall Market any morning before breakfast'. Despite the presence of numerous modern enterprises found on many a British high street, the market still retains some of its more traditional businesses such as fishmongers and butchers.

Where the dead were elevated above the living

Having continued ahead through what is without doubt London's most beautiful Victorian market, go over Gracechurch Street and keep ahead into St Peter's Alley. On the right is St Peter's-upon-Cornhill, the church of the 'great golden keys' as Dickens called it in *The Uncommercial Traveller*. Indeed, those keys still surmount the gateway to the peaceful churchyard in which local office workers while away their weekday lunch hours. The surroundings have changed beyond recognition since Dickens described the churchyard in *Our Mutual Friend* (1864–65) as having '... a paved square court, with a raised bank of earth about breast high, in the middle, enclosed by iron rails. Here, conveniently and healthfully elevated above the level of the living, were the dead, and the tombstones; some of the latter droopingly inclined from the perpendicular, as if they were ashamed of the lies they told... '

Below: Lizzie Hexam by the graveyard of St Peter's-upon-Cornhill.

Scrooge was here

Follow the alley as it bends right and at its end turn left along Cornhill where, in *A Christmas Carol*, Bob Cratchit 'went down a slide... twenty times in honour of its being Christmas-eve'. Continue, passing on the left the Church of St Michael, after which take the second left into Ball Court, where the everyday noise of the traffic is reduced to a murmur. Continue, passing the traditional city eatery of Simpson's, which has been expanding the midriffs of city gentlemen with its mutton chops and roast beef dinners since 1757. Hurry through the gloomy passageway to the left, out of which go left again. It was within this maze of alleyways that Dickens placed the counting house of *A Christmas Carol's* Ebenezer Scrooge. In this quaint, atmospheric backwater of twisting passageways and dark courtyards, time appears to have stood still, and it is not difficult to conjure up images of Scrooge's neighbours 'wheezing up and down, beating their hands on their breasts, and stamping their feet upon the pavement stones to warm them'.

The commodious George and Vulture

Further along the alley on the right you arrive at a 'very good old fashioned and comfortable quarters, to wit, the George and Vulture', a true landmark of Dickensian London. This charming old hostelry became Mr Pickwick's London base following the lawsuit brought against him by his landlady Mrs Bardell. Its main entrance is situated on the next right in St Michael's Alley. A well-polished brass nameplate, on which you can just about discern the name by which Dickens would have known it, 'Thomas's Chop House', adorns its outside wall. A timeless aura permeates its snug atmospheric interior, where portraits and photographs of Dickens, together with likenesses of many of his characters and scenes from his novels, adorn the walls.

The Royal Exchange

From the George and Vulture, go right along St Michael's Alley, then right through the arched brick passageway of Bengal Court, pass through an enclosed courtyard and keep ahead, turning right along Birchin Lane. On arriving back on Cornhill, go over the crossing, off which bear left, then first right into Royal Exchange Buildings. Opposite the bust of Paul Julius Reuter (1816–99), 'founder of the world news organization that bears his name', go left through the gates and step inside the Royal Exchange. An information board provides a detailed history of the building, which was founded in the 16th century by city Banker Sir Thomas Gresham. Queen Victoria opened the present building in October 1844; it was recently restored to its 19th-century splendour, and now houses exclusive shops.

Once inside, ascend any of the corner stairways and make your way round the walkway to view the canvasses by several Victorian artists, including **Lord**

Leighton, that show the 'rich and varied history' of the City of London. References to the Royal Exchange are to be found in many of Dickens's works, including *Sketches by Boz, A Christmas Carol, Little Dorrit* and *Great Expectations* (1860–61).

Dickens's first love

Having passed through the Royal Exchange, descend the steps of its magnificent portico and pause to look over at the sturdy, grey bulk of the Bank of England, which is mentioned several times in Dickens's novels. Bear left from the steps, cross Cornhill, and keep ahead through the narrow Pope's Head Alley to arrive at Lombard Street. It was here that Dickens's first great love, **Maria Beadnell** (1811–86), lived. In those days, the city hereabouts was residential as well as mercantile, and innumerable merchants, bankers, businessmen and their families lived in this bustling quarter. Maria's father, George, was manager of Smith, Payne and Smith's Bank at No 1 Lombard Street, and the family lived at No 2. It is not known how the 18-year-old Dickens met the dark-haired, dark-eyed and much admired Maria, but by 1830 he had fallen head over heels in love with her. She was 13 months his senior, capricious by nature, and for four years she toyed with his feelings, even – there is evidence to suggest – agreeing to a clandestine engagement. Maria's family, whilst welcoming the poor young reporter into their home, never considered him a serious suitor for their daughter – her mother never even managed to learn his proper name and referred to him as 'Mr Dickin' – and sent her out of his way to finishing school in France. When Maria returned, her attitude towards him had cooled considerably and, as their relationship entered its final throes, Dickens would walk to Lombard Street in the early hours of the morning just to gaze upon the place where Maria slept.

The Apple Riot

Continue right over Lombard Street to pass the Church of St Mary Woolnoth, where, in an infamous Friday morning sermon in 1868, Father Ignatius inflamed the sensibilities of the traders on Lombard Street, by declaring them far worse than Jericho. His remarks prompted hundreds of men to yell and hoot him as he left the church. This was followed a week later by the so-called 'Apple Riot', when thousands of people armed with apples arrived to pelt Father Ignatius and his congregation. They would have exacted a bruising reprisal had it not been for the timely intervention of the police.

A hungry Dickens

Cross over King William Street, go straight ahead along St Swithin's Lane, take the first right into Mansion House Place, and go left into St Stephen's Row. The towering walls of the Mansion House, home of the Lord Mayor of London rise along the right side. In his essay 'Gone Astray', Dickens recalled how, as a young boy, he had passed the kitchen here as dinner was being prepared and peeping 'in through the kitchen window... my heart began to beat with hope that the Lord Mayor... would look out of an upper apartment and direct me to be taken in... '

The place that Disraeli was too good for

Turn right into Walbrook (the church of St Stephen's on the left is well worth a visit), and continue ahead over Queen Victoria Street and Poultry via the two sets of traffic lights. Bear left, passing a blue wall plaque marking the site of the house where the writer **Thomas Hood** was born, and go first right into Grocer's Hall Court, left into Dove Court, right into Old Jewry, and first left into

Above: A society ball at London's Mansion House.

Frederick's Place. This hidden gem of bygone London is surrounded by a huddle of elegant terraced houses that were built by the Adams brothers – John, Robert and James – in 1776. Benjamin Disraeli (1804–81) worked for a firm of solicitors at No 6 in 1821. Destined to become one of the most colourful characters ever to lead a British political party, the young Disraeli's flamboyant style of dress set him apart from the firm's other clerks. 'You have too much genius for Frederick's Place,' he was told by one acquaintance, 'It will never do.' Leaving his employment here, he sought fame as a writer. But by the time his first novel *Vivian Grey* was published in 1826, he had run up huge debts, which would dog him until he was elected to Parliament as MP for Folkestone. His finances were further improved in 1839 when he married Mary-Ann Lewis, the wealthy widow of a former colleague. He served as Conservative Prime Minister in 1868 and also from 1874–80. Disraeli, despite his own literary talents, was not a great reader of contemporary fiction, and once confessed that he had 'never read anything of Dickens, except an extract in a newspaper'.

Guildhall Art Gallery

Exit Frederick's Place, go left along Old Jewry, left into St Olave's Court, left again onto Ironmonger Lane, and swing immediately right through the white-tiled Prudent Passage. Turn right onto King Street and keep ahead over

Gresham Street to enter the courtyard of the City of London's Guildhall. The magnificent frontage that greets you dates from the 18th Century. To its right is the Guildhall Art Gallery, opened in 1999 to display the Corporation of London's extensive art collection. On show are works by **John Everett Millais** (1829–1926), **Daniel Maclise** (1806–70), **Lord Leighton** (1830–96) and Sir Edwin Landseer (1802–73), who had been a friend of Dickens's since the 1830s. The collections do rotate, so it is worth phoning ahead if you want to be sure of viewing the works of the aforementioned artists. Be sure to pay a visit to the remains of the Roman Ampitheatre before you leave.

The Giants of the Guildhall

From the Guildhall Art Gallery, go straight across the courtyard, where you will have to clear security checks, before you enter the Guildhall. It was in the court that was then attached to the Guildhall that the case of *Bardell v Pickwick* was played out in *Pickwick Papers*. In his essay 'Gone Astray', Dickens mentions how as a small boy he had made up his 'little mind' to seek his fortune. 'My plans... were first to go and see the Giants in Guildhall... I found it a long journey... and a slow one... Being very tired I got into the corner under Magog, to be out of the way of his eye, and fell asleep.' Having entered the Guildhall, if you look back, you will see statues of the two giants guarding the west gallery, Gog (on the right) and Magog (on the left). Sadly, bombing in World War II destroyed the previous giants, to which Dickens referred.

The Museum of London

Exit the Guildhall, bear right across the courtyard, and continue through the barrier, keeping ahead onto Gresham Street. The second turning left is Wood Street, where the Cross Keys Inn once stood, and where Dickens as a small boy first arrived in London from Chatham. At the end of Gresham Street, go right onto St Martin Le Grand, over the pelican crossing, bearing right along Aldersgate Street to the roundabout where, on the left, is the stairwell up to the Museum of London. 'When a man is tired of London he is tired of life', said Dr Johnson, and the same could be said of this magnificent museum, which tells the story of London from pre-Roman times to the present day. The museum has a small Dickensian display on its lower level that includes the chair in which Dickens wrote *A Tale of Two Cities* (1859). On the same level there is a reconstruction of part of Newgate Prison; the Porter's Lodge from **Furnival's Inn**; and a 'Victorian Walk' containing shop fronts, pubs, and other 19th-century businesses.

Having perused the museum to your heart's content, backtrack to Aldersgate Street, bear left off the stairwell and walk straight ahead along Aldersgate Street to arrive at Barbican Underground Station where this walk ends.

CLERKENWELL TO CHANCERY LANE

Most of this walk is spent exploring the streets of Clerkenwell, a quirky little quarter of London that is perched on a hill above the valley of the River Fleet. In the 19th century it became one of the most impoverished and crime-ridden districts of the metropolis. Dickens knew its streets and alleyways intimately, and has left us with vivid descriptions of the filth and squalor found here before work commenced in the 1860s on a project to wipe out the slums once and for all. Known as the 'Holborn Valley Improvement' the scheme changed the face of the neighbourhood, and destroyed, amongst other places, Field Lane – the location of Fagin's Lair in *Oliver Twist*. Yet many places of that era survive today, and several locations are still redolent of the darker side of Victorian London.

Start:	Barbican Station (Circle, Hammersmith & City, and Metropolitan Underground lines).
Finish:	Chancery Lane Station (Central Underground line).
Length:	1¾ miles (2.8 km).
Duration:	1½ hours.
Best of times:	Anytime.
Worst of times:	At weekends St Andrew's Church and the Prudential Building are closed.
Refreshments:	One Tun PH, Ye Olde Mitre Tavern and Jerusalem Tavern. All are closed at the weekend.

Where Thackeray went to school

Exit Barbican Underground Station, turn left along Aldersgate Street, then left into Carthusian Street, and right through the gates into the quaint, historic Charterhouse Square. Follow the road left to pause on the right outside the gates of the Charterhouse. Originally founded as a Carthusian Monastery, the Charterhouse passed through successive owners following its dissolution by Henry VIII, before coming into the possession of the hugely wealthy Sir Thomas Sutton in 1611. Here, he established both the Charterhouse Hospital for aged men, and Charterhouse School for the education of the sons of the poor. By the early 19th century, Charterhouse had become a leading public school. However, the writer **William Makepeace Thackeray** (1811–63), an ex-pupil, was not impressed by the establishment, later recalling how he 'was lulled into indolence & when I grew older & could think for myself was abused into sulkiness and bullied into despair'. Although the school moved out of the area in the late 19th Century, the Charterhouse is still a hospital-cum-retirement home and can be visited at certain times of the year.

Smithfield Meat Market

Continue ahead and go through the gates onto Charterhouse Street. The Gothic frontage of the Fox and Anchor pub is worth noting as you pass, particularly the hideous grotesques that scowl down from its upper storeys.

Keeping to the right hand pavement, you pass the ornate Smithfield Meat Market on the left. It was built in 1868 to replace the old livestock market, whose closure in 1855 was no great loss. In *Oliver Twist*, the title character crossed it with Bill Sikes on market morning and found 'the ground was covered nearly ankle deep with filth and mire; a thick steam perpetually rising from the reeking bodies of the cattle'. In *Great Expectations*, Pip discovered the old market to be a 'shameful place being all asmear with filth and fat and blood and foam'. Nowadays, the cattle arrive pre-slaughtered in huge refrigeration trucks. The market, which works through the night, is a lively enclave and, although a lot cleaner than in Dickens's day, it can still prove somewhat gruesome.

St John's Gate

Go first right into St John Street, where several of the buildings still possess the lifting devices and loading bays as testimony to their market-related past. Cross over the zebra crossing, bear right and keep ahead, taking the left fork into St John's Lane. When you reach the end, go under St John's Gate, which was built in 1504 and is all that survives of the Priory of St John of Jerusalem. It was here that *Gentleman's Magazine*, which numbered **Dr Johnson** and **Oliver Goldsmith** amongst its contributors, was published in the 18th century. It later became the parish watch house, and by the mid-19th century was a popular public house known as the Old Jerusalem Tavern. In 1874, the Most Venerable Order of the Hospital of St John of Jerusalem acquired it, and three years later the St John's Ambulance brigade was launched from here. Today, a small museum is situated inside the old gatehouses and regular tours are given.

Jerusalem Tavern

Having passed through St John's Gate, you are suddenly confronted by a gloomy square of featureless office blocks. Hurry left along St John's Path, a dark, atmospheric passageway that eases between high walls to emerge onto Britton Street, where immediately on the left is the tiny Jerusalem Tavern. Although it has only been a pub since the 1990s, it occupies an 18th-century premises, and serves up a variety of real ales, including Old English Porter, which at 6.2% proof a pint might necessitate returning to complete the walk another day!

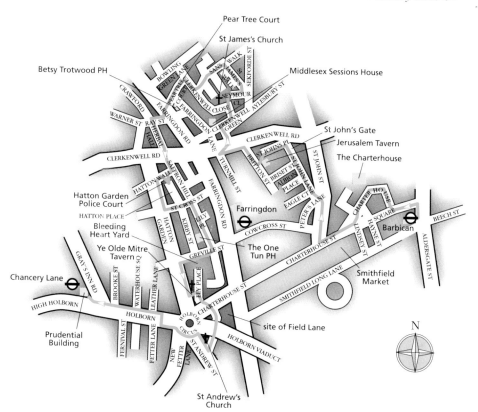

'Little Hell'

From the tavern, turn right onto Britton Street, then left along Clerkenwell Road. Having crossed Turnmill Street, pause on the corner. Although you can't see it, you are standing on the banks of the River Fleet, which flows deep beneath Farringdon Road on the other side of Farringdon Station. Throughout much of the 19th century, this area was considered one of the worst slums, or 'rookeries' in London. It boasted one of the capital's highest murder rates, and because Turnmill Street was seen as its centre, the locals knew it as 'Little Hell'. It was home to pickpockets, receivers, counterfeiters and child strippers – drunken women who would lure children away in order to steal their clothing.

'Driven amid palpable darkness'

The slums were finally swept away by the construction of Farringdon and Clerkenwell Roads in the early 1860s, and by the construction of the Metropolitan Railway line over the wall to your right. Work began on the line in 1860 to connect Paddington to Farringdon, and it was the world's first underground passenger railway. Despite serious misgivings at the time – notably from *The Times*, which considered it an 'insult to common sense to suppose that people... would ever prefer... to be driven amid palpable darkness through the foul subsoil of London' – it proved an instant success. Today, Turnmill Street has little of interest, except for a superb view of the dome of St Paul's Cathedral in the distance.

The Middlesex Sessions House

Backtrack to the pedestrian crossing, go over Clerkenwell Road, bearing right, then left onto Clerkenwell Green. The large building immediately on the left is the former Middlesex Sessions House, built in 1779 and the place that Mr Bumble, 'in the full bloom and pride of beadlehood... ', was bound for in *Oliver Twist* when he proudly boasted to Mrs Mann, 'And I very much question... whether the Clerkenwell Sessions will not find themselves in the wrong box before they have done with me.' The courts were closed in 1919 and the premises converted to offices. In 1979, the Masonic Foundation acquired the building and restored it to its former glory.

The Green that isn't green

Continue over Clerkenwell Green, which is notable for its lack of greenery. It was hereabouts in *Oliver Twist* that Mr Brownlow was reading a book at a stall as the Artful Dodger, Charley Bates and Oliver 'were just emerging from the narrow court, not far from the open square in Clerkenwell, which is yet called, by some strange perversion of terms "The Green"... ' Oliver watched in horror 'his eyelids as wide open as they would possibly go, to see the Dodger plunge his hand into the old gentleman's pocket; and draw from thence a handkerchief... ' Dodger and Bates escaped, leaving Oliver to take the blame.

Go clockwise, turning left at the Crown Tavern into Clerkenwell Close. Ahead of you is the church of St James, dating from 1778–82, the exterior of which has a dark gloomy air in contrast to its otherwise pleasant interior. One notable feature is the 19th-century iron 'modesty board', placed strategically around the base of the stairs to the left of the entrance, to prevent the gentlemen of the parish looking up the ladies skirts as they ascended the stairs! Also noteworthy are the huge blackboards that show charitable bequests from long-dead parishioners to the poor of the parish.

Go down the steps to exit the church, turn left through the gate and walk to the far steps that lead up to a bricked off doorway. To the right of these stairs

Opposite: The church and clock of St Andrew's, Holborn to which Bill Sikes referred in Oliver Twist. *It was the discovery of a dying woman on the church's steps that led Dr William Marsden to found the Royal Free Hospital in 1828.*

is the weathered tombstone of Ellen Steinberg and her four young children, who were stabbed to death on 8th September, 1834. The murderer was Johann Steinberg, Ellen's husband, and, as he then turned the knife on himself, his motive was never discovered. His wife and children were buried at St James's, their tombstone paid for by public subscription. The murderous husband was buried at night in a pauper's grave in nearby Ray Street, with a stake driven through his heart. This was the customary way of dealing with suicidal murderers in the early 19th century.

The Peabody Trust and Pear Tree Court

Go past the grave to exit the churchyard through the gates on the opposite side of the lawn. Turn left along St James's Walk, left into Sans Walk and keep ahead into Clerkenwell Close, at the end of which turn right to pass through the brown brick blocks of the Peabody Trust flats. American philanthropist George Peabody established the trust in 1862 'to ameliorate the condition of the poor and needy of this great metropolis and to promote their comfort and happiness'. Turn left into Pear Tree Court, thought to be the 'narrow court' from which the Artful Dodger, Oliver Twist and Charley Bates emerged onto Clerkenwell Green. Pear Tree Court runs onto Farringdon Lane where opposite, appropriately, is the Betsy Trotwood pub, named after David Copperfield's formidable aunt.

Where Oliver Twist appeared in court

Cross Farringdon Road via the pedestrian crossing on the right. Veer left then first right into Ray Street – beneath the surface of which Johann Steinberg may still be lying. Take the first left up Herbal Hill and cross Clerkenwell Road via the crossing, bear left, then take the first right into Saffron Hill. Turn right onto Hatton Wall, left under the covered passage into Hatton Place, and on arrival at the wall with the bricked up windows look through the grey gates. You have just walked the route along which the baying crowd brought Oliver Twist having captured him on suspicion of stealing Mr Brownlow's handkerchief. He was 'led beneath a low archway and up a dirty court' to be taken in through the back door of a 'very notorious metropolitan police office', where he was brought before the magistrate Mr Fang. It was also along here that Nancy came, at the request of Fagin, tapping the cell doors with her keys endeavouring to locate Oliver.

The original Mr Fang the Magistrate

Backtrack to Hatton Wall, go left and left again onto Hatton Garden. A little way along on the left pause outside No 54, which offers no hint that this was once the front entrance of the Hatton Garden Police Court, the original of the 'notorious' police office, to which Oliver was brought. Mr Fang was based upon Mr A S Laing, an infamous magistrate working here between 1836 and 1838.

According to **John L Forster**, on 3rd June, 1837, Dickens wrote to Mr Haines – a supervisor over police reports for the daily papers: 'In my next number of *Oliver Twist* I must have a magistrate; and casting about [for one] whose harshness and insolence would render him a fit subject to be *shown up*, I have... stumbled upon Mr Laing of Hatton-garden celebrity... it occurred to me that perhaps I might under your auspices be smuggled into the Hatton-garden office for a few moments some morning [in order to see him]... ' Forster records that, 'The opportunity was found; the magistrate... brought before the novelist; and shortly after, on some fresh outbreak of intolerable temper' Mr Laing was removed from the bench.

A notorious rookery

Continue along Hatton Garden, and go left into St Cross Street, noting the former charity school building on the corner, where a plaque gives its history. Turn second right into Saffron Hill and keep walking ahead. Now a shadow of its former crime-ridden past, Saffron Hill was, in the 19th century, a notorious rookery where crime and vice flourished. Theft was so common here that it was claimed you could have your handkerchief stolen at one end, and buy it back at the other! Bordered on its eastern side by the Fleet Ditch – in reality nothing more than a malodorous open sewer – the area was considered one of the most unwholesome parts of London, and few tears were shed when, in the 1860s, it was swept away. Towards the end on the right is the One Tun Pub, rebuilt in 1875, which claims to be the original of the Three Cripples, a favoured haunt of Fagin and Bill Sikes in *Oliver Twist*.

Mr and Mrs Plornish

Go right into Greville Street and take the first left into the wonderfully named Bleeding Heart Yard. Admittedly, it has changed beyond recognition since Dickens knew it, but it still has a secluded ambience. Mr Plornish and his wife, who was 'so dragged at, by poverty and the children together, that their united forces had already dragged her face into wrinkles', lived here in *Little Dorrit* and, in the same novel, the inventor Daniel Doyce had his factory 'over the gateway'.

Exit the yard, go left along Greville Street, left onto Hatton Garden and on arrival at the old gas lamp that leans over the pavement, turn left down the narrow alleyway. Pause alongside Ye Olde Mitre Tavern which was built in 1547, and is as timeless an old hostelry as you could wish for. Continue through the passageway and turn right into Ely Place. It was in one of the 18th-century townhouses of this charming enclave that Dickens set Mr Waterbrook's house in *David Copperfield*. Here the adult David renewed his friendship with his old school friend Thomas Traddles at a dinner party, which was also attended by the saintly Agnes Wickfield and the very 'umble Uriah Heep.

Above: Field Lane where Fagin's den of thieves was located in Oliver Twist.

Exit Ely Place, walk left along Charterhouse Street and first right into Shoe Lane – a grimy, shabby thoroughfare to the left of which once stood Field Lane where Fagin's den was located in *Oliver Twist*.

Go under Holborn Viaduct – it was in the construction of this bridge that Field Lane was obliterated; go sharp right onto St Andrew Street and at the top end, go right through the hedge and into the stunning interior of St Andrew's Church. Just inside the door is the tomb of Captain Thomas Coram who began the Foundling Hospital in 1742. Opposite is a memorial to surgeon **William Marsden** (1796–1867). In 1827, Marsden found a young woman dying on the steps of the church and was unable to get her admitted to any London hospital without a letter of recommendation. This led to him founding the Free Hospital in Greville Lane in 1828. Queen Victoria became its patron in 1837, and asked that it henceforth be known as 'The Royal Free Hospital', under which name it still operates in Hampstead.

Exit the church and cross over St Andrew Street, pausing by the trees to glance back at the church clock, just as Bill Sikes did in *Oliver Twist*, whilst telling Oliver it was 'hard upon seven! You must step out'. Turning your back on the clock, go right along St Andrew Street, cross the road and bear left over New Fetter Lane onto Holborn. Go over the crossing and veer left along the right side of the road until you arrive at the soaring red brick pile of the Prudential Building. Turn right through its gates and cross to the tiny porch on the opposite side. A somewhat raddled looking bust of Charles Dickens gazes dolefully out from a Perspex case. The Prudential Building stands on the site of Furnival's Inn, where Dickens lived from 1834 to 1837. During this time he began *Pickwick Papers* the work that set him on the road to literary fame. Whilst living here, he married **Catherine Hogarth**.

Return to Holborn, turn right and a little way along you will find Chancery Lane Underground Station where this walk ends.

CHANCERY LANE AND HOLBORN

This is one of my favourite Dickensian routes, packed with places that Dickens knew intimately and about which he wrote frequently. From the peaceful quietude of Staple Inn, through the timeless solitude of Lincoln's Inn, this walk has it all. It passes the home of Dickens's greatest friend, John Forster, provides the opportunity to visit two wonderful museums, and ends by a building where, Dickens, at the age of 15, worked for a firm of solicitors. All in all, this is Dickens's London at its very best, and if you have time to take only one walk, then this should be it.

Start & Finish:	Chancery Lane Station (Central Underground line).
Length:	2 miles (3.2 km).
Duration:	2½ hours.
Best of times:	Weekdays between 10am and 4pm when the Inns of Court and the museums are open.
Worst of times:	Weekends and evenings.
Refreshments:	Several pubs passed en route notably the Cittie of York PH.

'A little nook called Staple Inn'

Leave Chancery Lane Underground Station via exit three, which will bring you onto Holborn. Almost immediately on the right is the black and white timbered façade of Staple Inn, which, with its lattice windows set back in all sorts of angled gables, must surely be one of the most exquisite relics of old London. It dates from 1576, although it had to be repaired following considerable bomb damage in World War II, and it is so named because it once provided London accommodation for wool-staplers or brokers. 'Behind the most ancient part of Holborn', wrote Dickens in his last and unfinished novel *The Mystery of Edwin Drood* (1870), '... where certain gabled houses some centuries of age still stand looking on the public way... is a little nook... called Staple Inn. It is one of those nooks, the turning into which, out of the clashing street, imparts to the relieved pedestrian the sensation of having put cotton in his ears and velvet soles on his boots.'

To experience how little this secret niche has changed since Dickens wrote those words, go right through the ancient gateway and enter Staple Inn itself. As you do so note the warning just inside the wall on the left: 'The Porter Has

Orders to Prevent Old Clothes Men and Others From Calling "Articles For Sale" Also Rude Children Playing and No Horses Allowed Within This Inn.'

'Where smoky sparrows twitter'

Continue into the first courtyard and suddenly the rush and noise of modern Holborn disappears. Huge Plane trees tower over you, and 18th- and 19th-century redbrick buildings surround you. 'It is one of those nooks,' observed Dickens, 'where a few smoky sparrows twitter in smoky trees, as though they called to one another, "Let us play at country,"... Moreover it is one of those nooks which are legal nooks: and it contains a little Hall, with a little lantern in its roof... ' His description still holds true today.

The residence of Mr Grewgious

Keep ahead, passing through the arched passageway, and pause by the building immediately to the left. In *The Mystery of Edwin Drood*, this was the residence of the kindly lawyer Mr Hiram Grewgious, the guardian of Rosa Bud, Edwin Drood's fiancée. Note the stone above the doorway which is inscribed 'PJT 1747'. Dickens commented that Mr Grewgious had never 'troubled his head' as to its meaning, '... unless to bethink... that haply it might mean Perhaps John Thomas, or Perhaps Joe Tyler.'

'A disembodied spirit'

Follow the railing as it skirts the pretty little garden, go up the steps and bear right along the pedestrian walkway called Staple Inn Buildings. Turn right onto Holborn, continue onwards over Furnival Street, and a little way along, turn right through the iron gates into Barnard's Inn. Follow the passageways that lead you to an inner sanctum where Pip and Herbert Pocket had chambers in *Great Expectations*. It is a little confusing that so many enclaves in this area are known as 'inns', and Dickens has Pip ruminating upon this when first visiting Barnard's Inn. 'I had supposed that establishment to be an hotel kept by Mr Barnard... whereas I now found Barnard to be a disembodied spirit, or a fiction, and his inn the dingiest collection of shabby buildings ever squeezed together, in a rank corner as a club for Tom-cats.' Either Dickens was being a little unfair with his depiction, or the area has changed considerably, as this really is a lovely spot.

Took's Court

Backtrack, go left along Furnival Street, turn right into Took's Court, which Dickens renamed Cook's Court in *Bleak House* (1852–53). It was at No 15, now called 'Dickens House', situated on the left just after the road bears sharp left, that the meditative law stationer Mr Snagsby lived and worked.

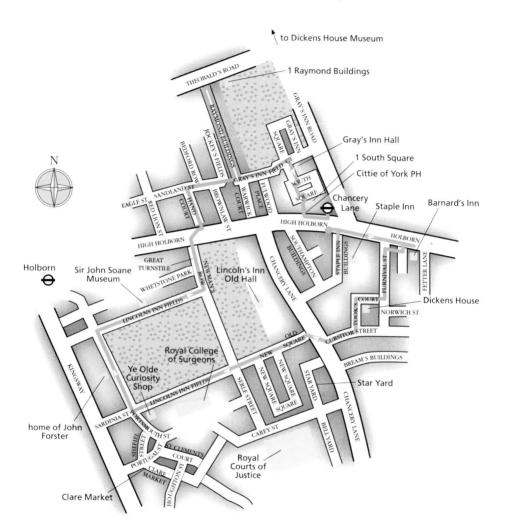

Dickens gets a black eye

Continue ahead, turn right along Cursitor Street, right onto Chancery Lane and cross to the Gatehouse (now rebuilt) of Lincoln's Inn. It was whilst crossing here on his first day working for **Ellis and Blackmore**, that the teenage Dickens, in a blue jacket and 'military-looking cap which had a strap under the chin' met 'a big blackguard fellow' who knocked off his cap and said 'Halloa, sojar'. 'Which,' Dickens later recounted, when he returned to the office sporting a black eye, 'I could not stand, so I at once struck him and he then hit me in the eye.'

The he Court of the Lord Chancellor

Go through the 16th-century gates and enter Lincoln's Inn, one of London's four Inns of Court. Immediately the surroundings change to a delightful combination of dark brick and light stone buildings. The redbrick building on the other side of the lawn is the Old Hall, dating back to 1489, and which, before the construction of the Law Courts on the Strand, was where the Lord Chancellor's Court met outside legal terms. It was here in 'Implacable November weather' that *Bleak House* began with its vivid images of a London fog. 'Fog everywhere... Chance people on the bridges peeping over the parapets into a nether sky of fog... as if they were up in a balloon, and hanging in the misty clouds. Gas looming through the fog in diverse places... shops lighted two hours before their time – as the gas seems to know, for it has a haggard and unwilling look... And in Lincoln's Inn Hall, at the very heart of the fog, sits the Lord High Chancellor in his high Court of Chancery... '

Jarndyce versus Jarndyce

Continue to the right of the hall and pause by its door on the left, which is occasionally open to provide a brief glimpse of the interior. This is where in *Bleak House* the legal suit of Jarndyce versus Jarndyce droned ever onwards, just as it had been doing for so long that no man alive could remember what it was about. Dickens considered the Chancellors Court '... the most pestilent of hoary sinners', and in *Bleak House* issued the following warning: 'This is the Court of Chancery; which has its decaying houses and its blighted lands in every shire; which has its worn-out lunatic in every madhouse, and its dead in every churchyard;... which so exhausts finances, patience, courage, hope; so overthrows the brain and breaks the heart; that there is not an honourable man among its practitioners who would not give – who does not often give – the warning, "Suffer any wrong that can be done you, rather than come here!"'

Opposite the door are the cloisters where the gravestones mentioned by Esther Summerson in *Bleak House* can still be seen. If open, the chapel above is worth a visit.

Miss Flite's bower

Keeping the cloisters to your right, walk into New Square, which given it was built in 1685 is anything but. The square has changed so little that it was used in the mid 1980s as a setting for the TV serialisation of *Bleak House*. Head towards the gates of Lincoln's Inn, passing the magnificent gardens to your right about which Miss Flite in *Bleak House* observes, 'I call it my garden. It is quite a bower in

Opposite: *Stepping through the gatehouse of Staple Inn you find yourself transported into an enclave that has changed little since Dickens's day.*

Above: Daniel Maclise's sketch of Dickens reading his Christmas story 'The Chimes' to a select gathering of literary greats in December 1844.

the summer-time... ' As you exit through the gates, the soaring redbrick gothic structure on the right is the New Hall, built in 1843.

Where lawyers' skulls should be arranged

Carry on ahead crossing Serle Street into Lincoln's Inn Fields, which is London's largest square, and where the Gordon rioters gathered in *Barnaby Rudge*. Keep ahead until you arrive at the classical, Ionic-columned frontage of the Royal College of Surgeons. Commenting on the lawyers of Lincoln's Inn, Mr Boythorn in *Bleak House* says that they should have their 'necks rung and their skulls arranged in Surgeons' Hall, for the contemplation of the whole profession, in order that its younger members might understand from actual measurement in early life, how thick skulls may become!'. Today, you can do likewise as all manner of gruesomely fascinating artefacts and anatomical specimens – lawyers' skulls excepted – are now on display and open to the public in the college's two museums.

Not the Old Curiosity Shop

Continue, turn left into Portsmouth Street and pause a little way along by the almost too-good-to-be-true 'Ye Olde Curiosity Shop'. This quaint little building dates from 1567 and was reputedly built from old ship timbers. The legend 'Immortalized by Charles Dickens' emblazoned on its wall is a bit of wishful thinking. Dickens emphatically states at the end of *The Old Curiosity Shop* (1841) that the building of which he wrote was 'long ago pulled down'. In a letter to *The Echo* in 1883, a Mr Charles Tesseyman confessed that his brother, who had dealt in old china, books and paintings from the premises between 1868 and 1877, had added the 'immortalized by' appellation to his shop front for 'business purposes'. He continued that, following his brother's death in 1877, the new tenant painted over his name but left the claim emblazoned on the wall. Around 1881, an American journalist writing about Dickensian landmarks arrived at the shop and 'straightway wrote an article in *Scribner's Monthly*... [assuring]... his readers that this was the old original Old Curiosity Shop of Dickens'.

The George IV pub on the right past the shop, rebuilt since Dickens's day, is thought to have been the original of the Magpie and Stump, where in *Pickwick Papers*, Jack Bamber tells Mr Pickwick bizarre and gruesome stories about the Inns of Court.

John Forster's house

Backtrack and continue clockwise around Lincoln's Inn Fields. Number 58 was, from 1834 to 1856, the home of **John Forster** (1812–76). Forster was Dickens's greatest friend and his first significant biographer. Dickens based Mr Podsnap in *Our Mutual Friend* (1864–65) on Forster, and later used his house for the residence of Mr Tulkinghorn – legal adviser to Sir Leicester Dedlock and evil blackmailer of Lady Dedlock – in *Bleak House*. Dickens was at his lawyer-bashing best when he wrote, 'The crow flies straight across Chancery Lane... into Lincoln's Inn Fields. Here, in a large house, formerly a house of state, lives Mr Tulkinghorn. It is let off in sets of chambers now, and in these shrunken fragments of its greatness lawyers lie in maggots in nuts.'

Dickens gives a private reading

On the 2nd December, 1844 Dickens, who had travelled especially from Italy for the occasion, gave a private reading at Forster's house from his new Christmas story 'The Chimes'. The select gathering included Forster, **Thomas Carlyle**, and **Daniel Maclise**. 'There was not a dry eye in the house', wrote Daniel Maclise to Catherine Dickens, who had remained in Italy. 'Shrieks of laughter – there were indeed – and floods of tears as a relief to them – I do not think that there ever was such a triumphant hour for Charles... ' Maclise also did a pencil sketch of the occasion (opposite), showing Dickens seated at the desk, the book open in front of him, surrounded by his enraptured audience. Forster considered it an accurate depiction of the event, although he did comment that there was a touch of caricature of which he considered himself 'chief victim.'

A second reading two evenings later was equally successful, and thus were sown the seeds of Dickens forays into amateur theatricals and, according to Forster, 'those readings to larger audiences by which, as much by his books, the world knew him in later life.'

The Sir John Soane Museum

Continue ahead, passing No 65 on the left. This was the home of **William Marsden** (1796–1867), one of the great figures of 19th-century healthcare and founder of both the Royal Free and Royal Marsden Hospitals. Keep going clockwise and pause outside the Sir John Soane Museum at No 13. Sir John Soane (1753–1837), architect of the Bank of England, reconstructed this house in 1792, and furnished it with a veritable treasure trove of all things beautiful, instructive and curious. Before he died, he succeeded in obtaining an Act of Parliament, which ensured that the houses – he expanded next door when his collection outgrew the original premises! – and their contents would be preserved as a public museum. Of particular Dickensian interest are the original paintings of **William Hogarth**'s (1697–1764) *The Rake's Progress* and *Election Campaign*. Hogarth was an astute observer and commentator on the social scene of 18th-century London. He was a favourite artist of the young Dickens whose style was greatly influenced by the narrative style of Hogarth's works. Later, he commented on Hogarth's compassion and praised him for his awareness of 'the causes of drunkenness among the poor'.

Ellis and Blackmore employ young Charles

Keep ahead past the museum. Turn left into Newman's Row, through Great Turnstile onto High Holborn, and go over the crossing. Bear right and take the first left into Hand Court. Turn right into Sandland Street and keep walking ahead past the disused water pump. On arrival at Jockey's Fields, go through the small gate, down the steps into Gray's Inn, turn left and walk past Raymond Buildings. Number 1, rebuilt after the bombs of World War II, was where Charles Dickens worked as a clerk for solicitors Ellis and Blackmore between December 1827 and November 1828. The desk at which he worked is preserved in the Dickens House Museum, to which you can now make a detour if you wish. It is at 48 Doughty Street and is reached by going right out of the gates, over Theobald's Road, left into John Street, and ahead into Doughty Street where you'll find it a little way along on the right.

Evidently the office comic, Dickens used to delight his fellow clerks with his talent for mimicry, whilst his knowledge of London, even at the age of 15, was both impressive and unrivalled. One of his amusements was to drop cherry stones from the second floor offices onto the hats of passers-by below. Should anyone complain he would confront them 'with so much gravity and with such an air of innocence, that they went away... ' It was whilst working here that Dickens began to learn shorthand and, by 1829, he had left their employ and become a shorthand writer in Doctor's Commons. But his experiences at Ellis and Blackmore would resurface time and again in his fiction. Indeed, in the firm's petty cash book, now preserved in America, can be found such names as Weller, Bardell and Rudge, all of which he would use later in his novels.

A depressing institution?

Backtrack past Raymond Buildings. Follow the path left, and turn left just before the covered passageway. Keep ahead, passing on the left the beautiful gardens of Gray's Inn; go through the long passageway to emerge onto Gray's Inn Square. To the modern eye this is a delightful piece of bygone London, but Dickens was particularly unimpressed by it. 'Indeed', he wrote in *The Uncommercial Traveller*, 'I look upon Gray's Inn... as one of the most depressing institutions in brick and mortar, known to the children of men.' Either there has been a great deal of change since he wrote those words, or else the drudgery of the 18 months he spent working as a clerk, clouded his judgement!

Bear right out of the passageway and continue ahead into South Square. Gray's Inn Hall, immediately on your left, dates from 1556. In *Pickwick Papers* Dickens mentions how 'Clerk after clerk hastened into the square by one or other of the entrances, and looking up at the hall clock accelerated or decreased his rate of walking according to the time at which his office hours nominally commenced'.

Dickens's portrait

Cross over to No 1 South Square, situated to the left of the exit. It was here that Ellis and Blackmore occupied 'a poor old set of chambers of three rooms... ' when Charles Dickens first came to work for them in May 1827. In those days it was No 5 Holborn Square, and it is the only building in the immediate vicinity to have survived the bombs of World War II. So little has changed that you can just picture the 'good looking and clever' young boy, his 'healthy pink – almost glowing' complexion, 'expressive eyes' and 'beautiful brown hair worn long, as was then the fashion... ' stepping across its threshold on his first day of employment. A copy of the **Daniel Maclise** portrait of him, painted in 1839, hangs on the wall of the corridor just beyond the doors to commemorate the building's associations with the budding author-to-be.

Leave Gray's Inn via the exit to the right, go left along Holborn to reach Chancery Lane Underground Station where this walk ends.

KING'S CROSS TO REGENT'S PARK

The coming of the railways in the 19th Century changed not just the face of England, but the way of life for its people. Vast swathes of London were destroyed to make way for the tracks, and little effort was made to re-house the tens of thousands of poor, whose tenement dwellings were swept away by the ceaseless onslaught. They simply drifted to other areas, and exacerbated the overcrowding in the slums around central London, to which the railways were forbidden by law to penetrate. Dickens wrote of the devastating effects of this expansion in *Dombey and Son* (1847–49). He even renamed one area of Camden Town Staggs's Gardens – 'stag' being Victorian slang for a speculator in railway stocks. The latter section of the walk takes in the air of Regent's Park and passes the house to which Dickens's wife, Catherine, retired after the breakdown of their marriage.

Start:	King's Cross Station (Circle, Hammersmith & City, Metropolitan, Piccadilly and Victoria lines).
Finish:	Great Portland Street Station (Circle, Hammersmith & City and Metropolitan Underground lines).
Length:	2 miles (3.2 km).
Duration:	1¾ hours.
Best of times:	Daytime.
Worst of times:	None.
Refreshments:	Camden Town has many cafés and pubs.

The King's Column

Leave King's Cross Underground Station via the Pancras Road and British Library exit. The large building to your right is the former Midland Grand Hotel opened in 1873. It stands on the site of Agar Town, a notorious shanty town about which Dickens wrote in 1851: it is 'a complete bog of mud and filth with deep-cart ruts, wretched hovels, the doors blocked up with mud... The stench of a rainy morning is enough to knock down a bullock.' Go right along Pancras Road, and make your way past the dingy railway arches. Battle Bridge Road, a little way along on the right, commemorates the name of the area before the coming of the railways in the 1830s. At this time, the nearby construction of the 60-foot (18.3-metre) high monument topped by a statue of George IV, led to the district being renamed King's Cross.

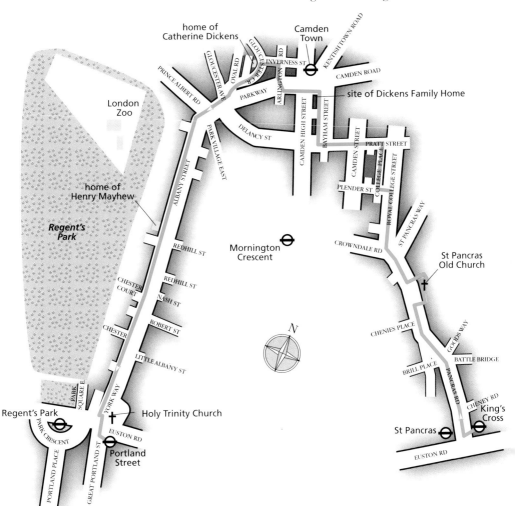

St Pancras Old Church

Pass under the three railway bridges, and go right over Brill Place. Continue along the still busy and unattractive Pancras Road. Behind the grimy windows of the shops and work places that occupy the railway arches, you catch glimpses of tailors, cobblers and picture-framers, beavering away seemingly oblivious to the 21st Century outside. When the arches give way to modern council housing, go over the zebra crossing, through the gates, and pause outside the tiny St Pancras Old Church. If the church is open, it is well worth a visit, particularly to admire its 6th-century altar stone, which legend holds belonged to St Augustine.

The Hardy Tree

Go through the gate to the left of the church, keep ahead and pause by the railings that surround the 'Hardy Tree', planted by Thomas Hardy (1840–1928) when, prior to becoming a novelist, he was studying architecture in London. Hardy was given the task of clearing the graves from Old St Pancras Churchyard during the construction of the Midland Railway in the 1860s. This ash tree that he planted on a domed mound of tombstones has now grown to maturity, and memorials cluster around its trunk or protrude from its roots – a bizarre, though curious sight. A few years before Hardy came here Charles Dickens had made use of Old St Pancras Churchyard as the burial place of the Old Bailey spy, Roger Cly, in *A Tale of Two Cities* (1859). It was also here that Jerry Cruncher and his son came 'fishing' in the same novel; although they were armed with a spade rather than a rod, for they were in fact body snatching.

Turn sharp left by the tree and cross the lawn to admire the Soane mausoleum, designed by architect **Sir John Soane** (1788–1830), following his wife's death in 1815 and where he too is also buried.

Dickens's teacher

Go clockwise around the railings that encircle the mausoleum, and seek out the crumbling gravestone to the left of the huge tree, where a weathered inscription commemorates Mr William Jones, 'for many years master of a respectable school in this parish' who died in 1836. The school in question was the Wellington House Academy, which stood on nearby Hampstead Road, and where Charles Dickens became a day pupil, following his father's release from the Marshalsea Prison. Dickens was somewhat disparaging of Mr Jones, later remembering him as 'by far the most ignorant man I have ever had the pleasure to know, [he was] one of the worst-tempered men perhaps that ever lived, whose business was to make as much out of us and to put as little into us as possible... ' Mr Creakle, the ferocious headmaster of Salem House in *David Copperfield* was based on William Jones.

A childhood home

With your back to the Soane mausoleum, cross to the elaborately gothic and very colourful Burdett-Coutts sundial, unveiled in 1879 by **Baroness Burdett-Coutts**. Exit the churchyard and go right along Pancras Road. Continue over Pancras Way and go next right into Royal College Street, passing the buildings of the Royal Veterinary College, after which go over the zebra crossing, and

Opposite: The Gothic extravagance of the Burdett-Coutts memorial stands in Old St Pancras Churchyard, and commemorates Angela Burdett-Coutts 'the Queen of the Poor,' and one of Dickens's closest friends.

forge ahead into Plender Street. Turn first right into College Place. In Dickens's childhood, College Place was known as Little College Street. When his mother and father were in the Marshalsea Prison, Charles lodged here with a friend of the family, Mrs Roylance. Later, he would remember sadly how he had had 'No advice, no counsel, no encouragement, no consolation, no support from anyone that I can call to mind, so help me God... ' The house in question has long since been demolished, and Dickens's description of the neighbourhood as 'a desolate place... surrounded by little else than fields and ditches... ' belongs to its dim and distant past. But his landlady lives on as Mrs Pipchin the 'marvellous ill-favoured, ill-conditioned old lady, of a stooping figure, with a mottled face like bad marble' who kept a children's boarding house in *Dombey and Son*.

The Dickens family arrive in London

Turn left into Pratt Street, continue over Camden Street and go next right along Bayham Street. The St Martin's almshouses, a little way along on the right, date from 1818. Cross cautiously to the left side of the street and, just before turning left into Greenland Road, pause alongside the light brown-brick Greenland Road Children's Centre. It stands on the site of No 16 Bayham Street, to which the Dickens family moved in 1823. Charles sank into despondency, longing for the fields and happy times of his former home in Chatham, Kent. Here, according to **John Forster**, Dickens took 'his first impression of that struggling poverty which is nowhere more vividly shown than in the commoner streets of the ordinary London Suburb, and which enriched his earliest writings with a freshness of original humour and quite unstudied pathos... ' The Micawbers in *David Copperfield*, and the Cratchits in *A Christmas Carol* lived in Camden Town. It is likely that Dickens based both their residences on his childhood home. If you want an impression of what the property looked like, a cursory glance at the row of three houses on the opposite side of the road must suffice.

Where Dickens's wife lived and died

Now turn left into Greenland Road, cross Camden High Street via the traffic lights. You might wish to take a break at Camden Lock and Market, both situated along Camden High Street to the right. Otherwise, keep ahead along Parkway, go over the zebra crossing and turn into Arlington Road. Take the first left into Inverness Street, at the end of which turn left into Gloucester Crescent, and cross to its right side to stop outside No 70. It was to this house that Dickens's wife, Catherine, moved in 1858, following the breakdown of their marriage. The house itself, set back from the road and now converted into flats, is ensconced behind a screen of trees and bushes that cast it into almost perpetual shadow. It was here that Catherine lived out the remainder of her days, a lonely figure. Whilst her estranged husband was alive, she rarely saw her children, with the exception of her eldest son, Charley. 'We were *all* very wicked not to take her part', their daughter Katy – whose wedding Dickens forbade Catherine from attending – later remembered. Yet, for all his cruelty towards her, Catherine never stopped loving Dickens and continued to avidly read his books. She died of cancer on 21st November, 1879. As Catherine lay on her deathbed, she handed Katy – who was nursing her through the long and painful illness – the letters that Dickens had sent her. 'Give these to the British Museum,' she said, adding poignantly, 'that the world may know he loved me once.'

Dickens talks to the animals

Continue to the end of Gloucester Crescent. Bear left onto Oval Road. Cross over the second set of traffic lights and keep ahead along Parkway. Continue over the next traffic lights. Go over the bridge and cross at the next lights to keep straight ahead into Albany Street. In Regent's Park to your right are the London Zoological Gardens of which Dickens was particularly fond. 'He knew the... address of every animal, bird and fish of any distinction,' recalled one friend. 'The delight he took in the hippopotamus family was most exhilarating. He entered familiarly into conversation with the huge, unwieldy creatures, and they seemed to understand him. He chaffed with the monkeys, coaxed the tigers and bamboozled the snakes, with a dexterity unapproachable'.

Henry Mayhew and the London poor

It is with this mental image of Dickens as a 19th-century Dr Doolittle that you continue along Albany Street until, quite a way along on the right, just after crossing Chester Gate, you pause outside No 55. Here was the home of **Henry Mayhew** (1812–87), journalist and founder of *Punch* magazine. A friend of Dickens, and a participant in his amateur theatricals, Mayhew is best remembered for his monumental study *London Labour and the London Poor* published in 1851. Costermongers, watercress sellers, crossing sweeps, water-carriers, nutmeg graters, rag gatherers and dog finders – are just a few of the struggling poor whose daily battles are highlighted in Mayhew's pages. His work still makes for uncomfortable reading, giving as it does a voice to this underclass whose lot it was to wallow in that dark and murky undercurrent that bubbled beneath the respectable surface of Victorian London.

This walk ends at the end of Albany Street where, having crossed Euston Road, you arrive at Great Portland Street Underground Station.

MARYLEBONE TO MARBLE ARCH

This is a pleasant stroll through a quarter of London that is rich in literary associations. The poet Elizabeth Barrett lived here at the time of her secret marriage to Robert Browning. Dickens himself lived at 1 Devonshire Terrace from 1839 to 1851 (it has since been demolished), and the surrounding streets featured in several of his novels, most notably *Barnaby Rudge* and *Dombey and Son*. His great friends William Wilkie Collins and William Macready both lived at houses passed in the course of the tour, and the route also goes past the place where Arthur Conan Doyle created another immortal Victorian character, Sherlock Holmes.

Start:	Great Portland Street Station (Circle, Hammersmith & City, and Metropolitan Underground lines).
Finish:	Marble Arch (Central Underground line).
Length:	2 miles (3.2 km).
Duration:	1½ hours.
Best of times:	Anytime, although the streets are quieter on Sunday.
Worst of times:	None.
Refreshments:	There are pubs, cafés and restaurants along the route.

Waterloo Church
Exit Great Portland Street Station onto Marylebone Road and cross to Holy Trinity Church. Designed by Sir John Soane in 1828, this was one of the 'Waterloo Churches' commissioned by Parliament in thanksgiving for the nation's deliverance from invasion during the Napoleonic Wars. Nineteenth-century parishioners included the **Duke of Wellington, J M W Turner** and **W E Gladstone**, whilst **Florence Nightingale** was a regular visitor. It is now headquarters to the Society for Promoting Christian Knowledge. The church itself can be visited through the bookshop, and makes a refreshing respite from the noise and bustle of the Marylebone Road.

Opposite: This stone relief on a modern office block remembers 1 Devonshire Terrace, Dickens's home from 1839 to 1851. Here he wrote several of his best-known works, the characters from which are featured upon this wall plaque.

WHILE LIVING IN A HOUSE ON THIS SITE
CHARLES DICKENS
WROTE SIX OF HIS PRINCIPAL WORKS.
CHARACTERS FROM WHICH APPEAR
IN THIS SCULPTURED PANEL

The actor who appeared with John Wilkes Booth

Behind the church, the modern Whitehouse Hotel stands on the site of 9 Osnaburgh Terrace, where the Dickens family lodged temporarily in 1844, and where Charles completed the last installment of *Martin Chuzzlewit* (1843–44), prior to leaving England to spend a year in Italy. Leave the church, turn right along Marylebone Road, go third right into Brunswick Place, then left into York Terrace East. A blue plaque on the wall of No 20, on the right, commemorates the actor manager Sir Charles Wyndham (1837–1919), who having trained as a doctor, volunteered to become a field surgeon during the American Civil War. He resigned in 1864 to act on the New York stage, where he appeared alongside the soon-to-be-notorious John Wilkes Booth, who assassinated Abraham Lincoln. Returning to England, he acted with both Sir Henry Irving and Ellen Terry, and in 1899 founded London's Wyndham's Theatre. He died in this house in 1919.

A great Shakespearean actor and friend of Dickens

Continue along York Terrace East, turning right into York Gate, at the end of which on the left is 1 York Gate, formerly the home of the actor manager, **William Macready** (1793–1873), who Dickens first met on 16th June, 1837. Of all his friends, Macready was one of the very few that Dickens never seriously fell out with – which given that Macready's temperament was every bit as prickly and egotistical as Dickens's, was a remarkable achievement. He was godfather to Dickens's daughter, Kate, and later advised Dickens on his amateur theatricals, considering him one of only two non-professionals 'with any pretension to theatrical talent'. Macready was manager of the Covent Garden Theatre (now the Royal Opera House) between 1837 and 1839 and instituted a policy of major Shakespearean revivals as well as presenting plays by contemporary dramatists. Dickens offered several of his own plays to Macready but they were all declined, as was Forster's suggestion that he stage a dramatization of *Oliver Twist*. However, this did not deter Dickens from dedicating *Nicholas Nickleby* (1838–39) to him. The Macreadys moved to York Gate in 1839 and two years later William became the manager of the Drury Lane Theatre. During this period, Charles and Catherine frequently dined with Macready and his wife, and when the Dickenses left for America in 1842, they entrusted the safe keeping of their children to the Macreadys. His management of the theatre, however, met with mixed success and, having suffered heavy financial losses he resigned in 1843 and moved from here to Soho.

St Marylebone Parish Church

Exit right from York Gate, cross Marylebone Road via the crossing to enter St Marylebone Parish Church. Here Robert Browning and Elizabeth Barrett were married on 12th September, 1846. It was also here that the second marriage of

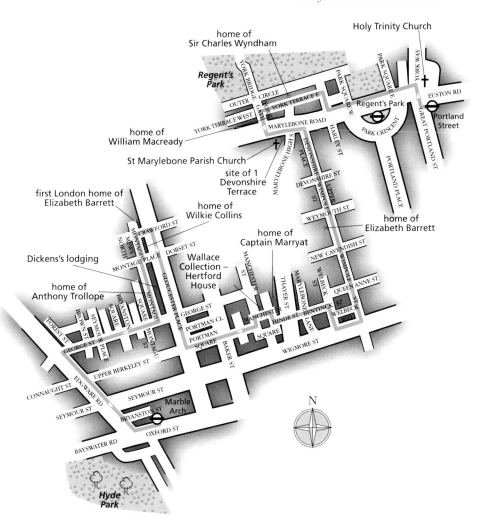

Mr Dombey took place and where little Paul Dombey was christened in *Dombey and Son*.

1 Devonshire Terrace – a home to Dickens

Go right out of the church and pause at the corner of Marylebone High Street, where a plaque on the wall marks the site of 1 Devonshire Terrace, Dickens's home from 1839 to 1851. It was whilst living here that he wrote *The Old Curiosity Shop*, *Martin Chuzzlewit*, *A Christmas Carol*, *Dombey and Son* and *David Copperfield*, characters from which are depicted on the stone relief that now adorns the wall of the modern office block on the site. Turn right into

47

Marylebone High Street and a little way along, on the right, another plaque marks where the entrance to the house stood. It has a quote from Dickens, 'I seem as if I had plucked myself out of my proper soil when I left 1 Devonshire Terrace and could take root no more until I returned to it.'

One of his neighbours here was a Mrs Jane Seymour Hill. A chiropodist, manicurist and also a dwarf, she was the inspiration for the untrustworthy Miss Mowcher, the dwarf beauty-specialist in *David Copperfield*. Recognizing herself in the portrayal, his neighbour fired off a pained missive complaining of his use of her 'personal deformities', and expressing her worry that 'should your book be dramatized and I not protected, madness will be the result'. Dickens sent a conciliatory reply, accepting the justice of her reproach, but assuring her that he had actually based the main part of the character on someone else. However, her solicitor responded, threatening to sue for the 'great mental torture and agony' he had caused her, unless changes were made. Thus Dickens, at the expense of storyline consistency, was compelled to transform Miss Mowcher into a fine upstanding character, allowed to lecture readers that they should not 'associate bodily defects with mental... except for solid reason'.

The birth of Sherlock Holmes

Backtrack and go right along Marylebone Road, and right again into Devonshire Place. Continue ahead into Upper Wimpole Street, the houses of which display

sundry blue plaques commemorating past residents, most of whom were connected with the medical profession. It was at No 2 (towards the end on the left) that Dr Arthur Conan Doyle (1859–1930) set up an ophthalmic practice. So few patients visited that he whiled away his working hours creating the character Sherlock Holmes.

Left: Crowds enjoy the Zoological Gardens at Regent's Park where Dickens used to talk to the animals.

48

Love among the rooms

Continue over Weymouth Street, and pause outside 50 Wimpole Street, the house to which Edward Moulton Barrett brought his family to live in 1838. His daughter, **Elizabeth Barrett** (1806–61), was a semi invalid and was almost constantly confined to her room, with only her pet spaniel Flush for company. To general critical acclaim, however, she embarked upon a productive period of writing poetry. Chief amongst her admirers was the poet **Robert Browning** (1812–89), who wrote to express his feelings for her work, and to tell a woman he had never met, 'I do... love these books with all my heart – and I love you too.' Elizabeth replied, 'I thank you Mr Browning, from the bottom of my heart.' So began 20 months of correspondence, during which the pair exchanged 574 letters. They became engaged shortly after their first meeting, five months after sending their initial letters, but had to keep the fact hidden, since Elizabeth's over protective father had forbidden any of his children to marry. On 12th September, 1846, the couple were married in secret at St Marylebone Church. A week later, accompanied by her faithful spaniel, Flush, they left for Italy where they lived, devoted to each other, until her death.

Continue along Wimpole Street. On the right is No 82 where the novelist **Wilkie Collins** died in 1889. Almost opposite, a blue plaque on the wall remembers former resident **Sir Frederick Treves** (1853–1923), the eminent Victorian surgeon who discovered **Joseph Merrick**, the so-called 'Elephant Man'.

Continue right into Wigmore Street, then first right into Welbeck Street. Number 64, which is second on the left, occupies the site of the London residence of Lord George Gordon in *Barnaby Rudge*. Go first left into Bentinck Street, where, at the long demolished No 18, the Dickens family lived in 1833. Continue ahead into Thayer Street, go right into Manchester Square, and right again into Spanish Place.

Captain Frederick Marryat

At No 4 on the right there is a blue plaque to novelist Captain Frederick Marryat (1792–1848). He had joined the navy at 14 and had become a commander by the age of 23. Following an adventurous career, he resigned in 1830 to dedicate himself to writing. He first made his name with nautical adventure stories, before turning his hand to children's novels, of which his most famous today is *The Children of the New Forest* (1847). He and Dickens became friends in 1841.

The Wallace Collection

Return to Manchester Square and immediately on the right is Hertford House. It is home to the Wallace Collection, assembled by several Marquises of Hertford, one of whom was immortalized by Thackeray as the mysterious and loathsome Marquis de Steyne in *Vanity Fair*. Sir Richard Wallace, after whom the remarkable art collection is named, was the illegitimate son of the 4th Marquess. When Richard died in 1890, he left his entire estate to his widow, who in turn bequeathed it to the nation, on condition it always remained in Central London.

Continue counter clockwise around Manchester Square, exiting right into Fitzhardinge Street. Cross over Baker Street into Portman Square – where the Podsnaps lived in *Our Mutual Friend* – and take the first right into Gloucester Place. Keep to the left side passing No 57, which Dickens rented in 1857 whilst working on *Our Mutual Friend*.

William Wilkie Collins – a favoured friend

A little further along, at No 65, you come to what was the home from 1867 of Dickens's great friend **William Wilkie Collins** (1824–89). Dickens had first met Collins in 1851 when they acted together in Bulwer Lytton's comedy *Not So Bad As We Seem* (*See* page 126). Despite his unusual appearance – Dickens once described his head as being 'triangular with a knob in the middle' – Collins was an enthusiastic and successful womanizer who, in addition to numerous one-night stands, maintained two mistresses and several illegitimate children in separate households. Collins, who was 12 years younger than Dickens, was seen very much as Dickens's protégé, and his two best-known works *The Woman in White* (1860) and *The Moonstone* (1867) were first serialized in *All the Year Round* (see page 138).

Their friendship appears to have deepened in 1857, around the time that Dickens was winning universal acclaim for his portrayal of the heroic **Richard Wardour** in the play *The Frozen Deep* (see page 128). It was at the time when, in Collins's memorable phrase, 'Dickens's domestic skeleton was becoming a pretty big one'. As Dickens became more and more besotted with **Ellen Ternan**, he persuaded Collins to tour the north of England with him, ostensibly to collaborate on *The Lazy Tour of Two Idle Apprentices*, but in reality to enable Dickens to visit Ellen Ternan who was appearing at the Theatre Royal, Doncaster. Collins's libertine lifestyle made him the ideal companion over these troubled years and he began to eclipse John Forster as Dickens's closest friend. Although Dickens did not approve of his daughter Kate marrying Collins's younger brother, Charles, in 1860, they still remained friends. But their relationship cooled considerably around 1867, possibly because Dickens was jealous of Collins's successes with *The Moonstone* and the play *No Thoroughfare*.

Although Collins wrote a further 15 novels, his ill-advised decision to switch from writing mystery and suspense novels to writing those with a social message led to a severe decline in his popularity. His health also began to suffer and, to ease the pain of both gout and neuralgic problems he took ever-increasing amounts of laudanum. It is said that one of his servants died after helping himself to half of his master's usual dose. Collins himself died in 1889 at the age of 65.

Sooty sparrows

Continue over Crawford Street to No 99, the first home of the Barrett family when they arrived in London from the countryside in 1835. Elizabeth Barrett was singularly unimpressed by the filth and pollution she found, and wrote to a friend complaining, 'we can't see even a leaf or a sparrow without soot on it'.

Make your way along Crawford Street. Go first left through Montagu Mews North. Turn right into Montagu Place and first left onto Montagu Square where at No 39 **Anthony Trollope** (1815–82) lived from 1873 to 1880. Turn right onto George Street and, having passed Bryanston Square on the right, near to which lived Mr Dombey in *Dombey and Son*, keep ahead and go left along Edgware Road.

Round about the Marble Arch

One day in 1849, Dickens and **Mark Lemon** were walking along Edgware Road when a youth named Cornelius Hearne picked Lemon's pocket. The two men gave chase, apprehended him and handed him over to the authorities. During the subsequent trial at which they gave evidence, Hearne accused them of being criminals who made 'their living by buying stolen goods'. He was also adamant that he recognized Dickens from a previous spell in prison 'where he was put in for six months, while I was their for only two'. Amid general courtroom mirth at the accusation, 19-year-old Hearne was sentenced to three months hard labour.

Continue to the end of Edgware Road, bearing left along Marble Arch. The Marble Arch itself stands marooned on its concrete island to your right, the London traffic flitting round it at ever-decreasing speeds. It was designed by **John Nash** in 1828 and originally stood in front of Buckingham Palace. Unfortunately, it proved too narrow for the royal carriages to pass through and was moved to its present location in 1851.

The Odeon Cinema on the left stands on the site of Hyde Park Place, where Dickens had his last London home. He wrote about it to his American friend J T Fields: 'we live here in a charming house, until the 1st of June... I have a large room here, with three fine windows overlooking the Park.' On Sunday, 22nd May 1870, John Forster dined here with him and they discussed the sudden death of Mark Lemon, news of which Dickens had received that day. He began reminiscing about other recently deceased friends lamenting that none were 'beyond his sixtieth year, very few even fifty.' Forster's suggestion that 'it is no good to talk of it' prompted the reply, 'We shall not think of it the less.' This was the last time that Forster saw Dickens alive.

Continue ahead over Great Cumberland Place and along Oxford Street. A little way down on the left is Marble Arch Station where this walk finishes.

HAMPSTEAD

Hampstead is a delightful village perched on a hill 440 feet (135 metres) above sea level. There has been a settlement here for over a thousand years, and since the Middle Ages Londoners have journeyed here to escape the often disease-ridden, certainly cramped and unimaginably filthy streets in the city below. Much of this walk centres on parts of Hampstead Heath's 800 wild acres (323.8 ha), which, thanks to a determined preservation battle fought by the local residents throughout much of the 19th century, was finally given over to 'the use of the public forever' by an Act of Parliament in 1872. Dickens knew the heath well, and was fond of walking here. All in all, the walk, though not brimming with sites, is a fascinating stroll through a delightfully rugged wilderness that affords some wonderful views across the London skyline.

Start:	Hampstead Station (Northern Underground line).
Finish:	Kenwood House from where you can take a bus to either Golders Green or Archway Stations (Northern Underground line).
Length:	2 miles (3.2 km).
Duration:	2½ hours.
Best of times:	Daytime and summer evenings.
Worst of times:	Winter evenings.
Refreshments:	Spaniards Inn.

Dickens's friend 'Stanny'

From Hampstead Station go left along Hampstead High Street, cross over the zebra crossing, and bear left to continue ahead until the pavement swings right into Prince Arthur Road. Number 86 on the right was the home of artist Clarkson Stanfield (1793–1867) from 1847 until his death.

At the age of 19, Stanfield was pressed into the navy for a number of years. Returning to civilian life, he became a professional designer of stage scenery, working at theatres in both London and Edinburgh. As an artist, he was renowned for his seascapes, and no less an authority than **John Ruskin** considered him one of the finest realists of all the English painters. Stanfield met Dickens (who came to know him as 'Stanny') in 1837, and the two soon became good friends. Stanfield provided illustrations for several of Dickens's Christmas

Opposite: The peaceful rural ambience of Old Wylde's farm has changed little since Dickens came here with his wife Catherine to mourn the death of his beloved sister-in-law Mary Hogarth; it was known as Collins's Farm in Dickens's Day.

books, and painted the scenery for many of his amateur theatricals. Their only real disagreement occurred when Stanfield, a devout Roman Catholic, refused to illustrate Dickens's *Pictures From Italy* (1846), on account of its satirical treatment of Catholicism. But their friendship survived and, following Stanfield's death in 1867, Dickens paid a moving tribute to him in *All The Year Round* (1859), recalling how, at their last meeting, the artist 'had laid that once so skilful hand upon the writer's breast and told him they would meet again "but not here"... '

Backtrack along the High Street. Go over the crossing by the post office, and bear right then left into Gayton Road, noting the Victorian 'Penfold' post box on the corner. Keep going, past the sturdy, late 19th-century houses, and continue ahead into Well Walk.

Constable's grief

Go over Christchurch Hill and a little further along on the right of Well Walk, No 40 has a plaque to the artist **John Constable** (1770–1837). He and his family moved here in 1827, and a year later his beloved wife, Maria, developed pulmonary consumption. A friend, who came to visit shortly before her death, found that Constable was his usual ebullient self in his wife's presence, but recalled how later, when the artist had taken him into a separate room, he burst into tears without speaking. Despite his grief, however, Constable retained his acerbic wit and, on one occasion, informed the local dairyman, 'In future we shall feel obliged if you will send us the milk and water in separate cans.'

The battle to save Hampstead Heath

Continue to No 44, then cross the road and go up the steps to the side of the Chalybeate Well. Bear right and continue along Well Walk. Cautiously cross the very busy East Heath Road, and go straight ahead onto the rough path for your first encounter with Hampstead Heath. The path becomes more rugged and rural with each step, and soon the noise of the traffic is negligible. Around you stretch 800 acres (324 ha) of wild and untamed heath, which as well as being a playground for Londoners provides a lush habitat for an abundance of wildlife.

However, was it not for a heroic battle fought by local residents in the 19th century, Hampstead Heath would have long since disappeared beneath a concatenation of Victorian developments. In 1829, Sir Thomas Maryon Wilson, Lord of the Manor, attempted to push the first of several Private Acts through Parliament that would enable him to build on the heath. Local residents, led by the banker John Gurney Hoare, were outraged, and began a campaign to save the heath that would last until Sir Thomas's death in 1869. On one occasion, Sir Thomas decided to order the planting of thousands of willows, turkey oaks and firs upon the open heath, an action that brought a howl of indignation from Dickens, who protested at 'such violation of virgin

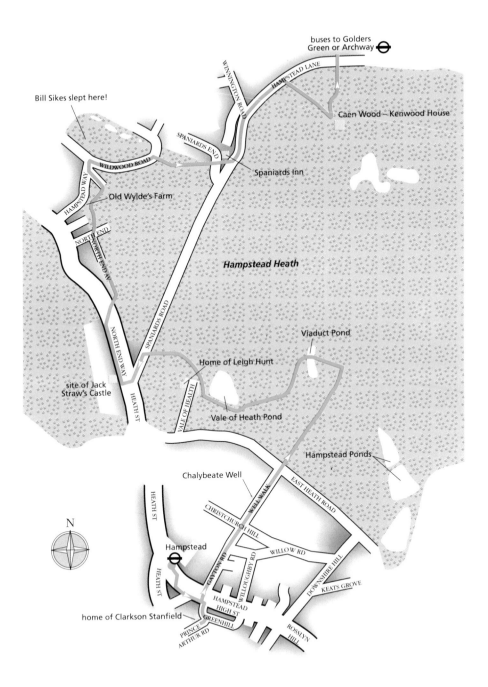

buses to Golders
Green or Archway

Bill Sikes slept here!

HAMPSTEAD LANE

WINNINGTON ROAD

SPANIARDS END

Caen Wood – Kenwood House

WILDWOOD ROAD

Spaniards Inn

HAMPSTEAD WAY

Old Wylde's Farm

NORTH END

NORTH END AV.

Hampstead Heath

SPANIARDS ROAD

NORTH END WAY

Viaduct Pond

Home of Leigh Hunt

site of Jack
Straw's Castle

HEATH ST

VALE OF HEALTH

Vale of Heath Pond

Hampstead Ponds

Chalybeate Well

EAST HEATH ROAD

WELL WALK

HEATH ST

CHRISTCHURCH HILL

N

Hampstead

GAYTON RD

WILLOUGHBY RD

WILLOW RD

DOWNSHIRE HILL

KEATS GROVE

HEATH ST

HAMPSTEAD
HIGH ST

home of Clarkson Stanfield

PRINCE
ARTHUR RD

GREENHILL

ROSSLYN
HILL

heathland'. However, Sir Thomas's brother and heir, John, proved more amenable to local opinion, and in 1871, sold his estates hereabouts to the Metropolitan Board of Works and the cause was won.

Viaduct Pond and Vale of Health

Keep walking straight ahead. Just before you arrive at a drinking fountain, turn left, and walk to the bridge to look down upon the lily-starred surface of Viaduct Pond. It was one of the Hampstead Ponds that was the subject of a learned paper, presented by Mr Pickwick to the Pickwick Club entitled, 'Speculations on the Source of the Hampstead Ponds, with Some Observations on the Theory of Tittlebats'. What Dickens meant by 'Tittlebats' is anyone's guess.

Go over the bridge. Turn left along the earth path, and bear left at the end. On arrival at a bench, strike out right across the grass and pick up the downhill path. Go straight as it passes into the undergrowth and becomes rather muddy, veering right where the log ramp intersects from the left. Head uphill between the trees. Cross over the clearing and follow another overgrown path that emerges at the Vale of Health Pond. Go straight across to ascend the stepped track to the left of the pond, and follow it as it forks left into the woodlands and leads to a road, along which turn right. You will pass a haphazard huddle of houses and alleyways, which originated in 1777 when a malodorous marsh was drained and the land developed. Its original residents were sweeps and washerwomen, but by the early 19th century it had become a fashionable enclave, and more houses were added until the success of the battle to save the heath ended its expansion. Famous former residents have included **D H Lawrence** (1853–1930) whose home at 4 Byron Villas you pass on the right.

A celebrated libel

Carry on walking ahead, and on arrival at the heath once more, follow the road to the left. Then go left past the two bollards to look over the second gate on the left, where according to the wall plaque, **Leigh Hunt** lived 'in a cottage on this site' from 1816 to 1821. At the time he was editor of *The Examiner*, which he had founded with his brother, John, in 1808, and in whose pages they championed the work of Keats, Shelley and Byron. They also used it as a vehicle for their own radical views, clashing dramatically with the Prince Regent (later George IV), whom they described as 'a corpulent man of fifty... a violator of his word... a despiser of domestic ties... who has just closed half a century without one single claim on the gratitude of his country... ' Called upon to refrain from further attacks, the brothers refused, and were sent to prison for two years.

A good 'ous

Continue along the alleyway, turn right and, on re-emerging at the road, cross back onto the heath to ascend the steep uphill track. At the end of the first incline, take the right rough path through the gorse. On arrival at a fence, veer left to head for the clearly visible main road, pausing first to look back at the view over the Vale of Health and across the London skyline. Go left along Spaniards Road. Cross at the pedestrian crossing, swerving left then right around the war memorial. Go over the next crossing and pause outside the castellated frontage of what was once Jack Straw's Castle, a favoured tavern of Dickens, who spent many a happy hour here. He once wrote to **John Forster** inviting him to 'muffle yourself up and start off with me for a good brisk walk over Hampstead Heath. I knows a good 'ous there where we can have a red-hot chop... and a glass of good wine... ' This, wrote Forster in his life of *Dickens* (1872–74), 'led to our first experience of Jack Straw's Castle, memorable for many happy meetings in coming years'. However, the bizarre fort-like building that greets today's visitor, which at the time of writing has been sold to a property developers for conversion into private flats, is a 1960s rebuilding of the original.

A financial scandal and political suicide

It was on the heath near to Jack Straw's Castle that the corpse of John Sadleir MP was discovered following his suicide in 1856. This ambitious Irishman arrived in London in 1846 determined to make his fortune. Within two years he had become a Member of Parliament and was chairman of the esteemed City Bank, London and County. By 1850 he was being hailed as one of the richest men in London and enjoyed a lifestyle to match. He rose to even loftier heights in 1853 when he became a junior treasury minister. And then it all went wrong. He was sacked from the Treasury for abusing his position for his own gain. This led to his being dismissed from the bank, causing the meltdown of his largely speculative and, as it transpired, totally fraudulent empire. In February 1856, having left a note confessing that 'I cannot live. I have ruined too many. I could not live and see that agony', he walked to Hampstead Heath, where he poisoned himself with prussic acid.

Dickens, who genuinely despised the mushrooming and frequently corrupt speculative commerce of his age, was at the time writing *Little Dorrit* (1855–57), and promptly immortalized Sadleir as the crooked financier Mr Merdle 'who was simply the greatest Forger and the greatest Thief that ever cheated the gallows'.

Where Dickens came to mourn

Turn right in front of Jack Straw's Castle and descend the delightfully rural North End Way. You arrive at the modern redbrick building where a black plaque marks the site near which John Gurney Hoare – 'the prime mover in the battle to save Hampstead Heath from development' – was born. Cross the busy road via the central bollards, and take the left path by the Hampstead Heath signboard.

Follow it as it swerves immediately right and keep ahead. At the convergence of several paths, take the left track, go down the hill and pass through the barrier onto North End Avenue. Continue ahead, absorbing the rustic ambience of this idyllic backwater, and keep going into North End, where the road soon becomes a gravel path and the buildings, though modern, blend agreeably with their surroundings. Just after the lane sweeps right, pause on the left where, nestling in quiet seclusion beyond the gates, is Old Wylde's. It was to this picturesque, white, weatherboard cottage, known then as Collins's Farm, that Dickens and his wife, Catherine, retreated in 1837, to spend two weeks recovering from the shock of **Mary Hogarth's** death. His description of it as 'a cottage of our own, with large gardens, and everything on a small but comfortable scale' still holds true today.

Spaniards Inn

It was to the fields hereabouts that Bill Sikes fled, having murdered Nancy in *Oliver Twist*, and here that 'he laid himself down under a hedge and slept'. The rugged wildness can hardly have changed since then and, as you continue along the path, you are struck by its pastoral timelessness. At the end of the path, bear left to descend the hill and go right along Wildwood Road. Just before it bends left, turn right past the green barrier, ascend the pathway, and at the end, turn left along Spaniards Road. Ease your way round what must be one of London's most precarious thoroughfares, and go left into Spaniards Inn to enjoy a well earned, calming draught.

This atmospheric, low-beamed, 16th-century hostelry is supposedly named after two Spanish brothers and joint proprietors, who argued over a woman and killed each other in a duel. Another regular haunt of Dickens, it was to the garden of Spaniards Inn that Mrs Bardell and her friends came to take tea in *Pickwick Papers*. Here she was arrested for debt and conveyed to the Fleet Prison by Mr Jackson of the legal firm Dodson and Fogg.

During the Gordon Riots of 1780, the rioters passed by the inn on the way to destroy Kenwood House, then the home of the Earl of Mansfield. The quick thinking landlord of the Spaniards offered them unlimited refreshment and managed to stall them long enough for the military to arrive and prevent the destruction of Kenwood.

It is here that this walk ends. You can, if you wish, make the long trek back along Spaniards Road, past Whetstone Pond and down Heath Street, to return to Hampstead Underground Station. Alternatively and highly recommended, leave the inn and continue along Hampstead Lane, where a little way along on the right is Kenwood House. This stunning heath-side villa, set in its own extensive grounds, contains the most important private painting collection ever given to the nation. From Hampstead Lane outside Kenwood, you can take buses to either Golders Green or Archway Underground stations.

HIGHGATE

This walk takes in the pleasing and atmospheric village of Highgate, its hillside location affording spectacular views across the London skyline. Despite the heavy traffic, the village still has a 19th century feel about it and remains much as it was when Dickens knew it. He first came here in 1832 and evidently liked what he found, coming back many times in later life. Indeed, it was to Highgate that he sent his most autobiographical character, David Copperfield, to live. Several members of his family, including his mother and father and his little daughter, Dora, are buried in Highgate's West Cemetery. In addition to this walk, Highgate has many other narrow alleyways and hidden nooks that are worth exploring.

Start:	Highgate Station (Northern Underground line).
Finish:	Archway Station (Northern Underground line).
Length:	2¼ miles (3.6 km).
Duration:	2 hours.
Best of times:	Anytime, although coinciding your walk to take in a tour of Highgate Cemetery is recommended.
Worst of times:	Winter evenings.
Refreshments:	Gatehouse PH, The Flask PH, and several cafés on Highgate High Street.

At the station take the exit marked Highgate Village and turn right onto Archway. Go left over the traffic lights, bear right then immediately left onto Southwood Lane. When you arrive at the point where Jackson's Lane joins from the left, cross over Southwood Lane, and keep walking ahead into the narrow pedestrian path called Park Walk.

Dickens's Highgate lodgings
Turn left onto North Road and stop outside the fourth cream-coloured building along, which is where the entire Dickens family lodged in the August of 1832, during one of John Dickens's attempts to avoid his more persistent creditors. 'The address is "Mrs Goodman's next door to the old Red Lion"', Dickens wrote to his friend Henry Kolle. 'If you can make it convenient to come down, write to me and fix your own day. I am sorry I cannot offer you a bed because we are so pressed for room that I myself hang out at the Red Lion, but should you be disposed to stay all night I have no doubt you can be provided with a bed at the same Establishment.'

Swearing on the Horns

The Old Red Lion, which was demolished in 1900, was just one of the 19 inns that served Highgate's small village population in the 19th century. At each one the ancient ceremony of Swearing on the Horns was religiously observed. Initiates had to kiss a pair of stag antlers that were dangled in front of them, whilst swearing on oath to drink only strong ale, 'never to kiss the maid when the mistress was willing' and so on and so forth. Successful candidates were then granted the Freedom of Highgate, and granted the right to kiss the most beautiful girl in the room. Times change and this venerable old custom is now only performed at a few local hostelries, one of which is the Wrestlers Inn, passed a few doors back.

'A very useful institution'

Continue along North Road, keep ahead over Castle Yard, and at the red brick buildings of Highgate School, go over the pedestrian crossing. The school, was founded in 1565, but by 1816 had fallen into 'complete decay'. Its fortunes were restored under the long Mastership of the Reverend John Dyne (1839–74), and a Royal Commission on secondary education in the 1860s applauded it as 'a very useful institution' doing 'very good work for the upper middle classes'.

After crossing, bear left and continue along North Road, the chapel of Highgate School soars over its somewhat cluttered, disused graveyard to your left. On arrival at Hampstead Lane go over the zebra crossing to enter the Gatehouse.

The Gatehouse

This rambling, part-timbered pub, rebuilt in 1905, is named after the gateway where travellers once paid tolls to cross the Bishop of London's lands. It was this 'high gate' that gave the village its name. The walls are adorned with prints and photographs of bygone Highgate as well as pages of history containing interesting snippets about past residents. Charles Dickens is said to have visited the previous pub on the site, and the first cartoon to appear in *Punch* magazine was sketched here.

Pond Square

Exit the Gatehouse and cross over Highgate West Hill via the pedestrian crossing. Pause to glance at the line of dwellings to the right, anyone of which could have been the little cottage to which David Copperfield brought his

Opposite: Although it bears the date 1663, Highgate's The Flask probably dates from the 18th Century. It was once one of the inns where the venerable custom of 'swearing on the Horns' was observed.

child-bride Dora to live. Pass through the bollards and walk down the slope into Pond Square. Although the water source from which its name is derived was filled in in 1864, the square still possesses a certain charm.

Steerforth's home

Keep to the left pavement and cross South Grove in front of the telephone box, where directly ahead of you is Church House, 10 South Grove. This is believed to have been the 'old brick house at Highgate on the very summit of the hill', where the Steerforths lived, and to which David Copperfield was invited to stay. David described it as '... a genteel old-fashioned house, very quiet and orderly. From the windows of my room I saw all London lying in the distance like a great vapour, with here and there some lights twinkling through it.'

Having admired the handsome façade, go right along South Grove, passing the white-fronted exterior of No 11, home to the Highgate Literary and Scientific Institute, founded in 1839 'for the promotion of useful and scientific knowledge'. The building contains a reading room, lecture hall, library and an excellent local history archive.

A Dickensian landmark where Coleridge lies buried

Continue along South Grove and turn left into the courtyard of St Michael's Church, which dates from 1832. No sooner had building work commenced, than the Vicar of St Pancras attempted to put an unholy spanner in the works by claiming that the church would be in his parish and should not be built. However, his objections were ignored and Highgate acquired its own parish church. In *David Copperfield*, Dickens wrote, 'The church with the slender spire, that stands on top of the hill now, was not there then to tell me the time. An old red-brick mansion, used as a school, was in its place; and a fine old house it must have been to go to school at, as I recollect... ' In 1961 the remains of **Samuel Taylor Coleridge** (1772–1834) were exhumed from his original burial place, the chapel at Highgate School, and re-interred under the central aisle of St Michael's.

The Flask

Retrace your footsteps along South Grove and cross over to pass The Flask, which bears the date 1663, although it most likely dates from the 18th century. **William Hogarth** (1697–1764) an artist whom Dickens admired, is said to have patronized The Flask, once sketching on the spot a fight between two other customers who set upon each other with their beer mugs.

Continue ahead. Cross over Highgate West Hill and go along the narrow road that runs between the railings. The structure atop of the green mound to your right is the reservoir, constructed here by the New River Company in 1854 when

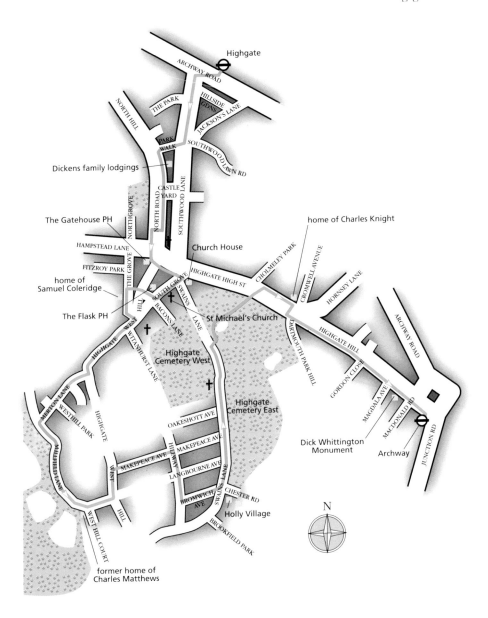

Highgate obtained its first piped water supply. Turn left into The Grove, lined with elegant, handsome houses, and pause outside No 3 where a plaque commemorates the residency of the poet Samuel Taylor Coleridge from 1823 until his death in 1834. Coleridge lived here with Dr James Gillman and his family, and had come to Highgate in the hope that the good doctor could cure him of his addiction to laudanum. A steady stream of eminent visitors, including **Thomas Hood**, **Dante Gabriel Rossetti** and **John Stuart Mill**, made the trek to listen to the brilliant conversation of the white-haired Coleridge. According to **Thomas Carlyle**, he lived 'on the brow of Highgate Hill looking down on London and its smoke-tumult, like a sage escaped from the inanity of life's battle'.

The publican who saved Queen Victoria's life

Continue along The Grove and turn right down Highgate West Hill. The huge building beyond the gates at the junction is Witanhurst, London's largest private residence after Buckingham Palace, and built in 1913 for soap millionaire Sir Arthur Crossfield (1865–1938). Number 40, set back from the road a little way along, stands on the site of the Fox and Crown inn whose landlord, James Turner, earned the nation's gratitude in 1837 for saving the life of Queen Victoria. Fourteen days after her accession, her carriage was descending the hill, when the horse suddenly bolted. Turner raced from his pub, grabbed the reins, and managed to bring the carriage to a halt. Victoria rested in his yard to recover from the shock, and later rewarded him with a Royal Coat of Arms.

Dickens's favourite comedian

Continue down Highgate West Hill and go right along Merton Lane, shaded by towering trees, and bordered on either side by large properties ensconced behind tall screens of leafy boughs. Turn left along Millfield Lane. Despite the presence of some unsightly blocks of flats, the lane, bordered to the right by the eastern section of Hampstead Heath, also boasts several delightful older residences and some quaint cottages. The white block of West Hill Court, on the opposite side as the road veers sharp left, stands on the site of Ivy Cottage, the home of the 19th-century comedian and actor **Charles Matthews** (1776–1835).

Charles Mathews was an idol of the early 19th-century theatre, 'the beau of elegance', as one contemporary described him. Appearing on stage, not in a role, but as himself, Matthews would enthral his audience with a description of a journey he had undertaken, interspersing the narrative with songs, recitations and character impersonations. Dickens claimed that he always went 'to see Matthews when he played', and as a young man, hoping to become an actor himself, intended to perform one of Matthews's routines for his audition at Covent Garden (*see* page 152). A newspaper once stated that Dickens was very much like Matthews in his manner, walk and voice – although adding that Dickens possessed an 'earnestness' that was lacking in Matthews. Dickens was much inspired by the staccato monologue perfected by Matthews for Thomas Holcroft's *The Road to Ruin* (1792). In fact, it was a style that Dickens immortalized with Alfred Jingle in *Pickwick Papers*, the first truly comic character he created.

'She saw with kind eyes'

Continue ahead. Turn left onto Highgate West Hill and a little way along go right through the iron gates into Makepeace Avenue. The Holly Lodge Estate through which you are now walking, was once described as 'London's loveliest garden colony'. It stands on the site of the Highgate home of **Baroness Angela Burdett-Coutts** whose philanthropic endeavours Dickens directed, saying of her charitable giving, 'she saw with kind eyes'. The house, where Dickens would often visit her, and which was a renowned centre of intellectual society in the 19th century, was demolished in 1920.

Holly Village

Go first right into Hillway and prepare to draw breath at one of the most amazing views so far. The London skyline stretches below you, a vista of tall towers peppered with such notable landmarks as St Paul's Cathedral, the London Eye, and the BT Tower. Turn second left into Bromwich Avenue and exit the estate via the gates to cross over Swain's (formerly Swine's) Lane, and pause by the eccentric huddle of Gothic cottages on the opposite side. Holly Village, as this eclectic collection of nine cottages is known, was built in 1865 under the auspices of Angela Burdett-Coutts to provide homes for her retired servants.

Highgate Cemetery

With your back to the village, cross Chester Road and brace yourself for a breathless ascent of Swain's Lane. Through the ivy-clad railings on your right, dark melancholic footpaths twist their way through Highgate's East Cemetery. Leaning tomb and memorial stones struggle to free themselves from a surging tide of creeping vegetation.

Sprawled across 17 hillside acres, and opened in 1839, Highgate Cemetery soon became the most fashionable Victorian necropolis in London. By the dawn of the 20th century over 100,000 people had been buried here in more than 52,000 graves. But, following World War II, there came a severe downturn in the cemetery's fortunes, and the whole place fell into decay until rescued in the 1980s by the enthusiastic and dedicated Friends of Highgate Cemetery.

The Dickens family grave

Pause from your assault on Swain's Lane by the gates of the Eastern Cemetery, which are to your right and where you can purchase a booklet that guides you to the graves of such contemporaries of Dickens as **George Eliot** and **Karl Marx**. To your left is the Western Cemetery, which can only be visited on tours conducted by the 'Friends'. Not normally on the tour, but possible to visit by special request, are the graves of Dickens's parents John and Elizabeth, his daughter, Dora Annie Dickens (1850–51) and his elder sister, Fanny (1810–48).

Original and brilliant genius

Take a deep breath and launch yourself once more up the relentless slope of Swain's Lane. Take the second gate on the right into Waterlow Park, turn immediately left and follow the pathway as it goes right past the tennis courts, and continues ahead to exit the park, where you bear left onto Highgate High Street. Go over the pedestrian crossing, veer right down Highgate Hill and pause outside the second building on the left, Ivy House, formerly the home of author and publisher Charles Knight (1791–1873). Knight praised Dickens publicly as 'a writer whose original and brilliant genius is always under the direction of kindly feeling towards his fellow-creatures'. The two became close friends in the early 1850s, and Knight participated enthusiastically in Dickens's amateur theatricals, as well as contributing 19 articles to *Household Words*. Much of the information in Dickens's *A Child's History of England* (1851–53) was derived from Charles Knight's *Pictorial History Of England*.

Turn again Whittington

Cross at the next traffic lights, bearing left over Dartmouth Park Hill, and continue down Highgate Hill. Once you have crossed Magdala Avenue, pause to admire the scruffy looking stone cat that casts a wary backward glance at London below, and which marks the site where Dick Whittington reputedly heard the bells of Bow Church urging him to 'turn again'. Bill Sikes passed this stone after the murder of Nancy in *Oliver Twist*; and Dick Swiveller, when taunted by the evil Quilp in *The Old Curiosity Shop*, threatened to run away 'towards

Highgate, I suppose. Perhaps the bells might strike up "Turn again, Swiveller".

Continue down the hill until, on the right, you arrive at Archway Underground Station and the conclusion of your stroll through Highgate village.

Left: Young Dick Whittington rests on Highgate Hill and hears the bells urge him to 'turn again'.

66

ISLINGTON AND HIGHBURY

This walk will take you through one of London's more chic neighbourhoods. It begins with a look at the life of Joseph Grimaldi, the clown whose antics Dickens admired as a boy and whose memoirs he later edited. It passes the homes of several people who had reason to regret their involvement with Dickens, and passes through the almost-rural Canonbury Square. There is also the opportunity to stand outside Park Cottage, where Ellen Ternan, the girl who may have been Dickens's mistress, lived. Had this secret become public during his lifetime, it would most certainly have destroyed his reputation, if not his career.

Start:	Angel Station (Northern Underground line).
Finish:	Highbury and Islington Station (Victoria Underground line).
Length:	2½ miles (4 km).
Duration:	2 hours.
Best of times:	Anytime.
Worst of times:	At night is not advised.
Refreshments:	Several pubs and cafés along the route.

Leave Angel Station and turn left along Islington High Street, cross Goswell Road at the traffic lights and continue ahead into St John's Street. A little way along, go over the pedestrian crossing where, as the road bears right and becomes Rosebery Avenue, you are greeted by a scruffy line of 19th-century townhouses.

The cheers of a clown
It brings you to the sleek, modern exterior of Sadler's Wells Theatre, the recent rebuilding of which belies the fact that it is one of London's oldest theatre sites, founded in 1683 by Thomas Sadler. In April 1781, at the age of three, Joseph Grimaldi (1778–1837) made his stage debut at Sadler's Wells, and went on to enjoy a successful theatrical career, during which he almost single-handedly laid the foundations for the pantomime tradition. Dickens had fond childhood memories of seeing Grimaldi perform at Sadler's Wells and, as a budding author, one of his first projects was to edit the *Memoirs of Joseph Grimaldi* (1837).

Continue along Rosebery Avenue, cross over the pedestrian crossing, bear right and go left by the ornate Finsbury Town Hall. Turn left into Garnault Place, follow it right, cross Tysoe Street at the zebra crossing, then veer left and ahead into Exmouth Market. A little way along on the left, a blue plaque above the doorway of 56A informs that 'Joseph Grimaldi, Clown', lived here from 1818 to 1828. This is the only one of his houses to have survived.

Dickens's friend and illustrator
Backtrack to Tysoe Street, go over the crossing, swinging left onto Rosoman Street, then over Rosebery Avenue and ahead into Amwell Street.

A fairly long walk brings you to Nos 69 to 71, where **George Cruikshank** (1792–1878) lived from 1824 to 1849. A leading caricaturist of his day, his long career spanned both the Regency and Victorian periods, and his work depicted the social and political changes of the age. Dickens first met Cruikshank on 17th November, 1835, and the two became close friends. As illustrator of *Sketches By Boz* and *Oliver Twist*, Cruikshank's depictions of 'Oliver asking for more' and of 'Fagin in the condemned cell' are two of the most memorable illustrations from all Dickens's books. But later in life, Dickens took exception to Cruikshank's zealous support of the temperance movement, and their relationship was permanently severed. When Dickens died, Cruikshank reportedly observed that 'One of our greatest enemies is gone' and in a later letter to *The Times* claimed that it was he, not Dickens, who had suggested the idea, plot and characters of *Oliver Twist*.

The death of a clown
Continue, keeping ahead into Claremont Square. Turn left along the busy and unattractive Pentonville Road. Go right at the next traffic lights into Rodney Street, and enter Joseph Grimaldi Park on the left. This peaceful oasis was formerly the churchyard of St James's Chapel, Pentonville, and a few tombstones lie hidden amongst the bushes. Straight ahead is the railed tomb of Joseph Grimaldi, where an information board gives a brief synopsis of the life of the father of modern clownery, in whose memory clowns are still known as 'Joeys'.

Thomas Hosmer Shepherd
With your back to the tomb turn left through the gap in the wall, pass to the right of the circular flower bed and exit the park through the gates in the far right corner. Go right over Rodney Street, along Donegal Street, and left into Penton Street. On arrival at the rustic looking Church of St Silas, cross the pedestrian crossing, bear left then right into Tolpuddle Street and hurry past the modern severity of Islington Police Station to go over the zebra crossing

Opposite: The houses that enclose the delightfully rustic Canonbury Square have changed little since the likes of actor Samuel Phelps and author George Orwell resided here.

and ahead into Cloudesley Road. Turn second right into Batchelor Street, where a row of pretty town cottages rescues you from the urban nightmare. Keep ahead passing No 26, which was once the home of Thomas Hosmer Shepherd (1793–1864) an artist and engraver whose work captured the rapidly changing and expanding landscape of 19th-century London.

'The emigrant's friend'
On arrival at the pedestrian crossing go over Liverpool Road, bear right, then first left into Bromfield Street. Go left into Parkfield Street, veer right along Berners Road and left onto Upper Street. Cross the pedestrian crossing, bear right and having passed Camden Passage on the left – where a veritable cornucopia of antique shops offer all manner of Victoriana for sale – go first left into the attractive Charlton Place. Number 32 on the right was the home of Caroline Chisholm (1808–77), known as 'the emigrant's friend'. It was here (then 3 Charlton Crescent) that she set up her Family Colonisation Loan Society to provide financial assistance for families wishing to seek new lives in Australia. Dickens, who was a keen supporter of the cause, visited Mrs Chisholm, but was most struck by the seemingly neglected appearance of her six children. 'I dream of Mrs Chisholm, and her housekeeping,' he wrote to Angela Burdett-Coutts, 'The dirty faces of her children are my continual companions.' The character of the philanthropic missionary Mrs Jellyby in *Bleak House* who 'had very good hair, but was too much occupied with her African duties to brush it' was partly based upon Caroline Chisholm.

'The original kind-hearted, veritable, Elia'
Continue to the end of Charlton Place, turn left onto Colebrooke Row and enjoy a gentle stroll along what is one of the most bucolic sections of the walk so far, to arrive at Bridal Mews. Opposite No 53, and well-hidden from the gaze of most, stands Colebrooke Cottage, where a plaque on the wall commemorates the fact that 'Charles Lamb 'Elia' (1775–1834), Essayist', lived here. Much revered by early Victorian men of letters, including Dickens, Charles Lamb described this as 'a white house with six good rooms', and lived here from 1823 to 1827. His eccentric wit – 'self-pleasing quaintness' as he termed it – was admirably demonstrated through a series of essays, which he contributed to *The London Magazine* between 1820 and 1823 under the pseudonym 'Elia'. These essays influenced some of Dickens's early work, and in 1838 he urged several acquaintances to read 'the original kind-hearted, veritable Elia'.

Tom and Ruth Pinch find themselves a house
Continue along Colebrooke Row, turn left into St Peter's Street, right along Essex Road and cross the pedestrian crossing, and bear left, then right onto Islington

Green. Veer right along Upper Street, pass over Gaskin Street, go over the pedestrian crossing, and bear right for what is a longish walk, passing a sequence of shops and offices. Keep walking ahead over Almeida Street. Turn left into the narrow Terrett's Place, where No 3 in the corner is said to be the 'singular little old-fashioned house, up a blind street', where Tom and Ruth Pinch, having spent hours house-hunting in *Martin Chuzzlewit*, 'discovered two small bedrooms and a triangular parlour, which promised to suit them well enough'.

Samuel Phelps, the great tragedian

Backtrack, turning left along Upper Street and cross the pedestrian crossing towards the grey bulk of Islington Town Hall. The Islington Museum to the right is well worth a visit. Veer left off the crossing, then turn right into Canonbury Lane. At the end of this road, proceed anti-clockwise around Canonbury Square, pausing at No 8, where a commemorative plaque remembers Samuel Phelps (1804–78), who lived here from 1844 to 1867. He was certainly an acquaintance, if not a close friend of Dickens.

Phelps was a renowned tragedian, whose performance as Macbeth at Sadler's Wells in 1844 amidst 'a hideous medley of fights, foul language, cat calls, shrieks, yells, oaths, blasphemy, obscenity, apples, oranges, nuts, biscuits, ginger beer, porter and pipes' illustrates the type of audience mid 19th-century actors had to endure. The fact that Phelps's daughter was expelled from her boarding school at the request of another parent who was outraged to discover that she came from a family of actors, also says much about the genuine contempt that 'decent' Victorians felt towards the acting profession. Phelps, however, remained actor-manager at Sadler's Wells for 20 years, transforming it into a well-thought-of and highly esteemed theatre, renowned for its productions of Shakespeare. In the early 1850s he employed the actress Mrs **Frances Ternan**, of whom we will hear more later on in the walk.

Continue down the steps, cross the busy Canonbury Road and keep going anti-clockwise until you arrive outside No 28 where George Orwell (1903–50) lived. His essay 'Charles Dickens' in *Inside the Whale*, 1940 was, according to *The Oxford Reader's Companion to Dickens* 'a milestone in the history of Dickens's reputation'.

Turn right out of Canonbury Square; continue into Canonbury Place and stop outside the dark brick Canonbury Tower, built around 1562 by the monks of St Bartholomew's Priory in the City of London. **Oliver Goldsmith** (1730–74) lived here between 1762 and 1764, and as a young man **Robert Seymour** (1708–1836) had rooms here.

Continue along Canonbury Place, keeping ahead into Canonbury Park South. Go right onto St Paul's Road, cross the crossing, bearing right and, after a short walk, turn left into St Paul's Place then left at the end into Northampton Park.

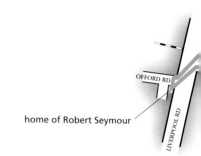

home of Robert Seymour

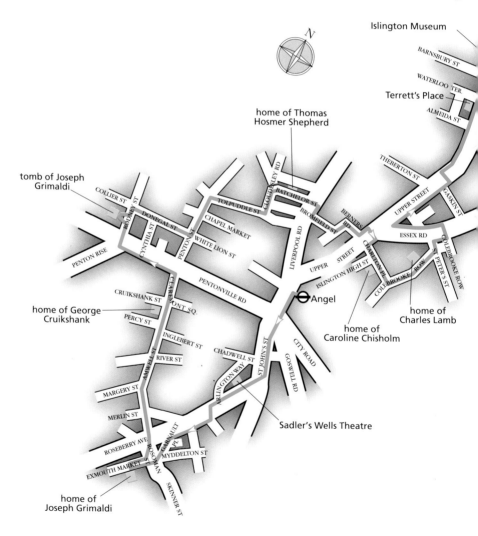

Islington Museum

home of Thomas
Hosmer Shepherd

Terrett's Place

tomb of Joseph
Grimaldi

home of George
Cruikshank

home of Caroline Chisholm

home of Charles Lamb

Angel

Sadler's Wells Theatre

home of
Joseph Grimaldi

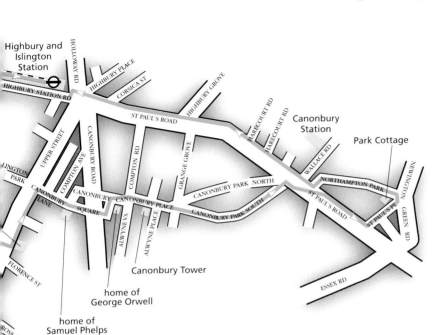

Highbury and
Islington
Station

HOLLOWAY RD

HIGHBURY PLACE

CORSICA ST

HIGHBURY STATION RD

HIGHBURY GROVE

ST PAUL'S ROAD

HARECOURT RD

HARECOURT RD

Canonbury
Station

WALLACE RD

Park Cottage

NEWINGTON

CANONBURY ROAD

UPPER STREET

COMPTON AVE

COMPTON RD

GRANGE GROVE

CANONBURY PARK NORTH

NORTHAMPTON PARK

ISLINGTON
PARK

CANONBURY
SQUARE

CANONBURY

CANONBURY PLACE

CANONBURY PARK SOUTH

ST PAUL'S ROAD

ST PAUL'S PL

GREEN RD

CANONBURY
LANE

ALWYNE VS

ALWYNE PLACE

FLORENCE ST

Canonbury Tower

home of
George Orwell

ESSEX RD

ROSS ST

home of
Samuel Phelps

A blot on Dickens's good name

Park Cottage, the squat grey building immediately on the left was, from the spring of 1855, the home of the widowed actress Mrs Frances Ternan and her daughters Fanny, Maria and Ellen. In 1857, Dickens was creating a sensation on the London stage with his performance as Richard Wardour in *The Frozen Deep* (1857) (*see* page 128). There were plans to take the production to Manchester's Free Trade Hall, and Dickens worried that his daughters and sister-in-law, who were acting in the smaller London venues, would be unable to perform in the larger arena. He therefore approached his friend, the actor and playwright Alfred Wigan, and asked if he could suggest an actress to play the female lead. Wigan suggested the Ternans. Thus, in August 1857, Charles Dickens met the family with whom he would develop a close personal relationship, albeit a relationship that became one of Victorian England's most closely guarded secrets.

When Dickens visited Park Cottage he was singularly unimpressed with the cramped conditions and pronounced them unhealthy and unwholesome. In time, he would become a generous patron to the Ternan family. But it is over the exact nature of his relationship with Ellen Ternan – Nelly to her family – that speculation has raged ever since it was first made public in the 1930s. There is no doubt that Dickens was besotted by her, and it is almost certain that it was meeting Ellen Ternan that led him to abandon his wife and break up the family home. But opinion is divided as to whether or not the two were actually lovers, and much has been written presenting compelling arguments both for and against. The facts strongly suggest the former. If this was the case, and their relationship had become public knowledge, it could so easily have created a scandal that would have ended the career of the author who, above all others, was worshipped as a staunch advocate of domestic harmony and the very embodiment of Christian virtue. However, since detailed analysis is beyond the remit of this book, I would suggest reading Peter Akroyd's masterful biography *Dickens*, and Claire Tomalin's excellent biography of Ellen Ternan, *The Invisible Woman* in order to reach your own conclusion.

The suicide of Robert Seymour

Continue along Northampton Park. Turn right onto St Paul's Road and just keep going until you arrive at Highbury Corner. Go over the crossing, bear left past Highbury and Islington Station, then turn first right along Highbury Station Road, at the top of which, go left onto Liverpool Road. Go over the crossing and continue along the opposite side until, just over Offord Road, you arrive at a concrete wall, behind which No 377 hides. This was the home of **Robert Seymour** (1798–1836), one of the most popular comic illustrators of the 1830s. In the autumn of 1835, he approached the publishers Chapman and Hall with a series of sketches he had drawn depicting the mishaps of a group of comical cockneys known as the 'Nimrod Club'. The publishers, who had asked several authors to write the captions without success, contacted the young journalist Charles Dickens, who was starting to make a name for himself with his *Sketches*. From the outset Dickens was determined to keep overall control of the project, which was re-named *Pickwick Papers*, much to Seymour's consternation.

On 17th April, 1836, Dickens invited Seymour to 'take a glass of grog' at his lodgings in Furnival's Inn. The meeting, the only time the two men actually met, was tense, as Dickens demanded that Seymour change one of his illustrations. Dickens tried to be conciliatory, but Seymour having suggested that a younger and more adaptable artist might 'suit Mr Dickens better', cut the meeting short and left. The next day, having worked on the new designs as requested, he left a note of apology to 'the best and dearest of wives', went into his garden shed, and shot himself through the head.

Dickens moved quickly to recover from the blow of Seymour's death and set about finding a new illustrator. Among those who expressed an interest was **William Makepeace Thackeray** (1811–63), who would later become Dickens's chief rival amongst the Victorian literati. However, the job went to **Hablot Browne** (1815–82) who, having adopted the pseudonym *Phiz* to match Dickens's *Boz*, remained Dickens's principal illustrator for the next 23 years.

Retrace your way along Liverpool Road. Go back down Highbury Station Road and turn left to arrive at Highbury and Islington Station where the tour ends.

BLOOMSBURY

It was in and close to the district of Bloomsbury that Dickens lived for much of his life. With the first flush of success that came with *Pickwick Papers*, he moved into a large house here, befitting his new-found status. It is now The Dickens House Museum and is a veritable shrine to his life and times, and the opportunity to visit what is his only surviving London home should on no account be missed. The walk also goes into the breathtakingly splendid British Museum Reading Room, which has recently been restored to its former glory and opened to the public. The section between Russell Square and Coram's Fields provides a glimpse of the way in which poor children were either abused, or simply forgotten by the higher echelons of 19th-century society.

Start:	Tottenham Court Road Station (Central and Northern Underground lines).
Finish:	Russell Square Station (Piccadilly Underground line).
Length:	1½ miles (2.4 km).
Duration:	2 hours.
Best of times:	When the British Museum and The Dickens House Museum are open.
Worst of times:	Evenings.
Refreshments:	The Lamb PH and several other pubs and cafés along the route.

Leave the station via exit three (marked Dominion Theatre) and keep ahead along Tottenham Court Road. Go first right into Great Russell Street and keep to the right side as far as No 14, where to the right of the door is a plaque stating that 'here lived Charles Kitterbell as related by Charles Dickens's *Sketches By Boz, The Bloomsbury Christening*'. It is unusual that the plaque should remember a fictional character as opposed to the author!

The founder of The Lancet
Proceed left along Adeline Place. On arrival in Bedford Square, pause outside No 35, where there is a wall plaque dedicated to surgeon Dr Thomas Wakley (1795–1862), founder of the medical journal *The Lancet* in 1823. He began it as a means of attacking medical malpractice and nepotism, an endeavour that involved him in numerous libel actions. Whilst serving as coroner for West Middlesex Hospital, Wakley often allowed Dickens to attend his inquests, thus providing him with some of the more gruesome material for his novels.

George Du Maurier

Go anti-clockwise round Bedford Square, which happens to be the only complete Georgian square left in Bloomsbury. Turn right into Bloomsbury Street and continue ahead. Upon arrival at the traffic lights, turn left into Great Russell Street. Number 91, the second door along, has a plaque to George Du Maurier (1834–96), who despite being almost blind in one eye, became one of the most admired black and white illustrators of Victorian England and was a regular contributor to *Punch* magazine. Later in life he also became a successful author and created the infamous character Svengali for his novel *Trilby* (1894).

'A masterpiece of absurdity'

Cross the road and take the second right into Coptic Street. Go left along New Oxford Street, and keep walking ahead over Museum Street to pause on the left outside the church of St George's, Bloomsbury, built between 1720 and 1730 by **Nicholas Hawksmoor**. Its bizarre pyramidical steeple, surmounted by a toga-clad statue of George I, was featured in Hogarth's *Gin Lane* (1750); Horace Walpole dismissed it as 'a masterpiece of absurdity', and *A London Guide* published in 1876 decried it as 'the most pretentious and ugliest edifice in the metropolis'. **Anthony Trollope** (1815–82) was christened in the church, and it was the scene in *Sketches By Boz* of the *Bloomsbury Christening*.

A Dickensian bookshop

Backtrack and turn right into Museum Street, which is lined with a pleasing mix of buildings occupied by cafés, pubs and antiquarian bookshops. Turn left into Great Russell Street and a little way along is No 46, the premises of the antiquarian booksellers Jardyce, named for the never-ending legal case in Dickens's *Bleak House*. Their speciality is 'Dickensiana', and they have a great selection of biographies and critical summaries, as well as many first editions of Dickens's novels.

The British Museum Reading Room

Backtrack along Great Russell Street, go over the crossing and go straight ahead into the British Museum. Keep straight ahead into the Great Court and enter the Reading Room. Since the British Library decamped to its new site at Euston, the famous Reading Room has been restored to its 19th-century splendour and is now open to the public for the first time since 1857. Scholars from **Thomas Carlyle** and **George Bernard Shaw** to Lenin and Marx have

Opposite: The Dickens House Museum is the author's only surviving London home, and it was whilst living here that Oliver Twist *and* Nicholas Nickleby *made his name famous throughout the world.*

studied beneath its huge copper dome, one of the largest in the world. Dickens acquired a reader's card for the British Museum Reading Room on 8th February, 1830 and, determined to lift himself out of the straitened obscurity that had marked his life thus far, launched into an intense period of self-education.

Where John Dickens died

Leave the Reading Room and follow the signs pointing north to exit the Museum onto Montague Place. Bear left, then right into Malet Street. At the junction with Kepel Street, go right through the gates to pass through the ground floor of Senate House, the principle building of the University of London, which stands on the site of the house in Keppel Street where **John Dickens** (1785–1851), Charles's father, died. Having gone through the doors on the other side, note the plaque on the wall to the right that marks the site of 16 Keppel Street where Anthony Trollope and his brother Thomas (1810–92) were born.

Dickens moves in

Go through the gates ahead and turn left into Russell Square. This is one of London's largest squares and was laid out in 1800. During the period that he worked in the blacking warehouse, Dickens used to walk across the square on his way to work each day 'with some cold hotchpotch in a small basin tied up in a handkerchief.' Walk clockwise round the square, then turn left into Bedford Way. Go right into Tavistock Square, over the traffic lights, and bear left. A little way up on the right there is a blue wall plaque marking the site of Tavistock House South where Charles Dickens lived from 1851 to 1860. Here he wrote *Bleak House, Little Dorrit*, parts of *A Tale of Two Cities* and *Great Expectations*. It was also whilst living here that he and his wife, Catherine, separated. The house itself was pulled down in 1901.

The sad plight of the climbing boys

Backtrack to the traffic lights. Go left into Tavistock Place, and first right into Herbrand Street, walking straight ahead through an unappealing section of buildings. Go over Bernard Street and take the next left into Guilford Street. Pass the line of dingy 18th-century houses on the left, go over the zebra crossing, keep straight into Queen Anne's Walk and follow it into Queen Square. Turn right into the square and go anti-clockwise until, on the other side of Cosmo Place, you

Left: Sweeps were a frequent site in Victorian London.

78

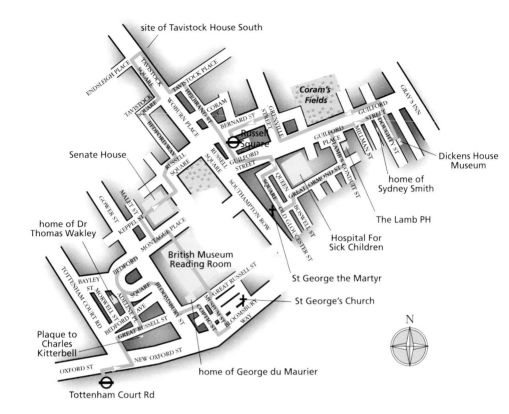

arrive at the church of St George the Martyr. Built in the 18th Century, it was radically altered in 1869 when the architect S S Teulon gave it the mock gothic look that it has today. In 1834, Captain James Smith left a bequest of £1000 for the church to provide an annual Christmas dinner for a thousand 'climbing boys'. These children, aged around nine and ten years old, worked for chimney sweeps, and were employed to crawl up and down chimneys using their tiny bodies to dislodge soot from the flues. It wasn't uncommon for them to get stuck, and many died of suffocation as a result. Those who survived would come down with their bare arms and legs raw and bloodied from chafing the sides. They would be made to stand against a hot fire to dry the blood and then the wounds were rubbed with brine to toughen the flesh. Many died miserably of cancers brought on by their workday environment. In 1840, the Climbing-Boy Bill made it illegal to employ children for this job, but the fury of fastidious householders ensured that the practice continued until The Chimney Sweepers Act (1875) made it illegal for anyone under the age of 21 to be sent up a chimney to clean it.

Above: *Thomas Coram established the Foundling Hospital to care for the huge numbers of children abandoned by their parents on the streets London.*

The Hospital for Sick Children

Continue round the square, noting the water pump that dates from the early 1900s when there was a reservoir in the square. However, times have changed and the pump now carries a warning: 'Unfit For Drinking'. Go right into Great Ormond Street, where on the left is the Hospital for Sick Children, founded by **Dr Charles West** in 1851. A Parliamentary commission in 1843 had revealed that of 2,363 patients in all London's hospitals only 26 of them were under the age of 10. Yet the annual mortality rate amongst children was an astonishing 21,000. In other words, children were being excluded from even the most basic medical treatments.

However, in its early years the hospital still attracted little public assistance and by the mid-1850s it still had only 31 beds. Indeed, its most enthusiastic benefactors were the poor themselves from whom £50 contributed in single pennies had been received every year since its opening. On 9th February, 1858 the hospital held a charitable dinner in the hope of securing better funding, and Dickens agreed to address the gathering. According to Forster 'he probably never moved any audience so much... ' and £3,000 was raised that night alone. A little while later, he also gave a public reading from *A Christmas Carol* on the hospital's behalf and, as a result of his efforts, the Hospital for Sick Children was properly endowed for the first time. Years later, Dr Charles West would recall, 'Charles Dickens, the children's friend... like the good fairy in the tale, gave her the gift that she should win love and favour everywhere: and so she grew and prospered.'

The Foundling Hospital

Continue along Great Ormond Street. Go left onto Lamb's Conduit Street, keep ahead into Guilford Place and go right onto Guilford Street. On the opposite side of the road is Coram's Fields once the site of the Foundling Hospital. It was established in 1742 by **Captain Thomas Coram** (1668–1751), to ease the plight of some of the huge numbers of abandoned children left by their parents (often unmarried mothers) 'to die on dung hills'. By the 19th century, thanks largely to the efforts of the composer Handel, its chapel had become a fashionable place of worship and Dickens, whilst living nearby at Doughty Street, was a regular member of the congregation. He was also a frequent visitor to the children in the hospital and corresponded with their chaplain, Mr Brownlow, whose name he immortalized in *Oliver Twist*.

The hospital moved to Berkhamsted in 1926 and its buildings here were demolished with the exception of the entrance arcades. Today a children's playground occupies the site and, in a nice reversal of the norm, adults are only allowed to enter if accompanied by a child.

The wit who Dickens conquered

Continue along Guilford Street and take the third right into Doughty Street, passing on the right No 14, the home of Sydney Smith (1771–1845). He was Canon of St Paul's Cathedral, an essayist, pamphleteer and brilliant conversationalist whom Dickens once called the 'great master of wit, and terror of noodles'. Smith confessed, '[I] stood out against Mr Dickens as long as I could' but, after reading *Nicholas Nickleby* was forced to concede that 'he has conquered me'. The two met in 1839 and became the best of friends and Dickens often quoted Smith approvingly. Following Smith's death, Dickens applauded him as 'the wisest and wittiest of the friends I have lost'.

The Dickens House Museum

Cross to the opposite side of Doughty Street, where a little further along on the left is No 48, now The Dickens House Museum. Dickens moved here in March

1837, just as he was starting to find success as an author. Whilst living here, he finished *Pickwick Papers*, wrote *Oliver Twist* and *Nicholas Nickleby* and began work on *Barnaby Rudge*. By the time he moved out, in December 1839, he was famous throughout the world. His daughters Mary and Kate were born here and it was whilst living here that he cemented his life long friendship with **John Forster**. It was the largest house he had lived in so far, and his domestic situation was, for a time, idyllic.

The death of Mary Hogarth

On 7th May, 1837 the idyll was shattered in a way that would affect him personally and professionally for the rest of his days. His sister-in-law, **Mary Hogarth** collapsed in the early hours of the morning – doctors later diagnosed heart failure – and died that afternoon in Dickens's arms. He took a ring from her finger and wore it for the rest of his life. In his extreme grief, it never seemed to occur to him that others might have felt her loss as keenly. Not her parents at losing a daughter. Not even his wife at the loss of a sister. 'Thank God she died in my arms,' he said shortly after her death, 'and the very last words she whispered were of me.'

Professionally, the immediate effect of her death on him was that he was unable to write the next instalments of *Pickwick Papers* and *Oliver Twist.* Instead Dickens and Catherine went to the wilder reaches of Hampstead to recover (See pages 57–8). But, in the years ahead, Mary Hogarth would be reincarnated time and again in his novels, becoming the all too perfect heroines such as Rose Maylie in *Oliver Twist,* Florence Dombey in *Dombey and Son,* Agnes Wickfield in *David Copperfield,* Lucy Manette in *A Tale of Two Cities* and, most famously Little Nell the unbelievably saccharine heroine of *The Old Curiosity Shop.* As an article in *The Dickensian Magazine* put it in 1937, on the centenary of her death, '[Mary Hogarth] is part of the world's literature'. Personally, her death may even have stunted his emotional growth leaving him with an idealized image of womanhood, which must have affected his relationship with Catherine. As time and years of child bearing took their toll on Catherine Dickens, she was more and more unable to live up to his ideal. For the rest of his life, Dickens would search for a new Mary Hogarth, and it could be said that the seeds of the later collapse of his marriage were sown in the room in Doughty Street where she died.

In 1922, The Dickens Fellowship rescued the house from demolition and, a few years later, opened it to the public. It is now a treasure trove of relics and articles that depict his life and times and is the perfect end to any tour of Dickensian London.

Exit the Dickens House Museum. Backtrack left along Guilford Street, turn right onto Grenville Street, and left along Bernard Street where a little way along is Russell Square Underground Station where this tour ends.

FITZROVIA

The district of Fitzrovia, with its shabby Georgian streets and buildings possesses a cosmopolitan and bohemian character that has, over the years, attracted an eclectic mix of, mostly impecunious, artists, writers and poets. Indeed the name 'Fitzrovia' wasn't given to the area until the 1940s, and before that it was simply known as Fitzroy Square. On this short walk, you will journey through the square and pass several of Dickens's childhood residences. Other sections, such as the journey along a featureless section of Gower Street must now, sadly, be walks of imagination. However, as you also come upon the possible real-life inspiration of Miss Havisham and learn a little more of Dickens's complicated private life, your imagination will, at least, have plenty to fire it!

Start:	Euston Square Station (Circle, Hammersmith & City and Metropolitan Underground lines).
Finish:	Tottenham Court Road Station (Central and Northern Underground lines).
Length:	1 mile (1.6 km).
Duration:	1 hour.
Best of times:	Anytime.
Worst of times:	None.
Refreshments:	Fitzroy Tavern, and many other pubs and restaurants passed on the route.

Leave Euston Square Station via the Gower Street exit and turn left along Gower Street, passing through the drab townscape, which 200 years ago formed the extent of London's northern border, and where a pastoral landscape of market gardens and green fields would have stretched behind you. Turn first right into Grafton Way, and pause immediately to gaze across at University College Hospital, Alfred Waterhouse's gothic extravaganza of red brick and terracotta, which was built between 1897 and 1906.

Mrs Dickens's establishment

In Dickens's childhood the section of road along which you have just strolled was known as Gower Street North, and the hospital stands on the site of No 4. The Dickens family moved to this address in 1823. With her husband John plunging more and more into debt, Charles's mother attempted to save the family fortunes by opening a school for young ladies. A brass plate, bearing the legend 'Mrs Dickens's Establishment', was placed outside the house, whilst Charles and the other children were sent to distribute advertising circulars around the neighbourhood. But, as Dickens later told **John Forster**, 'nobody ever came to the school, nor do I recollect that anyone ever proposed to come, or that the least preparation was made to receive anybody'.

A London gem
Continue to the end of Grafton Way. Turn right into Tottenham Court Road and then left into Warren Street. Keep ahead. Take the third left into Fitzroy Street and follow it into Fitzroy Square, a true gem amongst London squares. Begun in the 1770s, completed in the 1820s, and tastefully restored following bomb damage in World War II, it boasts an impressive list of former residents. They include **George Bernard Shaw** (1856–1950), Victorian Prime Minister Lord Salisbury (1830–1903) and Virginia Woolf (1882–1941), all of whom lived at No 29. In 1865, Pre-Raphaelite painter Ford Maddox Brown (1821–93) moved into No 37, which **Thackeray** had already immortalized as the residence of Colonel Newcome in his novel *The Newcomes* (1853–55). Here, Maddox Brown and his wife, Emma, entertained many luminaries of the age at their famous fortnightly evenings.

'A glass of punch and a cigar'
Leave the square along the continuation of Fitzroy Street, and towards the end pause outside No 25 on the right. Outwardly this house has changed little since 1832 when the Dickens family, attempting yet again to avoid John's creditors, came to live here. Fittingly, it has a genuinely down-at-heel air about it. Gazing up at its shabby, genteel, balconied windows, it is easy to picture Charles sitting behind any one of them; a young reporter, determined to escape the constraints that his father's improvidence had placed upon him, and writing to his friends inviting them to visit him here and enjoy 'A glass of punch and a cigar'.

Daniel Maclise
Continue, crossing Maple and Howland Streets and walk straight ahead into Charlotte Street. A little way along pause outside No 85, which was the home of the artist **Daniel Maclise** (1806–70) who lived here from 1835 to 1837. During this time he began to make his name providing line portraits of famous figures for *Fraser's Magazine*. He later illustrated several of Dickens's Christmas books.

Dickens's childhood home
Go next right into Tottenham Street, left along Cleveland Street and pause outside No 22 on the left. It was here, above a grocery shop kept by a certain John Dodd,

Opposite: Fitzroy Square was the address Dickens had printed on his business cards whilst he worked at Doctors' Commons. A hundred years later the square would lead to the district hereabouts being dubbed 'Fitzrovia'.

later to become one of John Dickens's many creditors, that the Dickens family lodged from 1814 to 1816. The family then moved from here to Chatham in Kent where Charles began what he would always remember as the happiest period of his childhood. The family returned to lodge at No 22 again in 1830, during his father's perennial attempts to avoid his creditors with a series of quick moves. This was the address that Charles gave when taking out his reader's ticket at the British Museum on his eighteenth birthday that year, and which he had printed on his business cards whilst working at Doctors' Commons (*see* page 6–7). The house has survived relatively unscathed and, although scarred and battered by age, it makes for a delightful flight of fancy to picture the young, eager and ambitious Charles Dickens hurrying in and out of its Georgian front door.

The white woman of Berners Street

Continue to the end of Cleveland Street. Turn right along Mortimer Street, passing on the right the imposing frontage of the Middlesex Hospital. Turn left into Berners Street, where a walk of the imagination is required. However, Dickens does come to the rescue, offering a literary morsel to mull over. This is the street with which Dickens associated the White Woman of whom he writes in his essay 'When We Stopped Growing':

> '*Dressed entirely in white with a ghastly white plaiting round her head and face inside her white bonnet… She is a conceited old creature, cold and formal in manner, and evidently went simpering mad on personal grounds alone – no doubt because a wealthy Quaker wouldn't marry her. This is her bridal dress.*'

He remembered this enigmatic woman from his boyhood days, and later she would become one of the sources for Miss Havisham in *Great Expectations*.

'The Berners Street affair'

In 1858, Ellen and Maria Ternan moved to 31 Berners Street (now demolished), which was a convenient address for both actresses to walk to and from work. Unfortunately, their unsociable hours brought them to the notice of the police who, believing them to be prostitutes, stopped them one night and subjected them to a barrage of insulting questions. Outraged, Dickens demanded an apology from Scotland Yard, and insisted that the officer in question be disciplined. Thereafter, he referred to the incident as 'The Berners Street Affair'.

A literary landmark

Turn left into Eastcastle Street, left again along Newman Street and, just after No 26 on the right, squeeze your way through Newman Passage, which becomes even narrower towards the end. It's not difficult to see why this was once

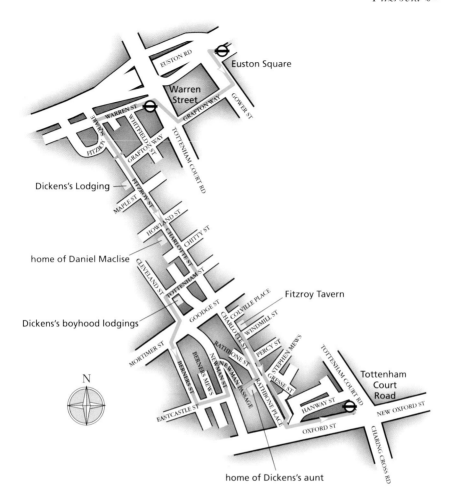

nicknamed locally 'Jekyll and Hyde Alley'. Having emerged onto Rathbone Street, cross over the road and through the slender Percy Passage at the end of which, bear right onto Charlotte Street. Cross to the Fitzroy Tavern, which began life as a Coffee House in 1833. Rebuilt as a magnificent Victorian pub in 1897, by the 1920s it had become a favourite of bohemian artists and writers. Its walls are adorned with its history, along with portraits of former drinkers.

Leave the pub, cross over Windmill Street and continue to the end of Charlotte Street. Number 7, on the right, stands on the site of the house where Dickens's aunt, Janet Brown, lived in 1829. Bear right, then left into Rathbone Place at the end of which turn left and allow the ceaseless surge of Oxford Street to sweep you to Tottenham Court Road Underground Station and the end of this walk.

SOHO

Dickens's first experience of this cosmopolitan neighbourhood was as a young boy when, newly arrived in London, he would visit his Uncle Thomas Barrow who was 'laid up' with a leg injury at a house in Gerrard Street. Later, the area would feature many times in his novels, most notably as the place where Dr Manette lived in *A Tale of Two Cities*. But the district was also at the forefront of the great Victorian battles to rid the metropolis of the scourge of epidemics, such as cholera, or of the crime and poverty that was endemic in what were some of London's worst slums. Thus the final section of the walk must, thankfully, be a walk of imagination, with only Dickens's words to illustrate the horrific conditions for which these quarters were once so notorious.

Start & Finish:	Tottenham Court Road Station (Central and Northern Underground lines).
Length:	2 miles (3.2 km).
Duration:	2¼ hours.
Best of times:	Anytime.
Worst of times:	None.
Refreshments:	Crown Tavern, Dog and Duck PH, John Snow PH, and many other pubs and cafés.

The House of Dr Manette

Leave the station via exit 1 (Oxford Street South) and turn right along Oxford Street. Go right into Charing Cross Road and take the fourth turning right (Foyles Bookshop is on the opposite corner) into Manette Street, formerly Rose Street but re-named after Dr Manette, who lived hereabouts in *A Tale of Two Cities*: 'In a building at the back, attainable by a courtyard where a plane tree rustled its green leaves, church organs claimed to be made, and likewise gold to be beaten by some mysterious giant who had a golden arm starting out of the wall... as if he had beaten himself precious...' The golden arm referred to is now preserved at The Dickens House Museum. However, a modern replica of it can be seen protruding from the wall a little way up on the left, whilst Artists' House, No 10 on the right, is a possible contender for the Manette residence.

Continue ahead as the road passes under the buildings and turn right onto Greek Street, passing to the left the Pillars of Hercules pub, an old-fashioned

Opposite: A modern replica of the Broad Street pump. In 1854 the handle was removed to prevent people drinking its water, and as a result ended the cholera epidemic in Soho, proving that the contagion was water-borne.

Soho hostelry, that was almost certainly the Hercules Pillars mentioned in *A Tale of Two Cities*. Continue to the junction with Soho Square and pause outside the House of St Barnabas, another possible contender for 'The quiet lodgings of Dr Manette'. According to Dickens, 'A quainter corner than the corner where the doctor lived was not to be found in London... It was a cool spot, staid but cheerful, a wonderful place for echoes, and a very harbour from the raging streets.' Nowadays, this mid-18th century building provides a temporary hostel for homeless women, although it is open to the public on Wednesday afternoons, and visitors can admire its intricately carved woodwork, rococo plasterwork and wrought-iron staircase.

With your back to the House of St Barnabas, cross over Greek Street and turn next left along Frith Street. Hazlitt's Hotel, a little way along on the left, occupies a premise built in 1718 where painter turned critic and essayist William Hazlitt (1778–1830) died with the words, 'Well, I've had a happy life'.

Doctor John Snow
Continue to the junction with Bateman Street where on the corner is the Dog and Duck pub, established here in 1718 and so little changed since the 19th century that the Victorian Society have applauded it as 'a rare if not unique

survival of a small Victorian town pub'. The building on the opposite corner sports a blue plaque on its Frith Street façade remembering **Dr John Snow** (1813–58), who lived in a house on this site whilst developing a theory that would save the lives of millions. Between 1831 and 1860 there were four major outbreaks of cholera in London. In the epidemic of 1849 53,293 people died, and John Snow became certain that infected

Left: The fact that these Soho brewery workers drank beer rather than water prevented them from catching cholera in 1854.

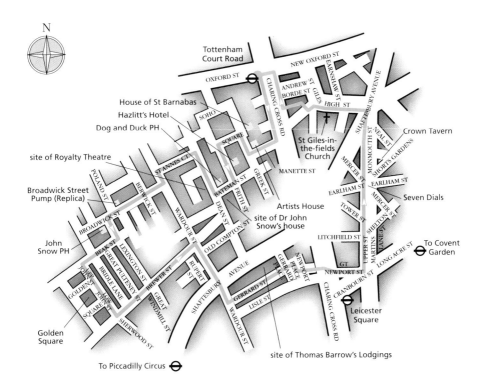

water was to blame. In August 1854, there was a particularly virulent outbreak and Snow began plotting on a map where the deaths were occurring. It became clear that the majority of the victims were drawing their water from the pump in nearby Broad Street. He also noticed that not one of the workers at the local brewery, who drank beer rather than water, died of the disease. On 7th September, Snow persuaded the authorities to remove the handle of the pump to render it unusable and, almost immediately, the epidemic ended.

'Poor little Dickens'

Go right along Bateman Street, then over Dean Street and pause outside Royalty House, which stands on the site of the Royalty Theatre, better known in Dickens's day as Miss Kelly's Theatre. It was here in 1845 that Dickens brought together a group of friends, including his brother Frederick, **Mark Lemon** and **John Forster** to perform Ben Jonson's *Every Man in his Humour* (1598). Dickens acted as stage manager and director as well as playing the part of Captain Bobadil. The play was performed before a specially invited audience on 21st September with, according to John Forster, 'a success that

that out-ran our wildest expectation; and turned our little enterprise into one of the small sensations of the day.' Not everyone, however, was impressed. 'Poor little Dickens!' exclaimed **Thomas Carlyle**, 'all painted in black and red, and affecting the voice of a man of six feet.'

Facing Royalty House, turn right along Dean Street, passing on the right Leoni's Quo Vadis, one of Soho's most famous restaurants, which occupies the house where **Karl Marx** (1818–83) and his family lived from 1851 to 1856 in two small upstairs rooms. A little further along on the left, the cream and redbrick offices of solicitors Allen and Fraser appear to have changed little since they first occupied the building in 1833.

The Broad Street water pump

Turn second left into St Anne's Court, once a haven for political refugees from France and Switzerland. You can read a history of the court on the wall of Clarion House a little way along on the left. Go left onto Wardour Street and first right into Broadwick Street. At its junction with Poland Street is a replica of the Broad Street (as Broadwick Street was then known) pump, the handle of which Dr John Snow removed in 1854. The original pump is believed to have been outside what is now the John Snow pub, located on the opposite side of Broadwick Street.

Go left by the John Snow pub and along Lexington Street, lined with a sequence of Victorian and Edwardian properties. On the upper floors bespoke tailors can be glimpsed going about their craft, whilst the atmospheric, candle-lit restaurants below give the impression of being of a bygone era. Take the first right into Beak Street, notable for how untouched by time it appears, and the third left into Upper John Street, which leads into Golden Square.

'The Guardian Genius'

Sadly, only a handful of houses in Golden Square, such as those at Nos 23 and 24 on the right, survive to give the impression of what it would have looked like in the 19th Century. In *Nicholas Nickleby*, Ralph Nickleby 'lived in a spacious house in Golden Square'. Dickens wrote, 'Although a few members of the graver professions live about Golden Square, it is not exactly in anybody's way to or from anywhere... Its boarding houses are musical, and the notes of pianos and harps float in the evening time round the head of the mournful statue, the guardian genius of a little wilderness of shrubs, in the centre of the square.' The statue in question still stands in the garden at the centre of the square and is reputed to be of **George II** (1683–1760).

Exit the square into Lower John Street and turn left along Brewer Street. Turn right into Wardour Street, noting the beer-barrel shape of the church tower on the left. This is all that remains of St Anne's Church, where Lucie Manette was married in *A Tale of Two Cities*.

Lord Shaftesbury – friend to the destitute
Continue over Shaftesbury Avenue, whose construction between 1877 and 1886 resulted in the demolition of some of London's most squalid slums, the dreadfulness of which Dickens strove to depict in his works. The new thoroughfare was named in honour of **Anthony Ashley Cooper**, the 7th Earl of Shaftesbury (1801–86). A largely forgotten figure today, Lord Shaftesbury was one of the most active philanthropists of the 19th Century. As a Member of Parliament he was responsible for several reforming acts designed to alleviate the suffering of the poor. Much of his work was aimed at highlighting the plight of the residents in the slums hereabouts, and their affection for him is illustrated by a delightful story. On one occasion, a gold watch that had been bequeathed him by his family housekeeper, Maria Mills, and which he treasured, was stolen. Shaftesbury advertised its loss, whereupon the local community found the boy responsible and left him, together with the watch, tied up in a sack on Shaftesbury's doorstep. He subsequently found the boy a place in one of his Ragged Schools. Dickens was one of his most vociferous supporters and applauded Shaftesbury's Lodging Houses Act of 1851 as 'the best law that was ever passed by an English Parliament'.

Continue over Shaftesbury Avenue along the continuation of Wardour Street and take the first left into Gerrard Street. The vivid colours and vibrancy of Chinatown now engulfs you. On the left, five doors after Macclesfield Street, is No 10, standing on the site of the bookseller's house where Dickens's uncle, Thomas Barrow, was laid up with a broken leg, and was visited by his ten-year-old nephew, Charles. Mrs Manson, who ran the bookshop, used to lend Dickens books to read, and for a time he was supremely happy. Thomas Barrow was attended by a very 'odd old barber out of Dean Street' who was forever 'reviewing the events of the last war, and especially of detecting Napoleon's mistakes, and re-arranging his whole life for him on a plan of his own'. Dickens later told how he had written a description of this old barber but had 'never had the courage to show it'. The house would later feature as the 'rather stately house of its kind, but dolefully in want of painting and with dirty windows' where the lawyer Mr Jaggers lived in *Great Expectations*.

The Victorian thieves quarter
Continue to the end of Gerrard Street. Turn right into the bustling Newport Place, left along Newport Court and, having crossed Charing Cross Road, keep going ahead into Great Newport Street. Turn left onto Upper St Martin's Lane and walk straight along Monmouth Street, whose buildings have an early 19th-century look to them. You have now entered Seven Dials which was the notorious slum district immortalized by **William Hogarth** in his *Gin Lane*. By the 1820s the streets of Seven Dials had a fearsome reputation. Prostitutes

would lure men into the warren of streets and alleyways, where their confederates would be waiting to rob and possibly even murder them. More than half the violent robberies that took place in London happened as a result of people inadvertently straying into what was the acknowledged 'thieves quarter of London'. As one commentator put it, 'The walk through Seven Dials after dusk was an act none but a lunatic would have attempted and the betting that he ever emerged with his shirt was 1000 to 60'. Central to this sordid nightlife was the Crown Tavern, situated at the junction where the modern replica of the original Seven Dials column now stands. This pub, then known as 'The Clock House' on account of the timeworn timepiece that it still displays, 'was a hot bed of villainy' where the 'King of the Pickpockets held his nightly court'. The police would stand outside, helpless to intervene, and would 'no more think of entering therein than into the cage of a cobra'.

Wild visions of wickedness
Typically, Dickens was fascinated by the sordid squalor of Seven Dials and neighbouring St Giles. According to **John Forster**, even as a young boy, he had a 'profound attraction of repulsion' to them. 'Good Heaven!', he would exclaim, 'what wild visions of prodigies of wickedness, want and beggary arose in my mind out of that place!'. The Crown Tavern, a delightfully snug hostelry resplendent with pictures and etchings of what the neighbourhood was once like, is the perfect environment in which to rest the feet and contemplate how much the reforming zeal of the Victorian slum clearances changed the metropolis for the better.

Where fashions are buried
Keep going along Monmouth Street to the left of the Crown Tavern. In his *Sketches By Boz* essay, 'Meditations in Monmouth Street', Dickens lauds the fact that, 'Through every alteration and every change Monmouth Street has still remained the burial-place of fashions; and such, to judge from all present appearances, it will remain until there are no more fashions to bury.' It is nice to see that the second-hand clothes shops (albeit selling 1960s and 1970s apparel) are still maintaining at least one tradition!

Thanks to the construction of Shaftesbury Avenue, most of the Monmouth Street to which Dickens referred was demolished, and it ends abruptly. As it does so, go left over the pedestrian crossings and into St Giles High Street. The lofty church of St Giles-in-the-Fields, passed on the left, whose name speaks volumes of the long gone rural past of this neighbourhood, has changed little since the 18th century and is worth a visit. Just past the church, go left into Denmark Street and first right into Denmark Place, a narrow thoroughfare that gives some idea of the unwholesome 'maze of streets, courts, lanes and alleys' that once gave the district a dubious notoriety. In *Nicholas Nickleby*, it was in the cellar of a house in the 'labrinth of streets which lies between Seven Dials and Soho', that Nicholas and his sister Kate, having lost their way, re-encountered Mr Mantalini, being scolded by his nagging wife to turn the mangle. 'I am always turning,' he wearily replied, 'I am perpetually turning, like a demd old horse in a demnition mill. My life is one demd horrid grind!'

Leaving him to his eternal task, go right along Charing Cross Road. Cross over the traffic lights, off which bear right, then left into Oxford Street to find Tottenham Court Road Station where this walk ends.

Below: Despite its high crime rate, Dickens was fascinated by the area known as Seven Dials. 'What wild visions of prodigies of wickedness arose in my mind out of that place', he once commented.

SLOANE SQUARE TO SOUTH KENSINGTON

This walk takes you through the quiet back streets of Chelsea where you will see a variety of buildings of all ages and styles. Highlights include the opportunity to visit the Royal Hospital, Thomas Carlyle's house, which is a genuine time capsule, and the airy St Luke's Church, where Dickens married Catherine Hogarth in 1836. You will also pass the house where George Eliot died, and the homes of Leigh Hunt, Tobias Smollett and George Gissing.

Start:	Sloane Square Station (Circle and District Underground lines).
Finish:	South Kensington Station (Circle, District, and Piccadilly Underground lines).
Length:	1³/₄ miles (2.8km).
Duration:	1¹/₂ hours.
Best of times:	Daytime.
Worst of times:	Evenings.
Refreshments:	Cross keys PH and Anglesea Arms PH. There are several cafés on the Kings Road and around South Kensington Station.

The Royal Hospital
Exit Sloane Square station, go over the crossing, bear left into Sloane Gardens and left along Lower Sloane Street. Cross to its right side and turn right at the traffic lights into Royal Hospital Road. There follows a long walk, the monotony of which is broken by the graceful façade of Sir Christopher Wren's majestic Royal Hospital on the left, founded in 1682 for men 'broken by war and old age.' It is still home to the Chelsea Pensioners, who can be seen about the area resplendent in their scarlet or blue uniforms and tri-cornered hats. You might like to visit the hospital before continuing with your walk.

Where George Eliot died
Continue along Royal Hospital Road. Keep ahead into Cheyne Place, passing on the left at the junction with Swan Walk, the Chelsea Physic Garden, which was established in 1673 by the Apothecaries Company to cultivate plants for medicinal usage. Cross Flood Street, go first right along Cheyne Walk and pause outside No 4, which bears a plaque informing you that **George Eliot** (1819–80) 'died here'.

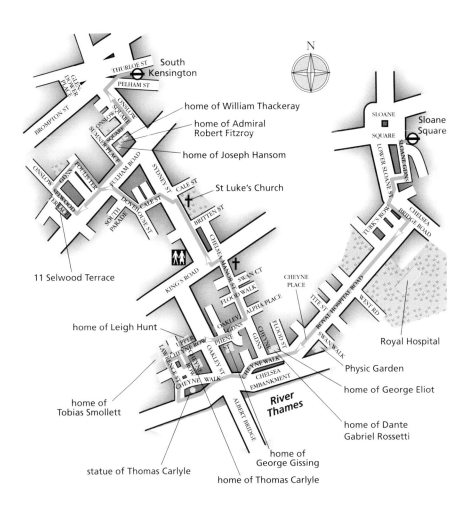

Mary Ann Evans becomes George Eliot

Mary Ann (or Marian as she later spelt it) Evans came to London from her native Warwickshire following the death of her father in 1849. She first met Dickens at a meeting of writers in 1852 and found him 'disappointing – no benevolence in the face and I think little in the heart... ' She had already met the journalist and critic George Henry Lewes (1817–78), a friend of Dickens and a keen participant in his amateur theatricals. By 1854 she and the already married Lewes were openly living together and their relationship, although accepted by their friends, scandalized polite society. In 1856 she began writing *The Sad Fortunes of the Reverend Amos Barton.* Lewes, needing to disguise the fact that the author was both a woman and a social pariah, approached the publisher John Blackwood on behalf of his 'clerical friend' and author of the work, George Eliot.

Dickens guesses the truth

Later published as *Scenes of Clerical Life* (1858), her early fiction won critical acclaim and the guessing game concerning this mysterious new author's true identity began. Dickens was fulsome in his praise, but was not fooled by the *nom de plume*, and quickly deduced that George Eliot was a woman. 'I believe that no man ever before had the art of making himself mentally, so like a woman since the world began' he wrote, and also commented that, if the *Scenes* had not been written by a woman, then 'should I begin to believe that I am a woman myself'. Later, having learnt the truth, Dickens invited George Eliot to contribute to *All the Year Round* and was frustrated by her repeated refusals. Following Dickens's death in 1870, it became a point of irritation to Eliot that **John Forster**'s life of *Dickens* outsold what is now her best-known work, *Middlemarch* (1871–72).

Lewes died in 1878. By 1880 Eliot was involved with the much younger John Cross whom she married on 6th May, 1880. They moved into 4 Cheyne Walk, formerly the home of Dickens's friend **Daniel Maclise**, on 3rd December, 1880. But their happiness here was short lived for at 10pm on 22nd December, George Eliot died. Cross was left to mourn. 'I am left alone in this new house we meant to be so happy in.'

Continue along Cheyne Walk passing No 16, which has a plaque to the artist and poet **Dante Gabriel Rossetti** (1828–82) and the poet Algernon Charles Swinburne (1837–1909). Keep walking ahead and cross over Oakley Street. Pass to the left of David Wynne's graceful statue 'The Boy with The Dolphin'. On arrival at the next section of Cheyne Walk, turn left along the grass fringed path to arrive at the seated statue of the great Victorian sage **Thomas Carlyle** (1795–1881), who lived in Cheyne Row from 1834 until his death.

An idol and a childhood favourite of Dickens

Dickens idolized Carlyle, once saying of him, 'I would go at all times farther to see Carlyle than any man alive.' The two were never close friends (Carlyle was not sure of the merits of what he referred to as 'fictioneering'), but they spent a great deal of time in each other's company. He was among the select gathering invited to hear Dickens read from 'The Chimes' in 1844 (*see* pages 34–35) and, together with his beloved wife Jane, frequently attended Dickens's amateur theatricals and later public readings.

Opposite: It was in St Luke's Church in Chelsea that Charles Dickens married Catherine Hogarth in 1836.

During a recital of *Pickwick Papers*, Carlyle sat in the front bench and laughed so hard that, according to one observer, 'I thought Carlyle would split... he haw-hawed... over and over till he fairly exhausted himself. Dickens would read and then he would stop in order to give Carlyle a chance to stop.' Dickens never tired of reading Carlyle's masterful tome *The French Revolution*, published in 1837 and used it in his research for *A Tale of Two Cities* (*see* pages 126–27). Jane Carlyle died in 1866, and Carlyle became a virtual recluse, occasionally venturing out to dine with Dickens and John Forster. When Dickens died, Carlyle wrote to Forster: 'No death since 1866 had fallen on me with such a stroke... The good, the gentle, high-gifted... noble Dickens – every inch of him an honest man.'

Continue along the path, taking the next right turn and cross over Cheyne Walk to keep ahead into Lawrence Street. Having passed the Cross Keys pub, proceed to the end where, on the left, No 16 has a plaque to **Tobias Smollett** (1721–71). Three of his novels *The Adventures of Roderick Random* (1748), *The Adventures of Peregrine Pickle* (1751) and *The Expedition of Humphrey Clinker* (1771) were amongst Dickens's favourite childhood books.

Carlyle's house

Turn right along Upper Cheyne Row and go first right onto Cheyne Row. Pause on the left outside No 24, the former home of Thomas Carlyle, now owned by the National Trust. Here, he was visited by Dickens, Forster, **Leigh Hunt** and many other literary and intellectual notables of the age. He and Tennyson would sit in the basement kitchen and smoke into the chimney in order to spare Jane Carlyle from the fumes. The house is truly atmospheric and you get the distinct impression, aided by touches such as his hat hanging on the clothes peg, that Carlyle might join you at any moment! He died in the first-floor drawing room, and the house's interior has altered little since.

Leigh Hunt

Backtrack and go right along Upper Cheyne Row to pause outside the pink frontage of No 22, where **Leigh Hunt** (1748–1859) lived from 1833 to 1840. Hunt and his almost permanent financial difficulties provided the inspiration for the impecunious Harold Skimpole in *Bleak House.* At first Hunt did not recognize himself in the portrayal, but when it was pointed out to him, it caused him a great deal of distress. Continue ahead, turning right onto Oakley Street. Go over the crossing and keep ahead into Phene Street. At the junction with Oakley Gardens note the blue plaque to the novelist **George Gissing** (1857–1903). One of Dickens's foremost early critics, he found much to admire in Dickens's works, but felt that his penchant for melodrama 'sadly led him astray'.

Where Dickens married Catherine Hogarth

Turn left into Oakley Gardens. Proceed clockwise and go left along Chelsea Manor Street. Turn left onto the busy Kings Road. Go right at the traffic lights and keep ahead along Sydney Street until you arrive at the lofty cathedral-like parish church of St Luke's built between 1820 and 1824. It was here on 2nd April, 1836 that Charles Dickens married Catherine Hogarth in what his best man, Thomas Beard, later described as 'altogether a very quiet piece of business'. As the bride was only 20 and technically a minor, Dickens had to revisit his old place of employment, **Doctors' Commons**, in order to obtain a special marriage licence.

Exit the church and continue right along Sydney Street. Go over the zebra crossing, straight ahead into Cale Street, right onto Dovehouse Street, left along Fulham Road and right at the traffic lights into Selwood Terrace. It is lined to your left side by a sequence of squat 18th-century houses. Prior to his wedding, Dickens moved into No 11 in order that he might be close to his bride's family, who lived nearby in, the now demolished, York Place.

The man who sailed with Darwin

Continue along Selwood Terrace. Go right into Onslow Gardens, right onto Foulis Terrace, left along Fulham Road and take the first left into Sumner Place. Number 28 was the home of Joseph Aloysius Hansom (1803–82), the man who invented the great Victorian conveyance the Hansom Cab. Turn first right into Onslow Square and a little way along pause outside No 38, which was the home of Admiral Robert Fitzroy (1805–65), commander of HMS *Beagle*, on board which the naturalist Charles Darwin (1809–82) sailed. Fitzroy lived here from 1854 to 1865, in which year he committed suicide, overcome by guilt for the part he had played in casting doubt upon the veracity of the Bible.

Where Thackeray lived

Onslow square's stylish stuccoed houses were built in 1846 to provide elegant town dwellings for the prosperous Victorian middle classes. Next along between Nos 32 and 38 there is an easily missed black wall plaque to William Makepeace Thackeray, who lived here from 1854 to 1862. Few who have moved house can fail to sympathize with his sentiments as he began the necessary alterations to his new house. 'O the upholsterers, the carpeters, the fenderers the looking glass people... O their bills their bills'. Whilst living here he wrote *The Virginians* (1857) and his last completed novel *The Adventures of Philip* (1861–2). His daughter, Anne, described the house as 'a pleasant bowery sort of home, with green curtains and carpets, looking out upon the elm trees'. Continue, turn left until you arrive at the traffic lights where on the opposite side of the road is South Kensington Station where this route ends.

SOUTH KENSINGTON TO HIGH STREET KENSINGTON

At the start of the 19th century Kensington was little more than a rural parish with a resident population of around 8,000. By 1881, the effects of the Great Exhibition (1851), The Exhibition (1862) and the subsequent establishment of museums and colleges in the district had sparked a westward migration of London's upper middle classes, and Kensington's population had mushroomed to around 163,000. The pastoral landscape was replaced by terrace after terrace of large houses, their columned porches and large rooms reflecting the supreme confidence and aspirations of their occupants. Although the area featured little in Dickens's works, it was home to several of his friends and acquaintances. The walk itself is one of contrasts, taking in quiet, almost rural, back streets, busy main roads and picturesque residential squares. A visit to the Victoria and Albert Museum, passed en route, is highly recommended.

Start:	South Kensington Station (Circle, District and Piccadilly Underground lines).
Finish:	High Street Kensington (Circle and District Underground lines).
Length:	1³/₄ miles (2.8km).
Duration:	1¹/₂ hours.
Best of times:	Anytime.
Worst of times:	None of note.
Refreshments:	There is a café at the Victoria and Albert Museum. Pubs and cafés line Kensington High Street.

Clever Mr Cole

Go up the steps from South Kensington Station. Turn right through the shopping arcade. Go right onto Thurloe Street and keep going ahead to go left into Thurloe Square. Turn right along Thurloe Place. Proceed past the line of

Opposite: *The ostentatious Albert Memorial commemorates the husband of Queen Victoria whose death in 1861 led Dickens to comment, 'England will do exactly the same without him as it did with him.'*

phone boxes and to the right pause outside No 33, now the Embassy of the Republic of Kazakhstan, but once the home of Sir Henry Cole (1808–82) campaigner and educator and first Director of the Victoria and Albert Museum.

The man who Queen Victoria described as 'Good Mr Cole with his, rough, offhand manner' was the driving force behind the Great Exhibition of 1851. He was personally chosen by Prince Albert, who punned that: 'If we want the exhibition to *steam* ahead, we must have *Cole.*' Cole rejected the original idea to house the exhibition in a dome, and settled instead on Joseph Paxton's Crystal Palace of iron and glass. The exhibition was a huge success, and with the surplus raised from ticket sales, he was able to realize his dream to build a complex of museums and colleges in Kensington, all of which still stand. He was also active in other areas of Victorian Reform, notably the introduction of the Penny Post. He came up with the ingenious ruse of having a pamphlet detailing its merits bound into one of the weekly instalments of Dickens's *Nicholas Nickleby,* thus getting the message across to 40,000 additional readers at a stroke. In 1843, he approached an artist friend asking that he design a special card that he could send out for Christmas. Three years later, he printed a thousand cards, sold each one for a shilling, and began the tradition and industry of the Christmas card.

The Great Exhibition
With your back to the house, bear left and cross the busy main road at the traffic lights to the left of the Victoria and Albert Museum. The museum's National Art Library is home to the Forster Collection, the largest collection of Dickens's manuscripts and proofs given by Dickens to his friend **John Forster**.

Walk along Exhibition Road, keeping to its left side. You pass by the Natural History Museum, the Science Museum and sundry buildings of Imperial College, all founded by Henry Cole. At the top, turn left into Kensington Gore. The Crystal Palace, in which the Great Exhibition opened on 1st May 1851, was situated in Hyde Park opposite. In February of that year, Dickens had been shown around the huge glass and iron structure, which was only partially roofed. He expressed his doubts that it could ever be ready in time, to which its designer Joseph Paxton replied, 'I think it will, but mind I don't say it will.' Despite homage being paid to Dickens's genius with prominently displayed statues of Oliver Twist and Little Nell, Dickens was unimpressed with the finished article and complained that his 'eyes refused to focus' on the 14,000 exhibits.

A literary hostess
Continue along Kensington Gore, pausing on the left by the Royal Albert Hall, opened in 1870 and funded from the profits of the Great Exhibition. It stands on the site of Gore House, home of Marguerite, Countess of Blessingdon (1789–1849), whose literary soirées attracted the cream of literary society,

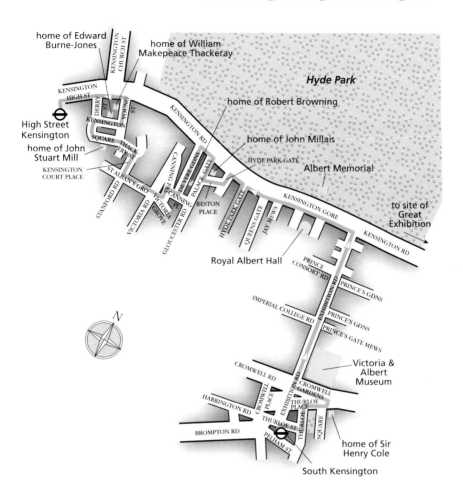

Dickens included. However, her extravagant lifestyle led to her bankruptcy and she abandoned England for Paris where she died in poverty.

The Albert Memorial

On the opposite side of the road to the hall is the ostentatious Albert Memorial. Prince Albert (1819–61), the consort of Queen Victoria, was until his death from typhoid, a driving force behind the Victorian age. His statue holds a copy of the catalogue from the Great Exhibition. Although Victoria was inconsolable at the loss of her husband, and polite society was shocked by his death, Dickens did not share in the general mourning for the prince. Indeed, he wrote that Albert 'was neither a phenomenon, nor the saviour of England; and England will do exactly the same without him as it did with him... '.

Continue along Kensington Gore, go over Queen's Gate, keep ahead into Kensington Road, and turn first left into Hyde Park Gate. Several blue plaques adorn the premises here, including that on No 9 to Robert Baden-Powell (1857–19141), founder of the Boy Scout movement; No 28, where statesman Sir Winston Churchill (1874–1965) lived and died, and No 22, home of Sir Leslie Stephen (1832–1904), father of Virginia Woolf.

The elder statesman of Victorian art

Return to Kensington Road. Go left, then first left into the next part of Hyde Park Gate and turn second right into Reston Place. Before you do, you may like to walk clockwise around Hyde Park Gate to admire the delightful buildings and gardens ahead. Keep straight ahead, and go through the gates of 8 Reston Place, which, despite its appearance to the contrary, is a pedestrian right of way. Keep left and go out onto Palace Gate, where on the wall of the stately No 2 on the right, is a plaque to the artist, **Sir John Everett Millais** (1829–96).

Millais, who was aged just 11 when admitted to the Royal Academy, was literally the *enfant terrible* of British art. Prodigiously talented, he first exhibited at the Academy when he was just 16, and in 1848 was one of the seven artists who formed the Pre-Raphaelite Brotherhood. In 1850 his *Christ In The House of His Parents* (now in Tate Britain) was universally vilified for daring to portray the Holy Family as ordinary. In *Household Words,* Dickens vehemently attacked Millais's infant Christ as a 'hideous, wry-necked, blubbering, red headed boy in a bed-gown'; whilst dismissing his depiction of Mary as 'so horrible in her ugliness', that she would 'stand out as a... Monster, in the vilest cabaret in France, or the lowest gin-shop in England'. However, five years later, following their first meeting at the dinner table of **Wilkie Collins**, Dickens wrote to Millais, assuring him of his admiration for his genius.

One of Millais's few supporters was author and critic, John Ruskin, until, that is, Millais fell in love with Ruskin's wife, Ellie, and married her in 1855, following the annulment of her first marriage on grounds of non-consummation. Thereafter, Millais's reputation evolved into that of principal statesman of British art, and he became one of the wealthiest painters of his age, famed for his historical narrative paintings and his portraits of the great and good. Following Dickens's death, Millais went to Gad's Hill and made a pencilled sketch of his bandaged head, which the author's daughter, Katey, believed showed 'a likeness to Tennyson'.

Turn right past Millais's house, continue to the traffic lights and go left along Kensington Road, where Kensington Palace is visible through the gates on the right. Go next left into De Vere Gardens, where at No 29, on the left, **Robert Browning** (1812–89) lived from 1887 to 1889. Following his death in Venice, his body was brought back here to await burial in Westminster Abbey.

A *literary calamity*

Continue to the end and go right into Canning Place, passing a little pocket of delightful mock-Tudor properties dating from 1846. Follow the road as it veers left. Go right into St Alban's Grove and keep ahead, turning first right into Kensington Court Place, then left into Thackeray Street. Continue ahead into Kensington Square. **John Stuart Mill** (1806–73), philosopher, lived at No 18. Dickens and Mill were never friends and had little personal contact, despite sharing many mutual acquaintances. Mill seems to have disliked Dickens, once describing his face as one of 'dingy black guardism irradiated with genius', and he was critical of Dickens's treatment of the rights of women in *Bleak House*. Mill was on more intimate terms with **Thomas Carlyle**, and it was in this house that one of the famous calamities of Victorian literature occurred. Having completed volume one of his epic *History of the French Revolution* (1837), Carlyle entrusted the only manuscript of it to Mill for his opinion. Shortly afterwards, a sheepish Mill was forced to confess to the author that his maid had 'taken it for waste paper' and burnt it in the fireplace. Carlyle had no choice but to re-write the whole thing from memory, confessing at the end that he felt like a man who had 'nearly killed himself accomplishing zero'.

Proceed clockwise round the square. Number 40 was the home of **Sir John Simon** (1816–1904), the great Victorian health and sanitary reformer. Artist **Sir Edward Burne-Jones** (1833–98), one of the second generation Pre-Raphaelites, lived at No 41 from 1865 to 1867.

Where Vanity Fair *was written*

Go next left into Young Street and pause on the left outside No 16, which from 1847 to 1854 was the home of **William Makepeace Thackeray** (1811–63). 'It has the air of a feudal castle,' wrote Thackeray on first beholding it, and it still possesses a certain timelessness. It was here, in the middle of one night, after months of racking his brain trying to think of a suitable title for his new work, that a flash of inspiration sent him leaping from his bed and running round his room crying, 'Vanity Fair, Vanity Fair'. It was with the publication of this, between 1847 and 1848, that Thackeray emerged as a major novelist, and Dickens was at last seen to have a serious rival. Nevertheless, Thackeray's daughters were not impressed by their father's success. On one occasion, as Alfred Tennyson sat reading his poetry aloud, he was interrupted by Minnie Thackeray who asked, 'Papa, why do you not write books like *Nicholas Nickleby*.' Years later, when passing the house with a friend, Thackeray suddenly bellowed: 'Down on your knees, you rogue, for here *Vanity Fair* was penned, and I will go down with you, for I have a high opinion of that little production myself.'

Leave Young Street, and go left along Kensington High Street, to force your way onwards until you arrive at High Street Kensington station.

HOLLAND PARK

Although not particularly long, this walk explores some utterly charming residential streets before plunging into the wilder reaches of Holland Park. You will pass the home of G K Chesterton, considered by many Dickensians to be the best of all Dickens's critics. The few remnants of Holland House, where the formidable Lady Holland held her famous dinners attended by leading political, diplomatic and literary figures of the day, are passed on a pleasing stroll through Holland Park. The latter section of the walk passes through the streets of what was a veritable colony of artists in the 19th century. Finally, the chance to visit the homes of Lord Leighton and Linley Sambourne, both of which are open to the public as museums, should not be passed up.

Start & Finish:	High Street Kensington Station (Circle and District Underground lines).
Length:	1¼ miles (2km).
Duration:	1½ hours.
Best of times:	Daytime.
Worst of times:	Evenings.
Refreshments:	There is a café in Holland Park. Pubs and restaurants line Kensington High Street.

G K Chesterton

Turn right out of High Street Kensington Station. Continue along Kensington High Street until, having passed Derry Street, cross to the church opposite. Bear left along Kensington Church Court and follow it as it becomes Kensington Church Walk, and twists its way to the west doorway of St Mary Abbot's church, which was rebuilt by Sir George Gilbert Scott between 1869 and 1873. Turn left onto Holland Street, first right into Gordon Place, and struggle up the long hill to go second left into Campden Grove. Take the next right into Hornton Street, the second right into Sheffield Terrace, and pause by No 42, where **G K Chesterton** (1874–1936) was born on 29th May, 1874.

Best known today for his 'Father Brown' books, the first of which was published in 1911, Chesterton's literary output was prodigious, covering virtually every topic of contemporary political, philosophical and social concern. He was also notoriously absent-minded and once, whilst on a lecture tour, reputedly telegraphed his wife, 'Am in Market Harborough. Where ought I to be?'. His study, 'Charles Dickens', was published in 1906 and established him as one of Dickens's finest critics. He followed this between 1907 and 1909 by writing prefaces for all Dickens's books, as they were reprinted in J M Dents *Everyman's*

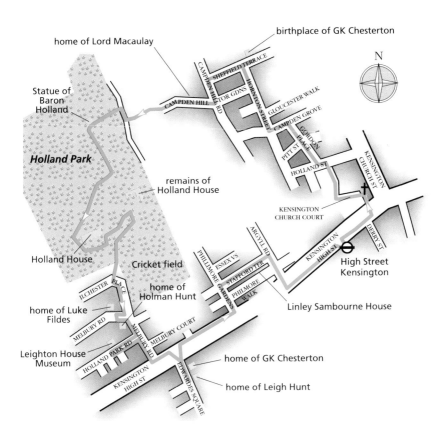

Library. In his 'The Victorian Age in Literature' (1931) Chesterton applauded Dickens as 'that most exquisite of arts... the art of enjoying everybody'.

The confident Lord Macaulay

Retrace your footsteps, then continue to the end of Sheffield Terrace. Turn right into Campden Hill Road and first right into Campden Hill. Queen Elizabeth College to the left stands on what was the site of Holly Lodge, the home of historian and Statesman **Thomas Babington Macaulay** (1800–59), whose monumental *History of England,* published in five volumes between 1849 and 1861, is still considered a classic. So representative was he of the supreme self-confidence that fired the Victorian era, that Lord Melbourne once commented, 'I wish I was as cocksure of anything as Tom Macaulay is of everything.'

The Baron and Lady Holland at home

Continue ahead to pass Holland Park School and go through the gate into

Holland Park. Bear right along the pathway. Take the first pathway left and pause on the right when you reach the seated statue of Henry Richard Fox, 3rd Baron Holland (1773–1840), where an information board provides a brief biography. Henry was married to Elizabeth Vassall (1770–1845), and they complemented each other well: he was affable and cultured; she was beautiful, vivacious and domineering. During their tenure, nearby Holland House became a great centre of social, literary and political life, with many famous visitors including William IV, Lord Byron (who complained that the house was too cold), Lord Macaulay, **Benjamin Disraeli** and Dickens. Towards the end of his life, Lord Holland was afflicted by gout, hence the walking stick in the statue's hand.

With your back to the statue, go straight ahead along the pathway (keeping a keen eye peeled for the peacocks). Bear diagonally right across the lawn, and pass through the small wooden gates on the right. Swing immediately left to veer right down the ramp, and go left down the steps, keeping ahead on the path as it descends past the beautiful gardens. Having gone through the archway, take the second pathway on your left (it has a sign for the 'Theatre'), and go up the grand set of steps a little way along on the left, to gaze at what little remains of Holland House. It was when Dickens received a summons – she rarely invited! – to one of Lady Holland's evening receptions that he knew he had been accepted into the higher echelons of the literati of his day.

It was said of Lady Holland that she was 'all assertion', and before she called upon the 26-year-old Dickens to attend one of her famous soirees at Holland House, she made enquiries as to whether 'Boz was presentable'. When they first met she had been reading the early instalments of *Nicholas Nickleby,* and Dickens, unable to resist her incisive questioning, found himself forced, against his will, to disclose the plot to her. She was impressed by the young author, and considered him 'modest and well-behaved', whilst her husband found him to be 'very unobtrusive, yet not shy, intelligent in countenance and altogether prepossessing'. Despite her haughty and overbearing manner, Lady Holland and Dickens became good friends, and he would often seek her advice and opinions, even though those opinions could often be, to say the least, contrary. Her dislike for Americans was intense, and when he came to say goodbye before leaving on his first visit to the United States, she tried desperately to dissuade him from going. 'Why cannot you go to Bristol,' she pleaded, 'and see some of the third and fourth class people there and they'll do just as well?'

Following her husband's death, however, the glory days of Holland House drew to a close. Lady Holland rarely used it, and when their son, the 4th Lord

Opposite: Little now remains of Holland House where the formidable Lady Holland held frequent soirées that were attended by the intellectual great of the 19th century. Dickens was first summoned here at the age of 26.

Holland, died in 1859, his widow ran into debt and the estate was greatly diminished. There was a brief resurgence of social grandeur in the Edwardian age, but after its almost total annihilation by the bombs of World War II, what little remained of the house was converted into the King George Memorial Youth Hostel. Fittingly, the vibrancy of youth now echoes through the remnants of the property where Dickens once wondered who would take the place of its rare personalities when they had 'stepped into the shadow'.

Go left off the steps and follow the road sharp left towards the youth hostel, where on the other side of the railings you can glimpse all that remains of Holland House's east wing.

The tide turns for Luke Fildes

Retrace your footsteps, and when you get to the 'Royal Borough of Kensington and Chelsea Notice Board', take the earth track that bears diagonally left, and follow it as it veers left onto the asphalt pathway. At the end keep to the right, then immediately left, and exit the park through the gates, walking straight ahead along Ilchester Place. Having taken a sharp right onto Melbury Road, pause by the gate of well-concealed No 31, immediately on the right, which was the home of the artist Sir Luke Fildes (1844–1927). It was **John Everett Millais** who, whilst staying with Dickens at Gad's Hill Place in 1869, suggested Fildes as a possible illustrator for *The Mystery of Edwin Drood*. When Dickens gave him the commission, an elated Fildes wrote to a friend, 'This is the tide! Am I to be on the flood? My heart fails me a little for it is the turning point in my career.' By the time of Dickens's death, however, Fildes had completed only six plates, although this didn't stop him being pursued by diehard Dickensians, who were convinced Fildes knew more about the intended ending of the novel than he was letting on. But perhaps Fildes's most lasting contribution to Dickens's memory was his watercolour *The Empty Chair*, painted shortly after the author's death, and which with its minimalist depiction of the chair in Dickens's study, summed up with a simple poignancy the void that his passing had left.

The man who saw the strain on Dickens

Backtrack, crossing to the right side of Melbury Road and follow it downhill passing No 18 where William Holman-Hunt (1807–1910) lived and died. A founder member of the Pre-Raphaelite brotherhood, Hunt had become the grand old man of British Art by the time he moved here in the 1880s. Holman-Hunt was best man at the marriage of his friend Charles Collins to Dickens's daughter Katey in 1860. His later comment on Dickens that 'all the bones of his face showed... and every line of his brow and face was a record of past struggle... ', provides a glimpse of the strain under which Dickens was labouring during the last decade of his life.

Lord Leighton

Go next right into Holland Park Road to arrive on the right at Leighton House Museum, where the Victorian artist **Lord Leighton** (1830–96) lived for the last 30 years of his life. Designed for Leighton in 1866 by George Aitchison, the building's plain brick exterior belies an interior that is nothing short of an Oriental extravaganza, and a lavish memorial to high Victorian taste. Its most striking room is the Arab Hall, added in 1879, with its mosaic floor, fountain, stained glass cupola and tiles from Greece and Egypt. Works of art by Leighton himself and also **Sir Edward Burne-Jones** are displayed.

Return to Melbury Road and go right, then left onto Kensington High Street. Cross over the traffic lights to bear right, then first left into Edwardes Square. Keep walking ahead passing No 1, home to G K Chesterton in 1901, and pause outside No 18 where **Leigh Hunt** (1784–1859) lived from 1840 to 1851.

Linley Sambourne's house

Go back across Kensington High Street by the traffic lights. Bear right, then left into Phillimore Gardens. Take the second right into Stafford Terrace, where a little way along on the right is No 18. The *Punch* cartoonist Linley Sambourne (1844–1910) lived here from 1874 until his death. The interior of this charming 19th-century house has been perfectly preserved, and provides a unique insight into late Victorian tastes in internal décor.

Continue along Stafford Terrace. Turn right into Argyll Road, left onto Kensington High Street where, a little way along on the right, the walk concludes at High Street Kensington Station.

Right: One of the famed garden parties that were often held in the grounds of Holland House.

KENSAL GREEN CEMETERY

All Souls Cemetery, Kensal Green, was founded in 1832 under the auspices of the General Cemetery Company, and was the first of the great commercial cemeteries to be opened in London. Today, it is the oldest surviving English cemetery in private ownership. It was the cemetery chosen by Dickens as the resting-place for his beloved sister-in-law, Mary Hogarth, and having purchased her grave, he was determined that one day he would be buried with her. The site was also chosen by many of the 19th century's great and good to be their final resting place and, since many of the mausoleums were constructed whilst their occupants were alive, they illustrate just how important some of those buried here considered themselves. It is fascinating, though slightly chilling, to stand by the graves of so many of those who dominated Victorian Society.

Start & finish:	Kensal Green Station (Bakerloo Underground line and Silver Link Rail North London Link).
Length:	1¼ miles (2 km)
Duration:	2 hours.
Best of times:	Anytime between 10am and 3pm, before the cemetery closes at 5.30pm. It is worth going on the first Sunday of the month, when you can visit the catacombs.
Worst of times:	Evenings when the cemetery is closed.
Refreshments:	There are no establishments offering refreshment in this area.

Exit Kensal Green Station. Turn left onto College Road, then right along Harrow Road, and go over the crossing. Veer left and follow Harrow Road until, some distance along on the right, you arrive at the Doric gateway that spans the entrance to the cemetery. Once inside, the noise of the traffic is immediately reduced to a distant murmur, and an amazing vista of wild and untamed woodland, punctuated with memorials and tombs fashioned in every possible architectural style, stretches before you.

Opposite: *Kensal Green Cemetery is a wild and untamed woodland and is where many of Dickens's friends and acquaintances lie buried. It is also the final resting place of his beloved sister-in-law, Mary Hogarth.*

IN MEMORY OF

WILKIE COLLINS
AUTHOR OF "THE WOMAN IN WHITE"
AND OTHER WORKS OF FICTION

The epitaph that Dickens composed

Keep ahead on the asphalt path to turn first right, then right again along North Avenue. Follow it left and, just after the seventh tree along on the right, pause by the grave of Dickens's revered sister-in-law **Mary Scott Hogarth** (1820–37), whose death on 7th May, 1837 had such a profound effect on Dickens. For months afterwards he dreamt of her every night, 'sometimes as a spirit, sometimes as a living creature, never with any of the bitterness of my real sorrow, but always with a kind of quiet happiness'. There is no doubt that he wished to be buried in the same grave as her, and when her brother George died in 1841, it was with great reluctance that he relinquished his claim. 'It is a great trial for me to give up Mary's grave,' he wrote to Forster, 'the desire to be buried next to her is as strong upon me now, as it was five years ago... and I *know*... that it will never diminish... I cannot bear the thought of being excluded from her dust...' The now weathered inscription was composed by Dickens himself: 'Young, beautiful, and good. God in His mercy numbered her with his angels at the early age of seventeen'.

Dickens's 'keepsakey impossible face'

Continue along the pathway. A little further along, more or less opposite the chest tomb of John Campbell, go left past the small clump of bushes, behind which is the slanting grey ledger tombstone of **Daniel Maclise** (1806–70). A close personal friend of Dickens, it was Maclise who, in 1839, painted the full-length portrait of the then 27-year-old author that is now in the National Portrait Gallery. Dickens described it as a 'face of me, which all people say is astonishing'; whilst Thackeray observed that 'a looking glass could not render a better facsimile...'. Only **George Eliot** demurred, deploring the 'keepsakey, impossible face'. When Maclise died in April 1870, Dickens paid a moving tribute in what would prove to be his last speech at the annual Royal Academy dinner, calling him 'the gentlest and most modest of men'.

'Discharged with good character'

Walk past Maclise's grave and pick your way through the neglected and overgrown tombs, to turn left along the grass track. Go past the holly bush and on arrival at the draped stone urn over the grave of Catherine Ann Smithson turn right. Make your way through the graves and keep going ahead over the asphalt roadway. Having crossed another grassy track, you arrive at a holly bush that overhangs the white flat gravestone of Charles Shirley Brooks (1816–74). Brooks was a member of the 'Punch Brotherhood' of journalists and a great admirer of Dickens, although he strongly disapproved of the way that Dickens treated his wife up to and following their legal separation. At the time, Brooks wryly observed that Mrs Dickens had been 'discharged with good character'.

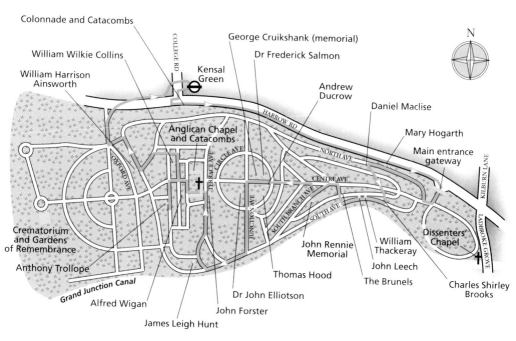

Colonnade and Catacombs

George Cruikshank (memorial)

Dr Frederick Salmon

William Wilkie Collins

COLLEGE RD

Kensal Green

William Harrison Ainsworth

Andrew Ducrow

Daniel Maclise

N

HARROW RD

Anglican Chapel and Catacombs

Mary Hogarth

OXFORD AVE

TERRACE AVE

CIRCLE AVE

NORTH AVE

Main entrance gateway

KILBURN LANE

CENTRE AVE

JUNCTION AVE

SOUTH BRANCH AVE

SOUTH AVE

LADBROKE GROVE

Crematorium and Gardens of Remembrance

John Rennie Memorial

William Thackeray

Dissenters' Chapel

Anthony Trollope

Thomas Hood

John Leech

The Brunels

Charles Shirley Brooks

Grand Junction Canal

Alfred Wigan

Dr John Elliotson

John Forster

James Leigh Hunt

'He kept his heart strings in a crystal case'

Continue ahead, bearing right onto the rough earth path. The moment that the wall to your left gives way to railings, turn right to the low-railed white tomb of **William Makepeace Thackeray** (1811–63). Thackeray's funeral took place in crisp, clear winter sunshine on 30th December 1863, and it was estimated that close on 2,000 mourners came to Kensal Green to pay their last respects to the man who, according to Anthony Trollope, 'kept his heart strings in a crystal case'. Dickens, who had only just been reconciled with the dead author (*see* pages 127–28), stood by the graveside with 'a look of bereavement in his face which was indescribable. When all others had turned aside from the grave he still stood there, as if rooted to the spot, watching with almost haggard eyes every spadeful of dust that was thrown upon it'.

The artist that Dickens mesmerized

Two graves along to the left, the inscription now illegible, is the grave of Thackeray's life-long friend, and principle *Punch* cartoonist, John Leech (1817–64). Leech also provided illustrations for *A Christmas Carol* and for successive Christmas books. In September 1849, whilst holidaying with Dickens on the Isle of Wight, he was knocked over by a giant wave and suffered a concussion that left him in constant pain and unable to sleep –

until, that is, Dickens hypnotized him into a 'magnetic sleep' and cured him of his affliction. When Leech died suddenly in November 1864, Dickens was deeply affected. 'This death of poor Leech' he wrote to Forster 'has put me out woefully.' For several days he found himself unable to work upon the book he was then writing – *Our Mutual Friend.*

Great engineers and crumbling angels
Continue along the path keeping the railings to your left, and just before you draw adjacent to the gas works, turn right onto the grass track and keep ahead past the pink marble obelisk of the Bentham family. Having crossed a second grass track, pause at the second grave on the right of the outstanding engineers Sir Marc Isambard Brunel (1769–1849) and his son Isambard Kingdom Brunel (1806–59). At the end of the path go left onto the asphalt surface and on arrival at the junction, take the left fork along the gravel footpath South Branch Avenue. Pause seven graves after the holly bush on the left at the memorial to **Sir John Rennie** (1794–1874).

'The Colossus of Equestrians'
With your back to Rennie's memorial, cross over to pass to the right of the Derville mausoleum, and keep going ahead towards the large mausoleum with a light brick door, which can be seen in the distance. When you reach it go left along Central Avenue to pause at the next left turn by the strikingly ornate tomb of Andrew Ducrow (1793–1842), guarded by two somewhat weathered sphinxes. This incredible Egyptian mausoleum cost £3,000 (around £150,000 today) to build and decorate. It commemorates an equestrian showman of astounding ability whose skill and daring captivated his audiences. 'The creatures were but the air on which he flew', wrote one critic. In his essay 'Early Coaches' in *Sketches By Boz*, Dickens writes of falling asleep on a coach journey and dreaming of 'exhibiting *à la* Ducrow'. A showman to the end 'the Colossus of equestrians' rests behind the humble inscription: 'This tomb erected by genius for the reception of its own remains'.

Dickens under the surgeon's knife
Continue ahead and pause by the sixth grave on the right by the tomb of Dr Frederick Salmon (1785–1868), who was founder of St Mark's Hospital, which was originally called 'The Infirmary for the Poor Afflicted with Fistula and other Diseases of the Rectum'. Salmon operated on Dickens for a fistula, a harrowing procedure that, given it was performed without anaesthetic, must have been excruciating. Indeed, when Dickens described the ordeal to his friend William Macready, Macready confessed to suffering '*agonies* as they related all to me, and did violence to myself keeping myself to my seat. I could scarcely bear it.'

Cruikshank's temperence remembered
Further along on the right is a memorial to **George Cruikshank** (1792–1878) cartoonist and illustrator of *Oliver Twist*. Although originally buried at Kensal Green, he was later exhumed and re-interred in St Paul's Cathedral.

Dickens learns to mesmerize
Continue along Central Avenue and take the next path left, pausing at the next junction on the right where, almost hidden by a tall tree, is the urn-topped obelisk of Dr John Elliotson (1791–1868). Dickens became acquainted with Elliotson in 1838, at a time when the physician was losing the confidence of his colleagues owing to his interest in hypnotism. Dickens, however, was fascinated by the subject and under Elliotson's tutelage, he too became proficient in the art of mesmerism. Elliotson later became the Dickens family doctor and was described by the novelist as 'one of my most intimate and valued friends'.

The song of the shirt
With your back to the Elliotson tomb take the left path, passing the tomb of the Paul family. A little way along on the left is the pink marble memorial to **Thomas Hood** (1799–1845), whose review of Dickens's *Master Humphrey's Clock* in the *Athenaeum on* 7th November, 1840 was one of the first favourable appreciations of Dickens's work. Hood's epitaph, 'He sang the song of the shirt', refers to his most famous poem *The Song Of The Shirt,* published in the 1843 Christmas issue of *Punch.* A morose denunciation of the northern mills where women were forced to work extremely long hours, it contained such melancholic lines as 'O God! That bread should be so dear, And Flesh and blood so cheap!'.

A Face Worth Meeting
Retrace your footsteps. Just before the Elliotson tomb, turn left. Go past the barrier. Turn right and take the second turning right along the grass track where, just before the second tree on the left, is a pedestal memorial to **James Leigh Hunt** (1784–1859). On first meeting Dickens in 1837, Hunt wrote to John Forster exclaiming, 'What a face is his to meet in a drawing room! It has the life and soul in it of fifty human beings'.

Continue along the grass track and go left when it intersects with the loose-stone pathway. Just before it changes to asphalt and climbs towards the Anglican Chapel, go right down the grass path where the third grave on the left is that of Dickens's great friend **John Forster** (1812–76).

Backtrack and go right towards the Anglican Chapel beneath where, in the catacombs that can only be visited on the first Sunday of each month, lie the remains of actor **William Macready** (1793–1873), and the surgeon, medical reformer and founder of *The Lancet*, **Thomas Wakley** (1795–1862). Just before the chapel – just past the men's toilet – go left and walk past the cloisters.

Go down the steps, and turn left. On the right you will find the grave of George Charles Todd Nailer. Just behind it, the inscription virtually obscured by the drooping branches of a large tree, is the grey, granite headstone of **Alfred Wigan** (1814–78), the man who introduced Dickens to **Mrs Frances Ternan** and her daughter, **Ellen**.

'Mr Popular Sentiment'

Go back to the main path and turn left (the cloisters and chapel will be to your right). Turn left along West Centre Avenue. Five graves after the red granite monument of Blondin (1824–97) – the most famous tightrope walker of all time – go left down the grass track, passing a series of mausoleums. Four graves after the broken and leaning column on the right is the solid pink and grey ledger tomb of **Anthony Trollope** (1815–82). Although chiefly remembered today for his chronicles of Barsetshire (1855–67), and famously satirizing Dickens as 'Mr Popular Sentiment' in his first successful novel *The Warden* (1855), Trollope was a life-long civil servant in the Post Office, whose legacy was the introduction of the pillar-box. Dickens and Trollope shared a personal connection in that Trollope's brother Tom married Fanny Ternan, sister of Ellen Ternan.

William Wilkie Collins

Backtrack past Blondin's grave and just before the two large mausoleums on the left, turn left down the narrow grass path, where a little after half way along on the left is the grave of **William Wilkie Collins** (1824–89). Collins was one of Dickens's closest friends and his most important literary collaborator.

The man who introduced Dickens to Forster

Keep ahead along the path. Turn left after the leaning tree and, at the end of that track, go left along the rough, gravel path where at the end on the right, surmounted by a very slender urn, is the tomb of Dickens's friend and mentor, William Harrison Ainsworth (1805–82). Ainsworth was a literary giant of the 1830s whose historical novels enjoyed immense success. He and Dickens first met around 1835, when Dickens was still a struggling literary hack. It was at Ainsworth's nearby house, Kensal Lodge, that Dickens first met his great friend and primary biographer, **John Forster**.

Continue ahead, turning next right to walk up the slight incline. Just before the path sweeps right, go left along the grass track. Go right onto Oxford Avenue, and exit through the green gates. Keep going ahead, turning right again onto Harrow Road. Go over the crossing, bearing right then immediately left into College Road where this walk ends at Kensal Green Station.

GREEN PARK TO WESTMINSTER

It is a mark of Dickens's sheer determination and strength of character that he overcame his humble beginnings and, by his early twenties, had been accepted into polite society. This walk explores the area where his transformation from lowly clerk to literary superstar took place. It includes the Houses of Parliament, in the predecessor of which Dickens worked as a reporter between 1832 and 1836. It goes past the houses of the great and good into which Dickens was welcomed as a guest when still only a young man. And finally, it provides the opportunity to stand alongside Dickens's grave and ponder the grief that gripped the world in the immediate aftermath of his death.

Start:	Green Park Station (Jubilee, Piccadilly and Victoria Underground lines).
Finish:	Westminster Underground Station (Circle, District and Jubilee lines).
Length:	2 miles (3.2km).
Duration:	1¼ hours.
Best of times:	Anytime.
Worst of times:	On Sundays and evenings Burlington Arcade is closed.
Refreshments:	Red Lion PH and several other pubs and cafés are passed en route.

Angela Burdett-Coutts

Leave Green Park Underground Station via the 'Piccadilly North Side' exit and turn right along Piccadilly. Continue over Stratton Street, on the corner of which used to stand the home of **Angela Burdett-Coutts** (1814–1906). In 1837, at the age of 23, Angela Burdett inherited the vast fortune of her maternal grandfather, the banker Thomas Coutts and added his surname to hers. Now the richest woman in England, with the exception of Queen Victoria, she was immediately inundated with proposals of marriage, but turned them all down. She met Dickens in 1839, and the two soon became close friends, a fact he made public by dedicating *Martin Chuzzlewit* to her in 1844. She reciprocated by paying for his eldest son, Charley, to be educated at Eton, and by arranging a cadetship with the East India Company for his second son, Walter.

But it is for her public philanthropy that Burdett-Coutts is best remembered today, and for which she was the first woman to be raised to the peerage in 1871. 'What is the use of my means but to try to do good by them,' she observed, and lived up to that ideal by giving away between £3 and £4 million during her lifetime. Dickens both advised her on, and oversaw the distribution of, many of these charitable bequests. He was particularly active in the founding and running of Urania Cottage, a home for fallen women in Shepherd's Bush. However, their friendship practically ended when he separated from his wife. Miss Burdett-Coutts, did not approve of the way he treated Catherine and attempted to forge a reconciliation. Dickens though, remained steadfast. 'Nothing on earth... no not even you,' he wrote, '... can move me from the resolution I have taken.'

Lord Palmerston

Continue along Piccadilly. Keep ahead over Bolton Street, Clarges Street and Half Moon Street to arrive on the right at the former home of Henry Temple, 3rd Viscount Palmerston (1784–1865), from 1857 until his death. Palmerston spent almost 60 years in Parliament, and 50 of those were spent in office. He was Foreign Secretary throughout the 1830s and again between 1846 and 1851. Dickens, along with many idealists, despised Palmerston, and once referred to him as 'the emptiest impostor... ever known'. But the ordinary people admired 'Lord Pumicestone's' energy, and appreciated the way his foreign policy, in particular his gunboat diplomacy, had made Britain respected internationally.

In 1855, when Lord Aberdeen's government was brought down due to the mismanagement of the Crimean War (1853–56), Palmerston became Prime Minister, his bluffness being seen as just what was needed. Fortunate to have come into office as the war entered its final throes, he claimed full credit when a successful conclusion was negotiated in 1856. His private life was just as colourful as his professional one and he was known for his womanizing even into his late seventies. His opponent, **Benjamin Disraeli**, refused to make political capital out of the rumours about Palmerston's affairs for fear the old man would become even more popular if his astonishing libido became public knowledge. Hale and hearty to the end, Palmerston died at the age of 81.

Dickens enters society

Backtrack and cross Piccadilly via the crossing. Bear left and keep ahead until, having passed Green Park Station, turn right after the telephone boxes and go along Queen's Walk, turning left through the passage that goes under the

Opposite: Westminster Hall is where Dickens walked for half an hour to gain control of his emotions following publication of his first story 'A Dinner at Poplar Walk'.

residential buildings. On emerging onto St James's Place, turn left and pause outside Nos 22 to 23, which stand on the site of the house of the poet Samuel Rogers (1763–1855). Rogers was the first person of literary note to acknowledge Dickens's genius, and it was at his famous breakfasts that Dickens first met with the intellectual great and good of the age. Dickens dedicated *The Old Curiosity Shop* to this early mentor, and later based Grandfather Smallweed in *Bleak House* on him.

The first person to be killed by a train

Walk along St James's Place, and as it veers sharp left, cross to No 28 on the right, where there is a blue plaque to William Huskisson (1770–1830). An able politician and statesman, his reforms of the unwieldy tax system, which had been a result of the Napoleonic Wars, enabled the Industrial Revolution to forge ahead. In 1824, Huskisson was Treasurer of the Navy, in which capacity he was petitioned from the Marshalsea Prison by John Dickens, who asked if he would recommend him for a pension on the grounds of ill health.

In 1830, Huskisson was attending the ceremonial opening of the Liverpool to Manchester Railway, when he was run over by Stephenson's Rocket. He died from his injuries a few hours later, thus achieving a posthumous immortality as the first person in history to be killed by a train.

Burlington Arcade

Walk to the end of St James's Place, turn left onto St James's Street, continue to the top and cross Piccadilly at the traffic lights. Bear right and continue ahead, turning left into Burlington Arcade. It was designed by Samuel Ware in 1819 for Lord George Cavendish, reputedly to prevent passers-by throwing oyster shells and other rubbish over the wall of his home, Burlington House. The arcade and its neighbourhood appear in *The Uncommercial Traveller.* It is still patrolled by top-hatted beadles who enforce its Regency laws forbidding you to whistle, sing or hurry.

Dickens suffers a strange experience

Amble past the exclusive shops, and at the far end, cross over Burlington Gardens into Cork Street. A little way down on the right, pause outside No 19, which in the mid-19th century was the Burlington Hotel. One morning in 1854, Dickens was walking along Cork Street when he was suddenly overcome by 'an icy coolness... accompanied by a general stagnation of the blood, a numbness of the extremities, great bewilderment of mind, and a vague sensation of wonder.' As he later recalled, 'on looking about me [I] found that I was in the frigid shadow of the Burlington Hotel. Then I recollected to have experienced the same sensations once before precisely in that spot...' Dickens remained

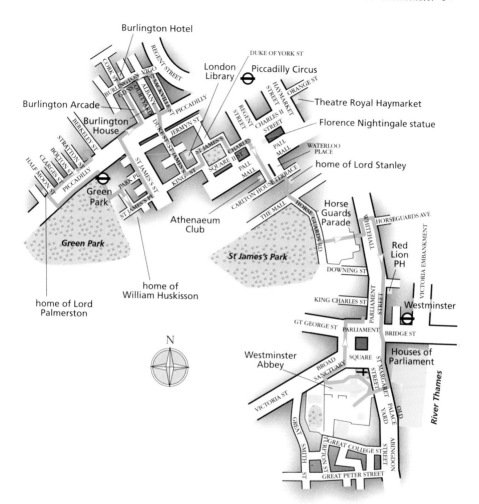

mystified as to what had occurred. It has been wondered if he may have suffered a mini seizure, a harbinger of the one that would kill him 16 years later.

Edward Bulwer-Lytton

Retrace your footsteps, turn left along Burlington Gardens, cross to the right side and pass the back of Burlington House, resplendent with several weathered statues. Keep ahead along Vigo Street; turn right into Sackville Street, right again onto Piccadilly, and then first right into Albany Courtyard. The elegant building ahead is Albany, built between 1770 and 1774, and converted into exclusive chambers for bachelors in 1802 and long considered one of the most distinguished addresses in London. **Edward Bulwer-Lytton** (1803–73), Dickens's friend and confidant had chambers here.

It was in Bulwer-Lytton's play *Not So Bad As We Seem* that Dickens performed before Queen Victoria in 1851. Although a successful novelist in his own right, Bulwer-Lytton's lasting contribution to English literature was persuading Dickens to change the ending of *Great Expectations.* In the original version Pip and Estella go their separate ways, she enduring widowhood and remarriage to a poor Shropshire doctor, he becoming successful in his own right, but remaining a bachelor. It was thanks to Bulwer-Lytton's intervention that, in the revised happy ending, the two met amidst the ruins of Satis House, beneath a moonlit sky, and Pip 'saw no shadow of another parting from her'.

The London Library
Continue along Piccadilly, you may wish to break your walk with a visit to the Royal Academy of Arts, at Burlington House on the right. Otherwise go over the crossing towards Fortnum and Mason, ahead into Duke Street St James's and take the third left onto King Street, keeping ahead to go left into St James's Square. A little way along on the left is the London Library, founded at the instigation of **Thomas Carlyle** (1795–1881), following his frustration at having to wait two hours for a book in the British Museum Reading Room, one morning in 1841. The library moved to this rather grand building in 1845, and it was from here in 1857 that Carlyle sent Dickens two cartloads of books, to assist with his research for *A Tale of Two Cities.*

Dickens's first publisher
Proceed clockwise round the square, passing Chatham House, where a plaque commemorates the residency of three Prime Ministers: William Pitt (1708–78), Edward Stanley (1799–1869) and **William Ewart Gladstone** (1809–98). Keep going straight ahead over Duke of York Street, and continue past the modern building at No 3, which stands on the site of the offices of John Macrone (1809–37), Dickens's first publisher and the man responsible for collecting *Sketches by Boz* into one volume.

J B Buckstone assists Dickens
Go next left into Charles II Street and, on arrival at Regent Street, pause by the crossing to look ahead at the graceful cream façade of the Theatre Royal Haymarket in the distance. Designed by **John Nash** between 1820 and 1821, this was where **Samuel Phelps** made his London debut as Shylock in 1837. It was between 1853 and 1878, however, under the inspired management of the popular comedian and actor, John Baldwin Buckstone (1802–79), that the 'Haymarket' enjoyed its most successful period. Buckstone was both a friend

of Dickens and an influence on his acting style. Indeed, Dickens claimed that, as a boy, Buckstone's acting had so moved him that he had gone home to 'dream of his comicalities'. In April 1857, **Ellen Ternan** began her career as an adult actress here in Buckstone's burlesque, *Atalanta.* This was the first of many roles, which Dickens appears to have been instrumental in obtaining for her since he later wrote to Buckstone saying, 'I shall always regard your remembering her as an act of personal friendship to me. On the termination of the present engagement, I hope you will tell me, before you tell her, what you see for her, "coming in the future".'

Florence Nightingale, the Lady of the Lamp
Turn right along Waterloo Place, where at the end in the centre of the road, is a statue of Florence Nightingale (1820–1910), depicting her in her legendary guise as the 'Lady of the Lamp'. This image of her as a gentle angel of mercy, drifting through the wards of Scutari military hospital during the Crimean War, dispensing compassion to cholera-stricken soldiers, belies a ruthless and able administrator. Her sheer force of will and recognition of the need for hygiene, greatly helped reduce the death rate in the conflict. Returning as a national heroine in 1856, her exertions had taken their toll and she remained a semi-invalid for the rest of her life. However, this did not quell her zeal, and she campaigned tirelessly for nursing and health reforms, both at home and abroad. In 1907 she became the first woman to be awarded the Order of Merit, allegedly accepting it with the words, 'Too kind, too kind'.

The Athenaeum Club
Cross Pall Mall via the pedestrian crossing, and keep ahead into Waterloo Place. Immediately on the right is the Athenaeum Club, founded in 1824 as a meeting place for the intellectual elite of London. Its elegant frontage is best appreciated from the island in the centre of the road. **Lord Macaulay** (1800–1869), **Anthony Trollope** (1815–1882), **Thomas Carlyle**, **Benjamin Disraeli** (1804–1881) and **William Makepeace Thackeray** (1811–1863) were all members, as was Dickens, who was elected at the relatively young age of 26.

Thackeray makes peace with Dickens
Glancing through the front doors into the clubs almost sepulchral interior, you can see the staircase where the famous reconciliation between Dickens and Thackeray occurred. In 1858, one of Dickens's young protégés, Edmund Yates (1831–1894), had included an unflattering profile of Thackeray in his gossip column *Town Talk.* Thackeray was furious and attempted to have Yates debarred from their club, The Garrick. Dickens, who was also a member, sided with Yates and, when the club expelled Yates, Dickens resigned in protest. Dickens and

Thackeray did not speak to each other for five years. In 1863, Thackeray was talking in The Athenaeum with Sir Theodore Martin (1816–1909), when Dickens entered and walked past them. As Dickens ascended the stairs, Thackeray broke from their conversation and caught up with him. Martin later recalled how 'Dickens turned to him... I saw Thackeray speak and presently hold out his hand... They shook hands, a few words were exchanged and immediately Thackeray returned to me saying "I'm glad I have done this".'

The tragedy behind The Frozen Deep

Continue along Waterloo Place, pausing by the statue of Sir John Franklin (1786–1847), whose expedition to find the fabled North West Passage in 1847 ended in tragedy when he and his fellow explorers disappeared. Thanks largely to the persistence of his widow, Jane, attempts were made to discover his fate and, eventually, one of the ships, together with a log of the expedition, was found. It was ascertained that after enduring one winter, their vessels had become ice-locked and several of the men, Franklin included, had died. Following another winter, the rest of the crew had abandoned ship, only to perish in the frozen wastes. Dickens was outraged by a suggestion that the survivors had resorted to cannibalism, and attacked the notion in an article in *Household Words*. The expedition inspired, on Dickens's suggestion, **Wilkie Collins**'s 1857 play, *The Frozen Deep*, in which Dickens played the part of the heroic and self-sacrificing Richard Wardour. For this role he grew the beard, which, for future generations, would become his most memorable feature.

Dickens proves himself

Continue to the end of Waterloo Place, turn left into Carlton House Terrace and pause outside No 11, formerly the home of Edward Stanley, Earl of Derby (1799–1869). In 1833, when Dickens was working as a Parliamentary reporter for his uncle John Henry Barrow's *Mirror of Parliament*, Stanley, who was then Chief Secretary for Ireland, brought his Bill for the Suppression of Disturbances in Ireland before the House. He gave a speech that was so long, that the *Mirror* reporters had to work in shifts to transcribe it. Dickens took down the first and last parts, and when it was published, all except these were found to be full of errors. Stanley, therefore, contacted Barrow and asked him to send the reporter responsible for transcribing these portions to his house, in order that he might copy down the whole speech, as it was to be printed for circulation in Ireland.

When Dickens arrived, he was ushered inside and Stanley, surprised by his youth, eyed him suspiciously, saying, 'I beg pardon but I had hoped to see the gentleman who had reported part of my speech.' Reddening, Dickens replied, 'I am that gentleman.' 'Oh indeed', said Stanley, half concealing a smile. He proceeded to pace up and down the room reciting his speech and, afterwards was fulsome in his praise of the young Dickens. Years later, Dickens came to dine here with the then Prime Minister, William Gladstone whose house this was, and was most amused to find himself in the very room where this youthful episode had occurred.

Did Dickens refuse a knighthood?

Backtrack and turn left down the steps, passing the Duke of York's column. Go over The Mall via the crossing. Looking right you catch a view of Buckingham Palace, where in March 1870 the only face-to-face meeting between Dickens and Queen Victoria took place. She found him '... very agreeable, with a pleasant voice and manner' and there were rumours afterwards that he had declined her offer of a knighthood.

A womanly kiss for young Master Dickens

Bear left along The Mall, right onto Horse Guards Road, and veer left over the gravel ground of Horse Guard's Parade, to pass under the arches and through the gates on the other side. Turn left onto Whitehall, go over the crossing, bear right, and keep ahead over Horse Guards Avenue. On the left, you will pass the Banqueting House, which is all that remains of Whitehall Palace. Here an information board provides a brief history of the building. Keep ahead along Whitehall, continue into Parliament Street, and pause at its junction with Derby Gate, to look up at the medallion bust of Charles Dickens above the second floor window of the Red Lion pub. The pub was rebuilt in 1900, but Dickens, according to an uncompleted autobiographical fragment, came to the premises at the age of 12, and ordered a glass of the 'VERY best ale... with a good head to it'. He was rewarded with a kiss from the landlady that was 'half admiring and half compassionate, but all womanly and good... '. Dickens introduced the episode into *David Copperfield* by having his autobiographical hero ask for a glass of the 'Genuine Stunning' ale.

Dickens works in Parliament

Continue to the end of Parliament Street, cross Bridge Street via the traffic lights and keep ahead with the Houses of Parliament (the New Palace of Westminster) on your left. Shortly after his 20th birthday, Dickens began working in the Gallery of the House of Commons as a parliamentary reporter for his uncle John's *Mirror of Parliament*.

Right: A woman selling oranges – a typical sight on the streets of 19th-century London.

Although the conditions were cramped and uncomfortable, he soon established himself as a first-class scribe, and had established a formidable reputation for speed and accuracy by the time he resigned to pursue his writing career in 1836. The Old Palace of Westminster had burnt down in 1834, and the current building designed by Sir Charles Barry (1795–1860), with help from Augustus Pugin (1812–52), was built and opened in 1852. The Clock Tower was completed in 1858 and a year later its world-famous bell, 'Big Ben', was installed.

Dickens's grave
Continue through Parliament Square, passing on the left Westminster Hall, which dates from 1097. It was inside this hall that Charles Dickens walked for half-an-hour to overcome his emotions on seeing his first story in print. Go over the crossing and keep straight ahead through the gates to enter Westminster Abbey on the left. Once inside, follow the route round the Abbey to Poets' Corner, where in the far right corner is the simple grave of Charles Dickens. Although Dickens had wanted to be buried in Rochester, Kent, it was decided that Westminster Abbey was the only fitting resting-place. However, his wishes for a private and unostentatious funeral were respected and, on Tuesday, 14th June, 1870, a small group of friends and family attended the

unadvertised service here. Nevertheless, afterwards thousands came to pay their respects, and the grave had to be left open for two days as, according to the Dean of Westminster, 'many flowers were strewn upon it by unknown hands, [and] many tears shed from unknown eyes...'.

Exit the Abbey, passing over the very simple grave of Baroness Burdett-Coutts by the doors. Go right from the gates, right into Parliament Square, turn left at the lights and go clockwise around the square into Great George Street. Continue walking ahead to its junction with Parliament Street, where you will find the entrance to Westminster Underground Station.

Left: Charles Dickens lies buried in Poet's Corner, Westminster Abbey.

WESTMINSTER TO HOLBORN

This eventful walk begins with a stroll from Westminster to Embankment where the horror of the River Thames before Sir Joseph Bazalgette built his remarkable sewer system is evoked. It then turns into the area where Dickens, as a young boy, had worked overlooking that stinking river, in a period that traumatized him for the rest of his days. Via a sequence of delightful streets, the walk ventures into Theatreland, passing landmarks that Dickens would recognize today. It follows Dickens through his final years as a successful magazine proprietor and finishes near a churchyard that he described vividly and gruesomely in *Bleak House*.

Start:	Westminster Station (Circle and District Underground lines).
Finish:	Holborn Station (Piccadilly and Central Underground lines).
Length:	2¼ miles (3.6km).
Duration:	2 hours.
Best of times:	Anytime.
Worst of times:	None.
Refreshments:	Several pubs passed en route. There are many cafés and restaurants in the Covent Garden area.

Leave Westminster Station via exit 1 marked Westminster Pier. Turn left and keep walking ahead along Victoria Embankment. The road along which you are walking is little short of a testimony to Victorian determination, confidence and ingenuity. It was the work of Sir Joseph Bazalgette (1819–91), a largely forgotten figure to whom London owes an eternal debt of gratitude.

London's population increases
Between the late-18th and the mid-19th century, the capital's population increased from around half a million to in excess of 2.5 million. The increased housing that sprang up to accommodate the citizens depended largely on an antiquated system of waste disposal that had changed little in 400 years. The effluent from the populace went into cesspools and privies, which invariably overflowed, sending reeking streams of raw sewage onto the streets, to pollute the wells and springs, *en route* to the River Thames.

Cholera epidemics

When the first cholera epidemic struck in 1831, medical opinion believed that the disease was caused by the smells that the capital's residents lived with on a day-to-day basis. In 1848, in an ill-conceived attempt to combat the stench from the sewage in the streets, Parliament passed an act instructing that all cesspits, privies and drains must be connected to a sewer that flowed into the Thames. Thanks to the Great Exhibition of 1851, people were introduced to flushing toilets. They began installing them in their homes, and the river, never pleasant at the best of times, became a fetid swamp, producing a stench which could, on occasions, be smelt from 30 miles (48.3 km) away. Newspapers such as *The Times* campaigned for Parliament to do something, but its members remained silent.

The Great Stink

Then, in 1858, one of the hottest summers on record caused the Thames to dry up and a stinking flat of slime was left behind. 'The Great Stink', as it became known, proved a highly efficient lobbyist. When Parliament, unable to halt the stench with curtains dipped in chloride of lime, was forced to rise early on several occasions, action was demanded. **Benjamin Disraeli** brought in an act giving the Metropolitan Board of Works the funds to resolve the problem.

Sir Joseph Bazalgette, the forgotten hero

Continue along Victoria Embankment and, just before you arrive at the Hungerford Suspension Bridge, pause on the right by the memorial to Sir Joseph Bazalgette. He was the Chief Engineer to the Metropolitan Board of Works, and thanks to his ingenuity, you are able to stand here without being violently sick! Bazalgette undertook what was, without doubt, the largest civil engineering project of the 19th Century. Twenty-two thousand labourers brought chaos to the horse-powered streets of the Victorian metropolis, laying out Bazalgette's network of over 1200 miles (1,931 km) of brick sewers. These criss-crossed London connecting with a further 82 miles (132 km) of main intercepting sewers that carried the effluent into the Thames far to the east of the city. Finally completed in 1875, the effect on the health of Londoners was immediate and dramatic. The cholera epidemics were brought to an end, and for the first time in centuries, the air at the heart of London ceased to be tainted with the fragrant aroma of human waste.

The Victoria Embankment, on which you stand, was designed by Bazalgette to carry the main west–east sewer, and was built between 1864 and 1870. It

Opposite: A knocker on the door of a house in Craven Street gave Dickens the idea for Marley's face appearing on Scrooge's door knocker in A Christmas Carol.

reclaimed 37 acres (15 ha) from the river Thames and connects Westminster with Blackfriars. Given his remarkable achievement and lasting contribution to the quality of life in London, it is a pity that Sir Joseph Bazalgette remains a neglected figure, and that only this dust-caked memorial remembers him.

Warren's Blacking Factory

Continue under the bridges, go over the pedestrian crossing, bear left and go past Embankment Station to turn next right into Northumberland Avenue. Keep ahead over Embankment Place, veer right into Craven Street, and just after the stage door of the Playhouse Theatre, turn right into the unnamed alleyway, to pause by the barrier. Charing Cross Station, which looms above you, stands on the site of Hungerford market, where Warren's Blacking Factory was situated. It was in this rat-infested, ramshackle, wooden building, abutting the river Thames, that Dickens came to work at the age of 12, sticking labels onto pots of boot blacking. His workmates mockingly referred to him as the 'Young Gentleman', and the humiliation of his experience traumatized him, the shame remaining with him throughout his adult life. 'Even now, famous and caressed and happy,' he later said, 'I often forget in my dreams that I have a dear wife and children; even that I am a man; and wander desolately back to that time of my life.'

The real-life Fagin and Dickens's fictional autobiography

The experience also affected his fiction. One of his work companions, for example, was an older boy named Bob Fagin, who was actually quite kind to the young Dickens, and certainly didn't deserve being immortalized in *Oliver Twist*. Later, whilst writing his autobiography, Dickens found this part of his life too painful to recall. Instead he created a fictionalized character, reversed his own initials, and published his thinly disguised autobiography as *David Copperfield*.

Marley was dead to begin with

Backtrack and go right along Craven Street. Lined by dark-brick, 18th-century houses. Number 40 was the home of **Dr Charles West**, founder of the Hospital for Sick Children. Legend holds that it was a grotesque old door knocker on one of these houses that gave Dickens the idea for Scrooge's knocker turning into Marley's face in *A Christmas Carol*. Unfortunately, when an enthusiastic photographer approached the owner for permission to photograph the knocker, she is said to have removed it and placed it in a bank vault for safe keeping. Its whereabouts are now unknown.

Continue to the top of Craven Street and go right along the Strand. Keep going, and on arrival at the pedestrian-crossing, turn right down the steps and into the uninspiring George Court.

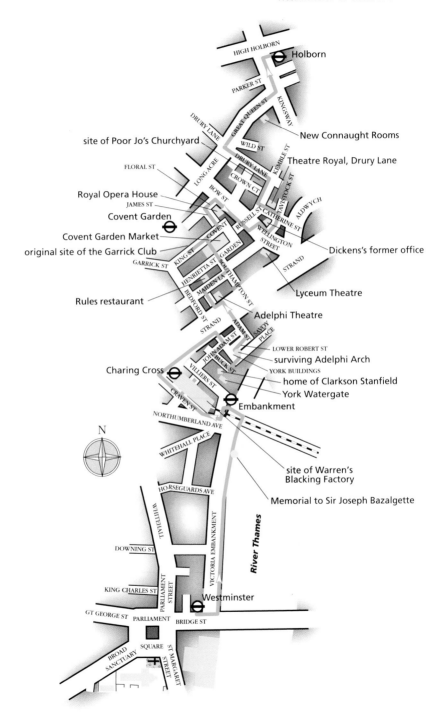

HIGH HOLBORN

Holborn

PARKER ST

GREAT QUEEN ST

KINGSWAY

DRURY LANE

New Connaught Rooms

site of Poor Jo's Churchyard

WILD ST

KEMBLE ST

Theatre Royal, Drury Lane

FLORAL ST

DRURY LANE

LONG ACRE

CROWN CT

TAVISTOCK ST

ALDWYCH

Royal Opera House

BOW ST

JAMES ST

RUSSELL ST

ST CATHERINE ST

Covent Garden

COVENT

WELLINGTON STREET

Covent Garden Market

KING ST

GARDEN

Dickens's former office

original site of the Garrick Club

HENRIETTA ST

SOUTHAMPTON ST

STRAND

GARRICK ST

MAIDEN LA

Lyceum Theatre

BEDFORD ST

Rules restaurant

STRAND

Adelphi Theatre

ADAM ST

SAVOY PLACE

LOWER ROBERT ST

JOHN ADAM ST

surviving Adelphi Arch

BUCK ST

Charing Cross

VILLIERS ST

YORK BUILDINGS

home of Clarkson Stanfield

York Watergate

CRAVEN ST

Embankment

N

NORTHUMBERLAND AVE

WHITEHALL PLACE

site of Warren's Blacking Factory

HORSEGUARDS AVE

Memorial to Sir Joseph Bazalgette

WHITEHALL

River Thames

VICTORIA EMBANKMENT

DOWNING ST

KING CHARLES ST

PARLIAMENT STREET

Westminster

GT GEORGE ST

PARLIAMENT

BRIDGE ST

BROAD SANCTUARY

SQUARE

ST MARGARET STREET

Left: A fly paper seller. Fly paper and net curtains were a useful way of ridding the Victorian household of flies.

Go right onto John Adam Street, and left into Buckingham Street, where a delightful combination of buildings of all ages and architectural styles greets you. At the end on the right a blue plaque on the wall of No 14 remembers the residence here of the artists William Etty (1787–1849) and Dickens's friend **Clarkson Stanfield** (1793–1867). It was at a house opposite (now demolished) that Dickens lodged in about 1834 whilst working as a reporter at the House of Commons.

The York Watergate

Go through the gates. Descend the steps and cross over to the York Watergate, dating from 1626, and long since left landlocked by the construction of the Victoria Embankment beyond. Indeed, gazing from here over to the Thames, which is now some way off in the distance, you begin to get the measure of Sir Joseph Bazalgette's achievement when you consider that, when Dickens lived in Buckingham Street, the river washed around the York Watergate. Having paused to read its history displayed on a board, go left along the pathway, up the steps and turn left into York Buildings. Three quarters of the way along turn right into the delightfully gloomy Lower Robert Street, and descend into one of only a handful of the surviving 18th-century arches, built to support the buildings of the Adelphi – a prestigious housing development by the Adams Brothers.

Dickens loved to explore this labyrinth of subterranean vaults where, according to one account, 'the most abandoned characters... often passed the night, nestling upon foul straw; and many a street thief escaped from his pursuers in these dismal haunts before the introduction of gaslight and a vigilant police.' In *David Copperfield*, doubtlessly remembering his own boyhood, Dickens wrote, 'I was fond of wandering about the Adelphi, because it was a mysterious place with those dark arches... '.

The Adelphi Theatre

Follow Lower Robert Street as it veers right. Go left through the gates at the end, ascend the seemingly endless stairs and keep ahead along Adelphi Terrace, bearing left along Adam Street. Continue on to the Strand. Cross to its opposite side and pause outside the Adelphi Theatre, twice rebuilt since the mid 19th-century, when popular, although piratical, dramatizations of Dickens's novels were staged here. Much to the author's consternation these plays were often put on long before the novels in question had been completed and often anticipated his endings!

A celebrated table for two

Facing the Adelphi, go left and turn into Exchange Court – the second alley on the right. Walk its splendidly atmospheric length and turn right onto Maiden Lane. A little way along on the right, a battered Royal coat of arms stands over the stage door of the Adelphi Theatre. Continue, pausing on the left where the road widens to admire the magnificent frontage of Rules, which is reputedly the oldest restaurant in London. Founded in 1798 by Thomas Rule, its interior is still furnished in grand Victorian style, with 19th-century prints and paintings on the walls and dark wood tables and chairs. Dickens used to dine here regularly and a special table was reserved for him in an alcove towards the back of the first floor. This is now a private dining room. Its walls are adorned with prints and a playbill for a performance that Dickens performed in, which he presented to the restaurant himself. Thackeray was also a regular, and, later, so too were the Prince of Wales (later Edward VII) and his mistress Lillie Langtry, whose private dining room was once the most celebrated 'Table For Two' in London.

The very breath of comic fiction

Continue to the end of Maiden Lane. Go left into Southampton Street and continue ahead to proceed clockwise around the piazza of Covent Garden Market, site of the famous flower, fruit and vegetable market from 1656 to 1974. It was a vivid description of the market in George Colman's *Broad Grins* that caused the young Dickens to venture here in 1822 to experience for himself 'the flavour of the faded cabbage-leaves as if it were the very breath of comic fiction'. In adulthood he mentioned the market many times in his novels. ˙

The Garrick Club

Keep going clockwise, passing on the left the portico of St Paul's church, dating from the 17th century, and where the opening of Shaw's *Pygmalion* (1913) was set. Take the next left into King Street and pause on the right outside No 35, where the Garrick Club was founded in 1831 as 'a society in which actors and men of education and refinement might meet on equal terms'. Dickens was elected to the club in 1837 and retained his membership until 1865.

Thackeray was also a member. One evening in May 1858, he was passing a group of members who were idly gossiping on the steps of the building. The subject of their conversation was Charles Dickens, who had formally and publicly separated from his wife. Rumour had it that the split was due to Dickens having an affair with his wife's younger sister, Georgina Hogarth, who had braved her family's displeasure and become her brother-in-law's housekeeper. To the Victorian mind, such a relationship was tantamount to incest, and it was this scandal that the group were discussing as Thackeray entered the club. 'No such thing,' he cried, 'it's with an actress.' When word reached Dickens of Thackeray's outburst, he sent him an angry denial. But Thackeray remained unconvinced, believing Dickens to be 'half mad about his domestic affairs'. It was later that year that the animosity between them erupted into the so-called 'Garrick Club Affair' (*see* page 127–8), which led to Dickens's resignation from the committee. The club eventually outgrew the intimacy of this first home and, in 1864, moved to its current location on nearby Garrick Street.

The Royal Opera House

Backtrack into Covent Garden Market; turn first left along James Street, right into Floral Street and right again onto Bow Street. Walk past the Royal Opera House, the current building dating from 1858 and which has recently undergone a costly state-of-the-art refurbishment programme. In the 19th century, it was known as the Covent Garden Theatre and it was to its stage manager, George Bartley, that Dickens wrote requesting an audition whilst working at Doctors' Commons (*see* page 152). From 1837 to 1839 the manager here was Dickens's great friend, the actor **William Macready**.

Where the Artful Dodger appeared in court

Continue along Bow Street. It was on the right before Russell Street that the old Bow Street Police Court was situated, and where the Artful Dodger appeared charged with theft in *Oliver Twist.* In 1879, the court moved across the road to its current location, opposite the Royal Opera House.

All the Year Round

Keep ahead into Wellington Street. Cross to the left side, and pause at the junction with Tavistock Street where a blue plaque states that 'this building housed the offices of Charles Dickens's Magazine *All the Year Round* and his private apartments from 1859 to 1870.' The magazine was a weekly publication and included serial fiction, essays, poetry and topical journalism. In its first 27 months the magazine serialized *A Tale of Two Cities, Great Expectations,* as well as Wilkie Collins's *The Woman In White* (1860), and became so successful that crowds would often gather in the street to await the next issue. It was also from here that his *Uncommercial Traveller* set out on his exploratory perambulations around London, the results of which were published in the journal between 1860 and 1869.

The Lyceum and Theatre Royal

Continue along Wellington Street and pause at the junction with Exeter Street to look across at the elegant cream portico of the Lyceum Theatre. It was here that a stage adaptation of *A Tale of Two Cities* was performed with Dickens overseeing rehearsals and, possibly, even directing the play. The novel's famed last words, 'It is a far, far better thing that I do, than I have ever done; it is a far better rest that I go to than I have ever known' were changed to the more succinct and melodramatic, 'Farewell Lucy, Farewell Life!' *Curtain.* **Ellen Ternan** also performed here several times in 1859. In 1863, Dickens's friend, the actor **Charles Fechter** (1824–79), became the manager of the Lyceum and celebrated by giving Dickens the Swiss Chalet that became the author's summer study for the remainder of his life (*see* pages 187 & 199). The offices of *Household Words*, a weekly journal that Dickens edited between 1850 and 1859, used to stand opposite the theatre on Wellington Street.

Turn left into Exeter Street, left into Catherine Street and continue to the top. On the right is the magnificent frontage of the Theatre Royal, Drury Lane, rebuilt in 1812 and managed between 1841–43 by William Macready who, although making a huge financial loss, added to the theatre's prestige.

Poor Jo's Churchyard

Go right along Russell Street, left into Drury Lane and a little way along on the left step through the gates to enter Drury Lane Gardens. This was formerly the burial ground for the church of St Martin's-in-the-Fields (the buildings on either side of the entrance were a mortuary and the keeper's lodge). By the 19th century it had become horribly overcrowded. Dickens used it in *Bleak House* as the original of Jo's Churchyard, where Captain Hawdon (Lady Dedlock's lover and Esther Summerson's father) was buried. It is described as 'a hemmed-in churchyard, pestiferous and obscene, whence malignant diseases are communicated to the bodies of our dear brothers and sisters who have not departed... '. It was on the steps of this churchyard that Esther found the dead body of Lady Dedlock.

Farewell to Dickens

Exit Drury Lane Gardens. Go left along Drury Lane, and turn right at the traffic lights into Great Queen Street. Keep going straight ahead past the huge entrance of the Freemason's Hall, which dominates the right side of the street, and pause outside the New Connaught Rooms on the right. These incorporate the surviving rooms of the Freemason's Tavern where a lavish farewell banquet was given prior to Dickens's departure on his last visit to America in 1867.

Continue to the traffic lights. Cross over Kingsway, bear left and keep going straight ahead to arrive at Holborn Underground Station where this tour ends.

TEMPLE AND FLEET STREET

This walk will take you along Fleet Street passing in and out of alleyways which, although changed considerably since Dickens's day, still bear a unique character ranging from the picturesque to the downright sinister. You will also visit the cloistered and enchanting Middle and Inner Temple. Take your time over this walk and make an effort to lose yourself in the labyrinths of hidden and historic places that are peppered along the route.

Start:	Blackfriars Station (Circle and District Underground lines).
Finish:	Temple Station (Circle and District Underground lines).
Length:	1¼ miles (2.8km).
Duration:	2 hours.
Best of times:	Mondays to Fridays 10am to 4pm.
Worst of times:	Weekends – much of the route is closed to the public.
Refreshments:	Punch Tavern, Ye Olde Cheshire Cheese PH, and the café at Somerset House.

Take exit eight from Blackfriars Station. Walk along New Bridge Street, passing No 14, where a plaque on the wall details the history of Bridewell Palace, founded here in 1523 by Henry VIII. It became a prison and hospital during the reign of Mary I, and by the 19th century had given its name to several hundred other penitentiaries, all of which were known as 'Bridewells'. Noah Claypole taunts Oliver in *Oliver Twist* by telling him that Oliver's mother was 'a regular right-down bad "un"' and 'it's a great deal better... that she died when she did, or else she'd have been hard labouring in Bridewell...'

Go left into Bride Lane, where the majestic 'Wedding Cake' spire of St Bride's Church rises before you, and go right along Fleet Street to arrive at the Punch Tavern.

Punch Tavern
Named after the satirical magazine *Punch*, which was reputedly conceived here in 1841, this snug hostelry is entered via a tiled passageway that leads

Opposite: *Pump Court, Inner Temple. Dickens's words – 'who enters here leaves noise behind' – still ring true of Temple especially during the evening.*

into a veritable time-capsule. Original cartoons and drawings from the magazine adorn the walls, as well as all manner of Punch and Judy memorabilia. The printers Bradbury and Evans published the first edition of *Punch* on 17th July, 1841 from their offices in nearby Crane Court. Despite the fact they later became Dickens's own publishers, and several of the so-called 'Punch Brotherhood' of journalists were close friends, he only ever submitted one article for publication, and that was rejected.

William Thackeray, a regular and prolific contributor, intended to include a good-natured parody of Dickens in his satirical series *Punch's Prize Novelists*. However, Dickens bristled at the prospect and let it be known through his friend **John Forster** that such articles 'did no honour to literature or literary men, and should be left to very inferior and miserable hands'. Nevertheless, he later complained to Thackeray that he was 'strongly impressed by the absurdity and injustice' of being left out!

Dickens the newspaper proprietor

Exit the tavern, turning left along Fleet Street. Pause outside the exquisitely ornate frontage of No 92, which stands on what was the site of the *Daily News* offices, a newspaper set up by Charles Dickens in January 1846. Continue along Fleet Street. Go left into St Bride's Avenue, where you will find St Bride's Church. It is worth visiting, particularly to descend into the crypt where the remnants of previous buildings on the site, including a Roman pavement, can be seen.

Mr Jerry Cruncher, the bodysnatcher

Follow the avenue as it bears right. Turn left along Salisbury Court, right into Salisbury Square, and go up the right-hand corner steps. Follow the paved walkway as it bears left through the grey offices and becomes Hanging Sword Alley. Here Jerry Cruncher, bank messenger and night-time body snatcher lived in *A Tale of Two Cities*. Go right along Whitefriars Street and cross Fleet Street. Keep going ahead into Wine Office Court, where the surging tide of modern urbanity is suddenly repelled by a time-worn step that delivers you into a true survivor of bygone London – Ye Olde Cheshire Cheese.

Ye Olde Cheshire Cheese

Rebuilt in 1667, this rambling tavern of creaking floors, cosy rooms and snug corners, possesses a timeless ambience that keeps the contemporary world firmly at bay. Portraits of those who have worked and supped here over the centuries gaze fondly down from its dark wooden walls. Dr Johnson, Oliver Goldsmith, Mark Twain, Alfred Tennyson and Sir Arthur Conan Doyle – to name but a few – have all ducked beneath its low beamed ceilings to absorb its 17th-century atmosphere. Dickens, too, was a regular, and the table to the right of the

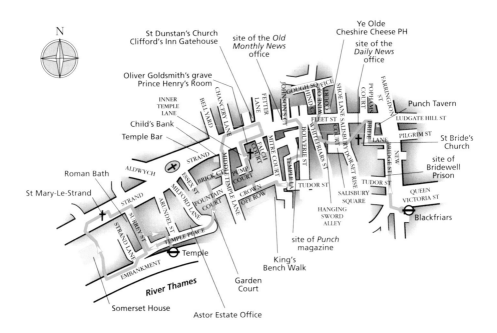

ground floor restaurant's fireplace is said to have been his favoured place. This is believed to have been the pub that Dickens had in mind when, following Charles Darnay's acquittal on charges of high treason in *A Tale of Two Cities,* Sydney Carton invites him to dine: 'Drawing his arm through his own' Sydney leads him to Fleet Street 'up a covered way, into a tavern... where Charles Darnay was soon recruiting his strength with a good plain dinner and good wine'.

Leave Ye Olde Cheshire Cheese and turn right along Wine Office Court. Bear diagonally left past the circular plant-bed, and keep ahead to turn left into Gough Square. Situated here is Dr Johnson's House, where **Samuel Johnson** (1709–84) laboured on his famous dictionary. It is now a museum dedicated to his memory and well worth a visit. Turn left into Johnson's Court, and follow it as it meanders between tall buildings of differing ages and styles. This twisting thoroughfare is perhaps one of the most important sites on the walk, for here stood the office of the *Old Monthly Magazine,* a small-circulation periodical in whose December 1833 issue Dickens's first published story 'A Dinner At Poplar Walk' appeared.

Dickens later recalled how 'stealthily one evening at twilight, with fear and trembling' he had dropped the story 'into a dark letter-box in a dark office up a dark court in Fleet – street'. When he found that they had published it, he was so overcome with emotion that he 'walked down to Westminster Hall, and turned into it for half an hour, because my eyes were so dimmed with joy and pride that they could not bear the street, and were not fit to be seen there'. Although he received no payment for his work, he wrote a further nine stories for the magazine and thus took his first tentative steps to becoming the 'inimitable Boz'.

Dickens falls out with Punch *magazine*

Exit Johnson's Court. Turn left, and cross Fleet Street via the pelican crossing, bearing right then left into Bouverie Street. Number ten on the right, a site now occupied by a modern office block, was home to *Punch* throughout much of the latter 19th Century. Its co-founder and editor **Mark Lemon** (1809–70) was one of Dickens's closest friends, and the Dickens children referred to him affectionately as 'Uncle Porpoise'. A prolific playwright, Lemon was also an enthusiastic participant in many of the amateur theatricals that Dickens delighted in staging, and was well known for his portrayal of *Falstaff*, a character for which his physique was amply suited! But, following Lemon's support for Dickens's wife, Catherine, after their legal separation, Dickens refused to have any contact with him and the two did not speak again for almost ten years.

'Who enters here leaves noise behind'

Turn right into Temple Lane, follow it left and, on arrival at Tudor Street, go right through the gateway into the Inner Temple. You have entered one of London's four Inns of Court, where barristers – the wigged and robed advocates of the legal profession – have their chambers. Immediately the blandness of late 20th-century architecture gives way to a tranquil oasis that has been left untouched by time and progress. 'There is yet a drowsiness in its courts and a dreamy dullness in its trees and gardens' wrote Dickens in *Barnaby Rudge.* 'Those who pace its lanes and squares may yet hear the echoes of their footsteps on the sounding stones and read upon its gates... "Who enters here leaves noise behind".'

Walk diagonally right over the main courtyard, pass the red post box and cross right towards the building with the clock above it. Squeeze through the narrow passage to its right. Turn right, then right again up the steps and bear left into the cloisters. Keep going straight ahead, passing on your right Temple Church, built in 1185. Proceed clockwise round the church and, having passed Goldsmith's Buildings, stroll by the tombstones of the churchyard to the railing where you will find the grave of **Oliver Goldsmith** (1730–74).

Oliver Goldsmith, a favourite author

Although Goldsmith was long dead by the time Dickens was born, he was one of his favourite boyhood authors and remained so for the rest of his life. Goldsmith's only novel *The Vicar of Wakefield* (1762) was a great influence on Dickens's early work, particularly *Pickwick Papers*. Dickens gave his youngest brother, Augustus, the nickname Moses, in honour of Moses Primrose the Vicar's son. Forster in his life of *Dickens* explains how, when this nickname was 'facetiously pronounced through the nose' it became 'Boses and being shortened became Boz', which was the pseudonym that Dickens adopted in 1836, and under which much of his early work appeared.

Backtrack past Goldsmith's Building and go right to exit the Inner Temple via the arched gateway. Almost immediately on the right is the entrance to **Prince Henry's Room**. This small yet beautifully preserved room dates from 1610, and was named after the eldest son of King James I. Originally a tavern called the Prince's Arms, in Dickens's childhood the building was occupied by Mrs Salmon's Waxworks, which Charles certainly visited and to which 'perspiring Wax Works' he later sent David Copperfield.

The weary giants of St. Dunstan's and the 'Demon Barber'

Exit Prince Henry's Room and turn right along Fleet Street. Pause outside the premises of the bankers Messrs Hoare and Co. to gaze across the road at St Dunstan's Church, whose magnificent clock, dating from 1671, is said to have been the first clock in London with a double-sided face, and the first to have the minutes marked on the dial. Its chief glory, however, lies in the two ancient giants that wearily lift their clubs every fifteen minutes and make half-hearted attempts to strike the bells. Sadly their efforts are frequently drowned out by the noise of the Fleet Street traffic. In *David Copperfield*, David and his aunt, Betsy Trotwood, make a special journey to witness the giants strike the bells,

and time their visit 'to catch them at it at twelve o'clock'. In 1830 the old church was demolished and the clock sold to the Marquis of Hertford who re-erected it at his house in Regent's Park. Over 100 years would pass before, in 1935, the clock was returned.

Continue to the traffic lights. Cross over Fleet Street and a little way along on the right, dive into the grim, dark passageway named Hen and Chickens Court. It admits you into a chilling, claustrophobic courtyard, where beneath your feet, hefty iron grilles cover precarious drops into mean

Right: *The church tower of St Dunstan's, Fleet Street, referred to in* The Chimes.

looking cellars where all manner of horrors might be lurking. You are standing at the rear of 185 Fleet Street where Sweeney Todd 'the Demon Barber' had his premises. His murderous, though fictional, escapades first appeared in print in 1847, and so captured the public imagination, that he became the most successful of all the Victorian melodramas. His habit of murdering his clients and conveying them by way of an underground tunnel to nearby Bell Yard, where Mrs Lovett kept a meat pie shop, struck a chord with a reading public who were far more dependent on outside caterers than we are today!

Return to Fleet Street. Turn right, and enter the gates of St Dunstan's. The present building dates only from 1829 to 1833, but is an excellent early example of Gothic Revival architecture. It was in the tower of this church that Toby Veck (known as 'Trotty' on account of his gait) was subjected to a sequence of visions in Dickens's second Christmas book *The Chimes.*

'A mouldy little plantation or cat-preserve'
Continue along Fleet Street. Take the next right and pause outside the 17th-century gatehouse, which is all that survives of Clifford's Inn. Dickens, in *Our Mutual Friend,* has left an enduring, albeit uncomplimentary, portrait of it. John Rokesmith, having followed Mr Boffin along Fleet Street, asks if he would 'object to turn aside into this place – I think it is called Clifford's Inn – where we can hear one another better than in the roaring street?' Mr Boffin 'glanced into the mouldy little plantation, or cat-preserve, of Clifford's Inn, as it was that day, in search of a suggestion. Sparrows were there, cats were there, dry rot and wet-rot were there, but it was not otherwise a suggestive spot.'

Backtrack, turn right along Fleet Street, and cross over Chancery Lane. Cross to the opposite side of Fleet Street at the traffic lights and, a little way along, pause outside Child's Bank, which appears as Tellson's Bank in *A Tale of Two Cities.* Although the bank that Dickens wrote of was pulled down in 1879, the interior of the present building has a decidedly antiquated feel. It is worth stepping inside to view the glass case on the wall opposite the door, in which ten guns are exhibited. The bank purchased the guns in June 1780 to defend the premises during the anti-Catholic Gordon riots so vividly described by Dickens in *Barnaby Rudge.*

Leaden-headed old obstruction
The unsightly memorial column in the centre of the road marks the site where Temple Bar stood until the increasing traffic and the resultant congestion necessitated its removal in 1877. In *Bleak House,* Dickens called it 'that leaden-headed old obstruction, appropriate ornament for the threshold of a leaden-headed old corporation.' Since 1888 the old gateway has lain forgotten at Theobald's Park, in Hertfordshire.

Back track along Fleet Street and turn right through the gateway into Middle Temple Lane. Elegant buildings of redbrick rise up on either side of the cobble-stoned byway, and Charles Lamb's sentiment that 'a man would give something to be born in such places' still holds true.

Dickens trains as a lawyer

Having passed Brick Court, turn right beneath the soaring London plane trees. To your left is Middle Temple Dining Hall, which was built in the 1570s and is occasionally open to the public, so a polite enquiry at the office just inside the door may well be to your advantage. Each of the four Inns of Court possesses its own dining hall in which aspiring barristers must eat a certain number of dinners during each law term. Despite heaping a goodly amount of scorn upon the legal profession, Dickens was not averse to participating in its traditions. In 1839 he enrolled as a student barrister at Middle Temple, hoping that the law would provide a safety net should his writing career end. However, he failed to eat the required number of dinners and subsequently resigned his membership in 1855.

Continue across the courtyard to the picturesque little fountain. In *Martin Chuzzlewit* (1843–44) Dickens wove a romance around this court involving Ruth Pinch and John Westlock. The area has changed little since Dickens wrote of it, 'Brilliantly the Temple fountain sparkled in the sun, and laughingly its liquid music played, and merrily the idle drops of water danced and danced, and peeping out in sport among the trees, plunged lightly down to hide themselves...'

Go down the steps to the left. Garden Court on the right is where Pip was living in *Great Expectations,* when the convict Abel Magwitch turned up one storm-tossed night to reveal himself as the source of Pip's good fortune. 'Alterations have been made to that part of the Temple since that time,' Dickens has Pip explain, 'and it has not now so lonely a character as it had then, nor is it so exposed to the river. We lived at the top of the last house, and the wind rushing up the river shook the house that night, like discharges of cannon, or breakings of a sea...' As you continue ahead to descend the next set of steps, remember that until **Sir Joseph Bazalgette** pushed back the line of the river and constructed the Embankment ahead of you in 1874, the Thames did indeed come right up to the walls of Garden Court.

Go through the gate, bear right, and leave the temple via the next gateway. Turn right along Temple Place, passing the ornate Astor Estate Office, built in 1895 for the 1st Viscount Astor, and noteworthy for its gothic exterior and pleasing weather vane, which depicts a golden caravel – the ship that took Columbus to the Americas.

Continue ahead, turning second right into Surrey Street. Halfway along turn left through the arch into Surrey Steps, and into a shaded walkway that has a sinister air. Go down the steps and turn right into Strand Lane, a narrow, sloping and astonishingly dingy alley that harks back to the darkest days of Victorian London. A little way along on the right you will find the Roman Bath.

Roman Bath
Although no one is sure exactly how old this 'antiquity' actually is, many writers, Dickens included, have referred to it as Roman. Dickens is said to have taken many a cold plunge in its icy waters, and sent David Copperfield to do likewise. The bath itself can be viewed through the window, and what is known of its history can be read on a board outside.

Backtrack along Surrey Street. Go right along Temple Place and turn right along the Embankment. Having turned right through the arches into Somerset House, keep ahead into the reception, where a detailed history of the building can be seen. Leave the room through the passageway to the right, and go up the 'Stamp' stairs. A 19th-century account of the basement through which you walk describes how 'in these damp, black and comfortless recesses the clerks of the nation grope about like moles... and doze and swear, as unconscious of the revolving sun as many miserable demons of romance condemned to toil for ages... '.

Dickens's improvident father
The stairs lead to the delightful courtyard of Somerset House, which was designed by William Chambers in the 1780s and intended to house government offices, including the Navy Pay Office where **John Dickens** (1785–1851) worked as a clerk in 1807. Employed in the same office was a young man named Thomas Barrow, with whom John developed a close friendship and whose sister he later married. In 1822, John was transferred back to Somerset House from the naval offices at Chatham. The resultant drop in salary, coupled with his inability to live within his means, led to his being incarcerated for debt in the Marshalsea Prison on 20th February, 1824 (*see* page 163–4).

Dickens's parents get married
Continue ahead past the line of fountains and exit Somerset House through the three arches. Go over the crossing and pause outside the church of St Mary-Le-Strand, which dates from 1711. It was here on 13th June, 1809 that John Dickens, who by this time had been transferred to the Navy Office at Portsmouth, married Elizabeth Barrow. He then took her back to their new home at Mile End Terrace, Portsmouth, and on 7th February 1812, their son, Charles, was born.

Leaving the church make your way to its rear. Cross back over the Strand, and go ahead into Surrey Street. Turn left along Temple Place, and a little further along on the right is Temple Underground Station where this tour ends.

MANSION HOUSE TO SMITHFIELD

This is a fascinating walk through places with which Dickens was familiar throughout his childhood and later life. The walk crosses the Thames where the first chapter of *Our Mutual Friend* is set. Following a brief riverside stroll, we go over the Millennium Bridge and then stray into a warren of streets laid out on their medieval pattern. Finally, although not included in the walk, you may wish to visit the Museum of London opposite Barbican Station.

Start:	Mansion House Station (Circle and District Underground lines).
Finish:	Barbican Station (Circle, Hammersmith & City and Metropolitan Underground lines).
Length:	2¼ miles (3.6km).
Duration:	2 hours.
Best of times:	When St Paul's Cathedral is open.
Worst of times:	When St Paul's Cathedral is closed.
Refreshments:	Several pubs and cafés are passed on the route.

Dickens in love

Exit Mansion House Station via The Queen Victoria Street/Garlick Hill exit and go left. Take the third left along Huggin Hill, the right side of which is bordered by Cleary Gardens. The churchyard of St Michael Queenhithe, demolished in 1896, was part of the last section of Cleary Gardens. Here the youthful Charles Dickens brought his coquettish first love, **Maria Beadnell**, during their courtship. He recalled in *The Uncommercial Traveller* how they had sheltered in a city church '... on account of a shower', and remarked on the coincidence, that it happened to be in Huggin Lane. Years later he would find it a painful pleasure to walk this way, remembering how 'for four years' he had 'hammered away at the maddest romance that ever got into any boy's head and stayed there... '.

Southwark Bridge

Go left along Upper Thames Street and pass to the left of the attractive church of St James Garlickhythe. Turn right onto Queen Street, left into Upper Thames Street, and cross over the traffic lights, keeping ahead onto Southwark Bridge. The iron bridge that Dickens knew, and over which Little Dorrit loved to walk because 'there is an escape from the noise of the street', was replaced by the

Left: Gaffer and Lizzie Hexam on the Thames from Our Mutual Friend.

present bridge between 1912 and 1921. It is on the stretch of river flowing to the left 'between Southwark Bridge, which is of iron and London Bridge, which is of stone' that *Our Mutual Friend* opens, with Gaffer and Lizzie Hexam making their grisly living fishing dead bodies from the murky waters of the Thames.

Bob Fagin's embarrassing act of kindness
Continue off the bridge, passing the grey bunker-like headquarters of the *Financial Times,* and pause on the left alongside the 18th-century line of houses called Anchor Terrace. One day, when young Charles was working at the blacking factory, he was taken ill and it was decided that he had best go home. Bob Fagin, 'who was much bigger and older than I', insisted on escorting him. Dickens later recalled how 'I was too proud to let him know about the prison; and after making several efforts to get rid of him, to all of which Bob Fagin in his goodness was deaf, shook hands with him on the steps of a house near Southwark Bridge, on the Surrey side, making believe that I lived there. As a finishing piece of reality in case of him looking back, I knocked at the door... and asked when the woman opened it, if that was Mr Robert Fagin's house'. The exact house where this little comic-tragedy was played out is not recorded.

Past and present collide
Go back along Anchor Terrace until you reach the bus stop, descend the steps and turn right onto Park Street. The site of Shakespeare's Globe Theatre is on the opposite side to the left and a display area details its history. Go under the bridge and take the second right into Bear Gardens, a cobbled street lined with dark, imposing warehouses, all of which were present when cargoes from all over the world were offloaded into these storehouses. The lifting mechanisms, still visible on several buildings, stand still, fastened onto walls. Turn left onto Bankside, keeping ahead to pass the modern re-creation of Shakespeare's Globe. Bear right up the ramp, and enjoy the magnificent view of St Paul's Cathedral on the opposite side of the river. You may wish to visit the Tate Modern, which

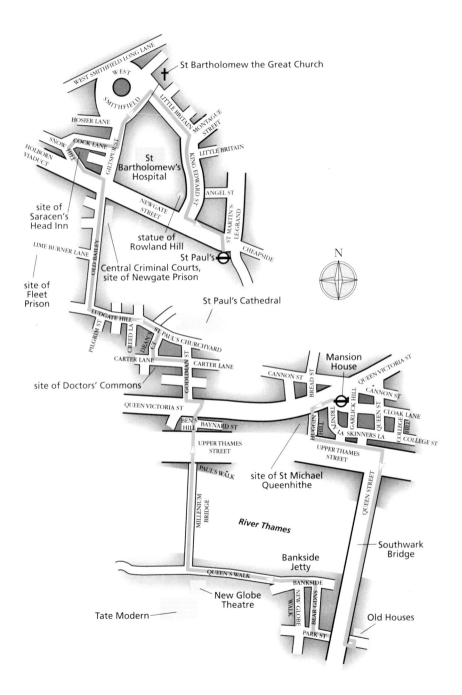

St Bartholomew the Great Church

WEST SMITHFIELD LONG LANE

WEST

LITTLE BRITAIN

SMITHFIELD

HOSIER LANE

MONTAGUE STREET

SNOW HILL

COCK LANE

GILTSPUR ST

LITTLE BRITAIN

HOLBORN VIADUCT

St Bartholomew's Hospital

KING EDWARD ST

ANGEL ST

NEWGATE STREET

ST MARTIN'S LE GRAND

site of Saracen's Head Inn

LIME BURNER LANE

statue of Rowland Hill

CHEAPSIDE

OLD BAILEY

St Paul's ⊖

N

Central Criminal Courts, site of Newgate Prison

site of Fleet Prison

St Paul's Cathedral

LUDGATE HILL

PILGRIM ST

CREED LA

DEAN'S CT

ST PAUL'S CHURCHYARD

GODLIMAN ST

CARTER LANE

CARTER LANE

CANNON ST

BREAD ST

Mansion House

QUEEN VICTORIA ST

CANNON ST

site of Doctors' Commons

QUEEN VICTORIA ST

BEN'S HILL

BAYNARD ST

HUGGIN HILL

⊖

QUEEN HL

GARLICK HILL

SKINNERS LA

QUEEN ST

CLOAK LANE

COLLEGE HILL

COLLEGE ST

UPPER THAMES STREET

UPPER THAMES STREET

PAUL'S WALK

site of St Michael Queenhithe

MILLENIUM BRIDGE

QUEEN STREET

River Thames

Southwark Bridge

QUEEN'S WALK

Bankside Jetty

BANKSIDE

New Globe Theatre

NEW GLOBE WALK

BEAR GDNS

Old Houses

Tate Modern

PARK ST

occupies the former Bankside Power Station, and is distinguished by its single soaring chimney, otherwise cross the river via the Millennium Bridge.

With each step St Paul's Cathedral seems to grow in stature before you: 'the great black dome' that Pip saw on his first visit to London in *Great Expectations;* the dome which to Little Nell in *The Old Curiosity Shop* loomed 'through the smoke, its cross peeping above the cloud', clear of 'the Babel out of which it grew'; the cross that in *Bleak House* is seen as the 'sacred emblem... the crowning confusion of the great, confused city... '. St Paul's dominates its surrounding today, just as it did then, and the modern buildings that line the approach form a guard of honour that complements rather than detracts from its splendour.

Doctors' Commons

Come off the bridge. Go over Queen Victoria Street, and veering left, pass on the right the 17th-century College of Arms, set back behind its ornate gates and railings. Turn right into Godliman Street and go up the hill. The monstrous grey building, which lines the left side, marks what, until 1859, was the entrance to a secluded collection of legal courts and buildings known as **Doctors' Commons**. This 'lazy old nook near St Paul's Churchyard', as Steerforth in *David Copperfield* describes it, was, according to *Sketches By Boz,* 'the place where they grant marriage-licences to love-sick couples, and divorces to unfaithful ones; register the wills of people who have any property to leave, and punish hasty gentlemen who call ladies by unpleasant names... '. In the spring of 1829, Dickens began working here as a clerk for a lawyer named Charles Fenton. He later spoke of this period as the 'usefullest of my life'. It gave him a fierce loathing for the machinery and furnishings of the British legal system, yet it also provided him with an array of characters and stories, which would later be used to such savage yet hilarious effect in so many of his novels.

Dickens's audition

Go left into Carter Lane, where on arrival at the marble columns of the white brick building, a fading sign commemorates the long vanished Bell Yard, where, in 1831, Dickens rented an office and set himself up as a freelance shorthand writer. It was whilst working here that he decided he wished to become an actor and so wrote to 'Bartley, who was stage-manager of Covent Garden Theatre and told him how... I believed that I had... a natural power of reproducing in my own person what I observed in others... '. The letter evidently made an impact, for Dickens was invited to audition and prepared to perform something from the repertoire of comedian **Charles Matthews**.

Opposite: *The dome of St Paul's Cathedral dominates its surroundings today just as it did in Dickens's day.*

But on the appointed day, he was unable to attend, owing to his being 'laid up with a terrible bad cold and inflammation of the face'. 'See how near I may have been to another sort of life,' he later wrote to **John Forster**.

Continue along Carter Lane and, just before the City of London Youth Hostel, which was originally the St Paul's Choir School – hence the bright ecclesiastical motifs and Latin inscriptions that adorn its façade – turn right into Dean's Court. As you emerge onto Ludgate Hill, the west face of St Paul's Cathedral soars majestically over you.

St Paul's Cathedral and the Duke of Wellington

Cross the road and make your way inside the cathedral. Dickens mentions St Paul's Cathedral many times in his novels and, of course, there are many more reasons to visit Sir Christopher Wren's masterpiece than to just seek its Dickensian connections. Having found your way down into the crypt, bear left. Go through the gates and stroll past an assortment of statues. Bear right and pause at the off-white tombstone of **George Cruikshank** (1792–1878), whose remains were transferred here from Kensal Green Cemetery. The memorial on the wall notes poignantly that it was placed 'by her who loved him best his widowed wife'.

Go right, and having passed the massive tomb of Lord Nelson, pause alongside the equally colossal tomb of Arthur, Duke of Wellington (1769–1852). Charley, Dickens's eldest son, was at Eton when the Duke died, and begged his father to take him to St Paul's for the funeral. Dickens, thanks to his friendship with the Duke of Devonshire, managed to acquire six permits for the ceremony. He was appalled by the ostentatious pomp that he witnessed. 'The whole public has gone mad about the funeral of the Duke,' he wrote to **Baroness Burdett–Coutts** (whose suggestion of marriage, incidentally, the elderly Duke had gently declined), and went on to express his disdain for the 'ruinous expenses that has beset all classes of society in connexion with death... '. In a subsequent article in *Household Words* entitled 'Trading in Death', Dickens protested that the Duke's funeral had been turned into a 'Public Fair and Great Undertakers Jubilee'.

Newgate Prison

Exit St Paul's Cathedral. Go straight to descend Ludgate Hill. Having crossed Ave Maria Lane, and passed the church of St Martin-Within-Ludgate, turn right into Old Bailey. Traverse its uninspiring length, and pause outside the Central Criminal Court located at the top end on the right. This courthouse, known the world over by the name of the thoroughfare in which its stands, Old Bailey, is on the site of Newgate Prison, which was demolished in 1902. A gaol has stood here since at least the 12th Century, although the one that Dickens knew was rebuilt, following the destruction of its predecessor by the Gordon Rioters in 1780.

Indeed, the description of the burning of Newgate Prison in *Barnaby Rudge* is a remarkable piece of writing that sees Dickens at his best. The square outside was thereafter used for public executions until their abolition in 1868. The prison held a 'horrible fascination' for Dickens and he visited it several times. It was the subject of one of his *Sketches by Boz*. It was behind its 'dreadful walls, which have hidden so much misery and such unspeakable anguish' that Fagin spent the night prior to his execution. And it was in its infirmary that Magwitch learnt on his death bed in *Great Expectations* that the daughter whom he had 'loved and lost' was Estella.

The Saracen's Head Inn
You may wish to take a break at the courts and attend one of the criminal trials. Then continue left onto Holborn Viaduct. Cross over the traffic lights, and pass the Church of

Above: A guard stands watch at Newgate Prison.

the Holy Sepulchre, dating in part from 1450 and added to over the centuries to create a cornucopia of architectural styles. It was from the tower of St Sepulchre's that the great bell was once rung as Newgate's prisoners were led out to their executions. Go first right down Snow Hill, and pause by the Police Station, where a blue plaque on the wall marks the old site of the Saracen's Head Inn, demolished in 1868. The inn was the chief coaching station for travellers bound for the north of England, and was frequently used as a base by visiting Yorkshire schoolmasters. Prior to the construction of Holborn Viaduct in 1868, Snow Hill was a major thoroughfare with a gradient so steep that 'Omnibus horses going eastwards seriously think of falling down on purpose, and... horses in hackney cabriolets going westwards not unfrequently fall by accident'. In *Nicholas Nickleby* Wackford Squeers advertised that he would be at the Saracens Head 'daily, from one till four... N.B. An able assistant wanted. Annual salary £5. A master of Arts would be preferred'. The title character, who was subsequently taken on as a master at Squeers's Yorkshire School, Dotheboy's Hall, answered the advert.

St Bartholomew's Hospital
Go first right along Cock Lane. Pause at the end on the left to look up on the wall at the cherubic Golden Boy, whose rotund shape marks the spot where the

Great Fire of London burnt itself out in 1666. Cross Giltspur Street, bearing left to pass the buildings of St Bartholomew's Hospital, which was founded in 1123, and is the oldest hospital in London to stand on its original site. Mentioned in *Martin Chuzzlewit* and *Little Dorrit,* the hospital also features in *Pickwick Papers* when Jack Hopkins, a medical student under the wonderfully named Mr Slasher the Surgeon, astonishes the Pickwickians with his story of the boy who stole his sister's beads and swallowed them one by one. 'He's in hospital now... and he makes such a devil of a noise when he walks about, that they're obliged to muffle him in a watchman's coat, for fear he should wake the patients!'

A little further along Giltspur Street, duck into the hospital grounds beneath the main gateway, which was built in 1702 by the stonemasons working on St Paul's Cathedral. Placed above it is London's only statue of King Henry VIII, whom Dickens in his *Child's History of England* called 'one of the most detestable villains that ever drew breath'. The church of St Bartholomew the Less is worth a visit, as is the little hospital museum, situated under the covered walkway ahead on the left. One of the chief glories of Barts is the magnificent staircase to the Great Hall, which can be seen from the museum and where two large paintings by **William Hogarth** (1697–1764) are hung, *The Pool at Bethesda* and *The Good Samaritan.* It is said that Hogarth used patients from the hospital as his models and, such was his attention to detail, that modern doctors can still look at the individual subjects and diagnose the diseases from which they were suffering.

Where Oliver Twist was christened

Backtrack out of the main gate and go right to continue ahead into West Smithfield. **Smithfield Market** is away to your left. Having passed the wall memorial to Sir William Wallace, executed here in 1305, pause to look up at the black and white timbered gatehouse, dating from 1595. Beyond it is London's oldest Parish church, St Bartholomew the Great, dating from 1123 and brimming with atmosphere. It is often used as a film location, and it was here in the recent television adaptation that *Oliver Twist* was christened.

Mr Jaggers, Rowland Hill and the Penny Post

Before the gatehouse, turn right into Little Britain. It was here in what Pip, in *Great Expectations,* described as 'a gloomy street' that the lawyer Mr Jaggers had his office. The street still warrants this description. Go along its right side until it becomes King Edward Street and you arrive at the frock-coated, roadside statue of Sir Rowland Hill (1795–1879). This man who, in the face of determined government and postal service opposition, introduced the penny post in 1840.

Continue along King Edward Street, passing the World War II bomb damaged ruins of Christchurch Greyfriars on the left. Go over Newgate Street via the traffic lights, bear left and a little way along is St Paul's Underground Station.

SOUTHWARK

Dickens first came to know Southwark in the traumatic days of his childhood when his father, John, was incarcerated for debt in the Marshalsea Prison. He was left alone and unhappy in lodgings in Camden Town, but after pleading with his father, he was found new lodgings in Lant Street, close to the prison. There is no doubt that this period of his childhood affected his later life profoundly, both personally and professionally. References to debt and debtors prisons crop up time and again in his novels, most notably in *Little Dorrit* ('The child of the Marshalsea'), and in *David Copperfield*, where John Dickens appears as Mr Micawber, and Charles's memories of the Marshalsea are transferred to the nearby King's Bench Prison.

Start:	Monument Station (Circle and District Underground lines).
Finish:	Borough Station (Northern Underground line).
Length:	2 miles (3.2km).
Duration:	2¼ hours.
Best of times:	Daytime.
Worst of times:	Evenings.
Refreshments:	The George Inn on Borough High Street.

Monument
Leave Monument Station via the Fish Street Hill exit. Turn right and walk to the Monument itself, which is 202 feet (61.6 metres) high, and the tallest isolated stone column in the world. It was built between 1671 and 1677 to commemorate the 'dreadful visitation' of the Great Fire of London (c.1666), which began in Pudding Lane, which is the adjacent street. Dickens mentions the Monument several times. In *Martin Chuzzlewit*, Tom Pinch gets lost in London and then finds himself 'hard by the Monument'. He is about to ask the attendant for directions when a couple arrive and pay their 'tanner' (sixpence) to ascend to its viewing platform. Having let them in through the 'dark little door', the attendant sits down and laughs, 'They don't know what a many steps there is! It's worth twice the money to stop here.' Should you be considering a similar ascent, the spiral stone staircase has 311 steps, but the view from the top is worth the effort.

The giant warders
Continue down Fish Street Hill. Cross Lower Thames Street, bear right and pause alongside the church of St Magnus the Martyr, which was constructed between 1671 to 1676. Before the rebuilding of London Bridge (1823–31), during which its

Left: The 19th-century London Bridge is now an incongruity in the Arizona sun.

location was moved upriver, the churchyard had formed its roadway approach. In *Oliver Twist*, as Nancy heads for her secret meeting with Mr Brownlow and Rose Maylie on London Bridge, Dickens notes how the tower of old Saint Saviour's Church (passed later), 'and the spire of Saint Magnus, so long the giant warders of the ancient bridge, were visible in the gloom... '. A few remnants of the old bridge can be seen in the churchyard, whilst a detailed model of it is displayed inside the church.

Across London Bridge with Dickens

Exit left from the churchyard. Walk under the bridge. Go left up the steps and follow the signs marked 'London Bridge West Side'. Arriving on the bridge, go right at the bus stop and cross the bridge, about which Dickens wrote many times, sometimes referring to the old one and sometimes to the 1832 reconstruction. It was over the former that Pip in *Great Expectations* walked in agonies of despair upon hearing that Estella was to marry Drummle. *David Copperfield* was 'wont to sit, in one of the old stone recesses watching the people going by, or to look over the balustrades at the sun shining in the water and lighting up the golden flame on top of the Monument'.

On arrival on the opposite side, take the stairs on the right (an arrow points to Glaziers Hall), and at the bottom, pause to look at the only remaining arch of **John Rennie**'s 19th-century bridge. The rest was shipped off to America when the present structure was built between 1967 and 1972. It was on the steps of the old bridge that Nancy's fateful meeting with Mr Brownlow and Rose Maylie took place in *Oliver Twist*. Here she betrayed Fagin, Sikes and Monks and was overheard by Noah Claypole. When Sikes learnt what she had

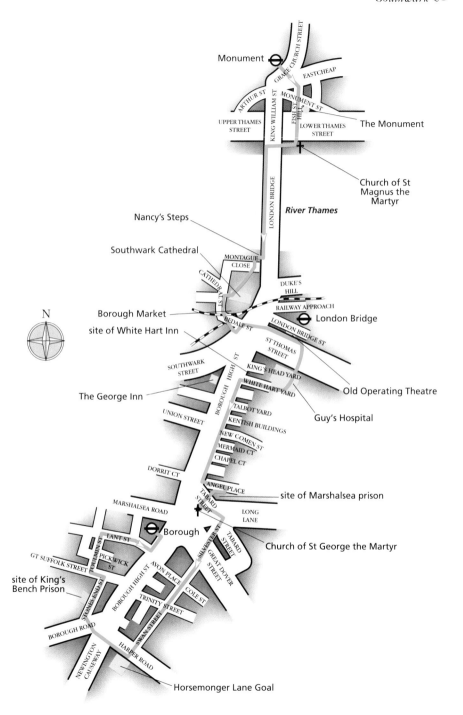

Monument

GRACE CHURCH STREET

EASTCHEAP

ARTHUR ST

KING WILLIAM ST

MONUMENT ST

FISH ST HILL

UPPER THAMES STREET

LOWER THAMES STREET

The Monument

Church of St Magnus the Martyr

LONDON BRIDGE

River Thames

Nancy's Steps

Southwark Cathedral

MONTAGUE CLOSE

CATHEDRAL ST

DUKE'S HILL

RAILWAY APPROACH

N

Borough Market

BEDALE ST

London Bridge

LONDON BRIDGE ST

site of White Hart Inn

ST THOMAS STREET

SOUTHWARK STREET

BOROUGH HIGH ST

KING'S HEAD YARD

WHITE HART YARD

Old Operating Theatre

The George Inn

TALBOT YARD

KENTISH BUILDINGS

Guy's Hospital

UNION STREET

NEW COMEN ST

MERMAID CT

CHAPEL CT

DORRIT CT

ANGEL PLACE

site of Marshalsea prison

MARSHALSEA ROAD

TABARD STREET

LONG LANE

Borough

LANT ST

SILVESTER ST

TABARD STREET

Church of St George the Martyr

GT SUFFOLK STREET

TOULMIN ST

PICKWICK ST

AVON PLACE

GREAT DOVER STREET

site of King's Bench Prison

BOROUGH HIGH ST

STONES END ST

TRINITY STREET

COLE ST

BOROUGH ROAD

NEWINGTON CAUSEWAY

SWAN STREET

HARPER ROAD

Horsemonger Lane Goal

159

done, he murdered her at his house in Bethnal Green, not on the steps of the bridge, as the plaque on the wall here states wrongly.

When Dickens was profoundly ignorant

Go right off the steps. Keep ahead and go left through the gates into Southwark Cathedral. Once inside, go left along the side aisle and pause alongside the tomb of John Gower (d.1408). The church did not become a cathedral until 1905, so Dickens would have known it as St Saviour's. In his essay 'City of London Churches' in *The Uncommercial Traveller* he wrote that he was 'profoundly ignorant' of the names of 'at least nine-tenths' of London's churches, 'saving that I know the church of Old Gower's tomb (he lies in effigy with his head upon his books) to be the church of St Saviour's, Southwark...' Today Gower's colourful effigy still reclines, exactly as Dickens described, and an information board details his achievements as the first English poet.

With your back to Gower, cross to the opposite aisle and, having paused to admire the memorial to William Shakespeare and the window above, resplendent with sundry characters from his plays, go right and exit the church through the glass doors.

Bob Sawyer doesn't live here

Ascend the steps to the right. Go left along Cathedral Street and, opposite 'Fish' restaurant, go right into Borough Market, said to be the oldest fruit and vegetable market in London. Take the first passage left and walk between the fenced-in stalls. The market has retained its steel and glass structure, dating from 1851, and still has a decidedly Victorian air. Dickens used it as the setting in *Pickwick Papers*, when a very drunk Bob Sawyer, attempting to find his way home, 'double knocks at the door of the Borough Market Office' and takes 'short naps on the steps... under the firm impression he lived there and had forgotten the key'.

At the time of writing, plans were underway to re-erect the magnificent portico of the Floral Hall, which once stood in Covent Garden, on the Stoney Street side of Borough Market.

England's oldest operating theatre

Continue through Borough Market and exit left onto Borough High Street. Go right at the traffic lights into St Thomas Street, and enter the red brick tower of St Thomas's Church on the left. Ascend the winding wooden stairway to the roof space of the church, which was once used as the herb garret of St Thomas's Hospital, and from 1822 until 1862 as its female operating theatre. Rediscovered

Opposite: The George Inn, dating from 1677, is the only one of a plethora of coaching inns that once lined Borough High Street that still stands.

in 1956, it was restored, and is now one of the most unique and atmospheric of London's museums. The displays provide vivid glimpses of the science of surgery in the days before anaesthetic or even basic hygiene were an accepted ingredient of medical practice. This informative exhibition gives the history of both England's oldest operating theatre and St Thomas's hospital, where **Florence Nightingale** (1820–1910) founded her School of Nursing. It also provides a lot of detail on the surrounding area when, in the 19th century, it was one of the capital's worst slums.

A recess where David Copperfield sat
Thankful that you were born into a more medically advanced age, go left from the church, and continue along St Thomas Street. Go over the crossing. Bear right and turn left through the gates into Guy's Hospital, where a statue of the founder, Thomas Guy, greets you. Cross to the covered passage ahead, and pause by the quad on the left, where you will find one of the recesses from the old London Bridge, in which David in *David Copperfield* was wont to sit. A brief history is displayed.

Where Mr Pickwick met Sam Weller
Continue down the steps. Go right, then right again. Pass left under the arch; bear left, and turn right into White Hart Yard. Nothing, save the name of the yard, survives of what was, until its demolition in 1889, the largest of the coaching inns that lined Borough High Street. It was to the White Hart Inn that Mr Pickwick

followed Alfred Jingle and Rachel Wardle, following their elopement, and in so doing first met with Sam Weller in *Pickwick Papers*.

Hundreds of ghost stories
Exit the yard left along Borough High Street. Long ago, the voracious appetite of the railways swallowed up the character of this busy thoroughfare, and it is to Dickens we must turn to recapture it. 'In the Borough' he wrote in *Pickwick Papers* 'there still remain some half

Left: In Pickwick Papers *a drunken Bob Sawyer fell asleep in Borough Market thinking he lived there.*

dozen old inns... Great rambling, queer old places... with galleries, and passages, and staircases, wide enough and antiquated enough, to furnish materials for a hundred ghost stories...'

The George Inn
However, all is not lost, for if you turn in through the sturdy black gates next on the left, you will find London's only surviving galleried coaching inn, The George, which was built in 1677. Although Dickens only makes one very brief mention of the pub in *Little Dorrit*, 'if he [Tip Dorrit] goes into the George and writes a letter', the place itself is a true time capsule. Turning into the yard from the busy rush is to be transported back to a bygone age. You can picture the long ago travellers and forgotten inn-workers, gazing down from the one surviving gallery as the coaches clattered into view. You can almost hear the whinnying of the horses, the cursing of the stable-hands and the banter of the coachmen. The inn's interior is as antiquated as its exterior, and on the wall to the right of its middle bar, Dickens's life insurance policy is displayed.

Exit The George and continue along Borough High Street. Almost every yard off it is named after an old inn. Some retain a few of their cobblestones, and several possess the scarred granite blocks set at the width of a wagon axle, the purpose of which was to protect the gate posts from the damage the coaches caused as they turned into the yards.

John Dickens goes to prison
Having passed the John Harvard Library, turn immediately left into Angel Place, lined on the right by a dismal brick wall, which is all that remains of the Marshalsea Prison, where John Dickens was incarcerated for debt in 1824. Before being taken, he turned to his 12-year-old son and told him tearfully, 'the sun was set on him for ever'. 'I really believed at the time,' Dickens later told **John Forster**, that these words 'had broken my heart.' Dickens recalled how, when he first visited his father here he 'was waiting for me in the lodge... and [we] cried very much... And he told me, I remember... that if a man had twenty pounds a year, and spent nineteen pounds nineteen shillings and sixpence, he would be happy; but that a shilling spent the other way would make him wretched.' Mr Micawber would later give the same advice to *David Copperfield* in the most autobiographical of all Dickens's novels.

The Marshalsea Prison
For the rest of his life Dickens was haunted by Marshalsea Prison. It dominates *Little Dorrit*, the heroine of which is a debtor's daughter, born and raised within its confines. And Dickens was speaking from personal experience when he wrote about 'the games of the prison children as they whooped and ran, and

played at hide-and-seek, and made the iron bars of the inner gateway "Home"'. He wrote in the same novel that the Marshalsea 'is gone now, and the world is none the worse without it'. But, as he neared the book's completion, spurred on by letters from readers of the serialization enquiring what had become of it, he returned to look upon what remained.

The dark secrets of his miserable childhood would not become universally known until after his death. Thus, his readers would not have known that he was referring to personal memories when, in the preface to the first edition of the book, he wrote that anyone who turned out of Angel Court [now Place] 'will stand among the crowded ghosts of many miserable years'.

Little Dorrit's Church
Backtrack to go left along Borough High Street and, on the other side of Tabard Street, is the church of St George the Martyr. Built between 1734 and 1736 it is also known as 'Little Dorrit's Church', since it was here that the heroine of Dickens's novel was christened. It is also in this church that, on returning to the Marshalsea Prison, she finds herself locked out and so spends the night in the vestry of the church, using the church register as a pillow. Later, she marries Arthur Clennam here. There is a depiction of *Little Dorrit* in the church's east window, behind the altar, on which her kneeling figure is shown wearing a poke bonnet.

Exit right from the church. Go right into Tabard Street and, towards the end on the left, go through the gates into the gardens, where opposite is the other side of the Marshalsea Prison wall, which has a truly sinister air when viewed on a cold, wet, winter's day.

Horsemonger Lane Gaol
Backtrack, turning left along Tabard Street. Continue over the crossing and ahead into Tabard Street's continuation. Take the first right into Sylvester Street. Cautiously cross Great Dover Street. Keep ahead into Swan Street, at the end of which, turn left onto Trinity Church Square. The houses that now line your way date from the 1820s and, as you turn first right, you pass on the left Trinity Church itself. Follow the square as it veers left. Go first right into Brockham Street. Continue over Harper Road and into Newington Gardens, where there is a board giving a history of Horsemonger Lane Gaol, which stood on this site until 1878.

Dickens watches an execution
Dickens came to the gaol on 13th November 1849, to see the public execution of Frederick and Maria Manning – a husband and wife who had conspired to murder Mrs Manning's young lover. Dickens had come specifically to watch the

behaviour of the crowd, and was disgusted by the 'wickedness and levity', 'the brutal mirth or callousness' that he witnessed. In a subsequent letter to *The Times* he concluded, 'I do not believe that any community can prosper where such a scene of horror and demoralization... is presented at the doors of good citizens...'

King's Bench Prison

Leave the gardens. Go left along Harper Road, crossing diagonally right over Newington Causeway, using the crossings wherever possible, and keeping ahead towards Borough Road. Turn first right into Stones End Street. The Scovell Estate, to the left, occupies the site of the King's Bench Prison, where Mr Micawber – the character based on John Dickens – was imprisoned for debt in *David Copperfield.*

Turn left into Great Suffolk Street, first right into Toulmin Street, passing Pickwick Street on the right, and go next right into Lant Street.

Dickens in paradise

The Charles Dickens Primary School, immediately on the right, stands on the site where the 12-year-old Charles lodged in the house of one Archibald Russell, an agent for the Insolvent Court, during his father's incarceration in the Marshalsea. 'A back attic was found for me,' he later recalled, 'A bed and bedding were... made up on the floor... and when I took possession of my new abode, I thought I was in paradise.' He could take breakfast with his parents and brothers in the prison before setting out to walk to work at Warren's Blacking Factory, via one of the most squalid and unsavoury parts of London. Everything he saw lodged in his childhood memory, and in later life, he would draw upon these experiences time and again in his novels. By his own admission he later immortalized Mr and Mrs Russell as the Garlands in *The Old Curiosity Shop.*

A melancholy street

Bob Sawyer, a medical student at Guy's Hospital, and 'a carver and cutter of live people's bodies' had lodgings in Lant Street in *Pickwick Papers.* Although it is now a modern thoroughfare with none of its 19th-century character, it has a curious, almost forgotten feel about it. In *Pickwick Papers* Dickens relates what this area was like. 'There is a repose about Lant Street... which sheds a gentle melancholy upon the soul... its dullness is soothing... The majority of the inhabitants either direct their energies to the letting of furnished apartments or devote themselves to the healthful and invigorating pursuit of mangling... The population is migratory... His Majesty's revenues are seldom collected in this happy valley, the rents are dubious and the water communication is very frequently cut off.'

With these utopian thoughts of a bygone age, go left along Borough High Street where a little way along is Borough Station and the end of this walk.

THE EAST END

This walk is a journey for your imagination where the urban landscape bears no resemblance to the eastern quarter of the city that Dickens wrote of. But the section that passes through Spitalfields, with its 18th-century weaver's houses and memories of the varied groups of immigrants that have settled here, is genuinely enthralling. The area was once renowned for its dire poverty, where children grew up surrounded by squalor and vice. Dickens was all too familiar with the dreadful conditions that prevailed in the crowded slums and warned his readers that they ignored the dangers posed by this sordid underbelly at their peril. 'Turn that dog's descendants loose,' he wrote, 'and in a very few years they will so degenerate that they will lose... their bark – but not their bite.' His prophesy appears to have been realized when, 18 years after his death, this area became Jack the Ripper's murderous hunting ground.

Start:	Aldgate Station (Circle and Metropolitan Underground lines).
Finish:	Whitechapel Station (District and Hammersmith & City Underground lines).
Length:	2 miles (3.2km).
Duration:	1³/₄ hours.
Best of times:	Daytime.
Worst of times:	Undertaking this walk at night is not recommended.
Refreshments:	Several pubs along Whitechapel Road. Note that the Nags Head has exotic dancers for much of the day. Try one of the Indian restaurants on Brick Lane.

The Aldgate Pump

Exit Aldgate Underground Station and go right along Aldgate High Street, passing on the right the church of St Botolph's, dating from 1740. This is the 'easterly parish church of Houndsditch' where in *A Tale of Two Cities* 'Cruncher... on the youthful occasion of his renouncing by proxy the works of darkness... had received the added appellation of Jerry.' In other words, he was christened here!

Keep ahead over the two sets of traffic lights and continue over Mitre Street. At the next lights, go left over Leadenhall Street and pause at the weathered Aldgate Pump. The present stone pump with its dog-head spout, dates from only 1870, when it replaced the one that Dickens had written about (which actually stood a few feet to the west) in *Dombey and Son, Nicholas Nickleby* and *The Uncommercial Traveller.* Today it sits rather incongruously alongside its modern neighbours, a little piece of old London that many who pass hardly notice.

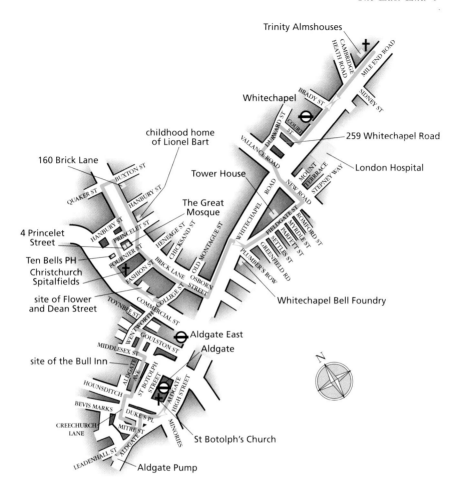

Trinity Almshouses

CAMBRIDGE HEATH ROAD

MILE END ROAD

Whitechapel

BRADY ST

SIDNEY ST

COLET ST

childhood home
of Lionel Bart

DURWARD ST

VALLANCE ROAD

259 Whitechapel Road

160 Brick Lane

BUXTON ST

Tower House

MOUNT TERRACE

STEPNEY WAY

London Hospital

ROAD

NEW ROAD

QUAKER ST

HANBURY ST

The Great
Mosque

WHITECHAPEL

ROMFORD ST

4 Princelet
Street

HANBURY ST

PRINCELET ST

HENEAGE ST

CHICKSAND ST

OLD MONTAGUE ST

FIELDGATE ST

MYRDLE ST

PARFETT ST

SETTLES ST

GREENFIELD RD

Ten Bells PH
Christchurch
Spitalfields

FOURNIER ST

FASHION ST

BRICK LANE

OSBORN STREET

PLUMBER'S ROW

site of Flower
and Dean Street

TOYNBEE ST

COMMERCIAL ST

COLLEGE ST

Whitechapel Bell Foundry

WENTWORTH

GOULSTON ST

Aldgate East

MIDDLESEX ST

Aldgate

site of the Bull Inn

ALDGATE AVE

ST BOTOLPH STREET

ALDGATE HIGH STREET

HOUNSDITCH

BEVIS MARKS

DUKE'S PL

MINORIES

N

CREECHURCH LANE

MITRE ST

St Botolph's Church

LEADENHALL ST

ALDGATE

Aldgate Pump

From Jack the Ripper to Mr Pickwick

Backtrack, turning left along Mitre Street, then right into Mitre Square. Here the flower-bed covers the site where the body of Jack the Ripper's fourth victim, Catherine Eddowes, was discovered on 30th September 1888. Go diagonally right over the cobbled square, passing through Mitre Passage. Veer right along Creechurch Lane, and over Duke's Place via the crossing. You might wish to make a detour to visit Bevis Marks Synagogue, which, founded in 1701, is England's oldest synagogue. It is situated a little way along on the left before you cross. Carry on ahead onto Stoney Lane, right into White Kennett Street, and pass through the modern posts onto the cobbled through way. Having ascended the ramp in the far-left corner, bear left onto St Botolph's Street. On arrival at the second bus stop, swing left down the steps and go right into

Aldgate Avenue, where the Bull Inn stood until 1868. It was from here that Mr Pickwick set out for Ipswich: 'away went the coach up Whitechapel, to the admiration of the whole population of that pretty densely populated quarter.'

Turn left into Middlesex Street, known as Petticoat Lane until the 1830s owing to the second-hand clothes market that stood here. In the 1820s Ikey Solomon, 'the Prince of Fences', operated from Gravel Lane, the now featureless thoroughfare passed on the left. He is often identified (wrongly as it happens) as being Fagin's real-life original.

Dickens enjoys some working class fare
Go right into New Goulston Street, left onto Goulston Street, passing the large tenement buildings on either side, which were built in the 1880s to replace the unsavoury hovels that had formerly lined the road. Go right along Wentworth Street, where on most days you will find a bustling market. Cross Commercial Street via the crossing, and bear left to reach the junction with Lowther Close. This was formerly Flower and Dean Street, and on its corner stood the 'Self Supporting Cooking Depot for the Working Classes'. In the chapter entitled 'The Boiled Beef of New England' from *The Uncommercial Traveller,* Dickens related how he had come to dine here and commented how, for a mere fourpence-halfpenny, he had 'certainly never eaten 'better meat, potatoes and pudding'. A few days later, he continued he had dined at his club in Pall Mall 'for exactly twelve times the money, and not half as well'. His only objection was that the Cooking Depot didn't serve beer!

An East End time capsule
Continue along Commercial Street and pause to gaze up at the solid, soaring tower of Nicholas Hawksmoor's masterpiece, Christ Church Spitalfields, which dates from 1720. On the corner of Fournier Street is the Ten Bells pub, built in the mid-19th Century. Its fine tiled panel from that era, depicts the area's more rural past. Turn right along Fournier Street, which along its latter length is lined with many splendidly restored 18th-century houses. Go left along Wilkes Street and first right into Princelet Street. The buildings that you have passed and those that now stretch before you, have a genuine timelessness about them. Built in the 18th Century for the Huguenot silk merchants and master weavers, they had by the mid 19th Century become common lodging houses, offering miserable living conditions to the poverty-stricken and partly criminal populace. Number 4, on the right, which has a distinctly down-at-heel look

Opposite: These old Almshouses on Mile End Road sit uneasily alongside their more modern neighbours. They were the inspiration behind the Titbull's Almshouses in The Uncommercial Traveller.

about it, does in fact preserve much of its 18th- and 19th-century paintwork and fixtures and fittings. Indeed, so unchanged is its character that recent television adaptations of *Great Expectations; Nicholas Nickleby* and *Oliver Twist,* as well as several biographical films on Dickens's life, have been filmed here. However, it *is* a family home and not a film set so please respect their privacy.

Stroll along Princelet Street. Number 19, on the left, dates from 1719. It became a synagogue in 1870 and remained so until 1980. Plans are afoot to turn the building into a museum of immigrant life. On arrival at the junction, pause to look over at No 106, which was the childhood home of Lionel Bart (1930–99), whose stage musical *Oliver!,* and its subsequent film, provided a melodious, foot-stomping score to one of Dickens's best-known and best-loved stories.

The Ebenezer Temperance Association

Turn left along the bustling and vibrant Brick Lane. Cross to the right side, keeping ahead over Buxton Street. A little further along on the right is No 160, which featured in *Pickwick Papers* as the Mission Hall, where the Brick Lane Branch of the 'United Grand Junction Ebenezer Temperance Association' held their monthly meetings. Here the members 'sat upon forms, and drank tea, till such time as they considered it expedient to leave off... '

The London Society

Backtrack along Brick Lane and keep going past Princelet Street. Pause at the junction with Fournier Street on the right, where the large building on the corner has a history that is reflective of the neighbourhood's changing demographics. Built in 1743 as a Huguenot School and chapel, the building was acquired in 1809 by the London Society – a group of evangelical Christians dedicated to converting Jews to Christianity. The society was one of several such bodies that offered £50 to any proselyte who would resettle in a Christian district. These societies became a joke amongst the émigré community, as it was well known that certain perpetual converts, were simply going from one society to another proclaiming their changes of faith and collecting their rewards on Earth rather than in Heaven! When the London Society disbanded in 1892, they reported having spent thousands of pounds on conversions, but could only claim sixteen bona fide successes. They were certain of these because they had sent them to China as Christian Missionaries. However, the Society had long before given up their tenure here, for in 1819 the building became a Methodist Chapel, remaining so until 1897, when it became the Spitalfields Great Synagogue. In 1975, it was converted into a Mosque.

Oysters and poverty

Continue along Brick Lane, passing on the right Fashion Street, which was the childhood home of writer and Hollywood scriptwriter Wolf Mankowitz (1924–98), who wrote the book of the Broadway musical *Pickwick*. Keep going ahead along Osborne Street, and go left along Whitechapel Road. The garden on the right was formerly the site of St Mary's Church. It was from the lime-washed exterior of this church, known as the White Chapel that this area derived its name. In the early 19th Century, Whitechapel Road, one of the poorest parts of London, was noted for its array of oyster stalls. As Mr Pickwick and the loquacious Sam Weller make their way along here, en route to Ipswich, the latter comments how 'It's a wery remarkable circumstance... that poverty and oysters always seem to go together... Blessed if I don't think that ven a man's wery poor he rushes out of his lodgings, and eats oysters in reg'lar despration... '

Big Ben and the 'Monster Doss House'

On arrival at the crossing, go over Whitechapel Road, veer left and pause outside the Whitechapel Bell Foundry, which has been casting bells on this site since 1783 and is where Westminster's Big Ben was cast in 1858. Go right into Fieldgate Street and follow it as it sweeps left to pass the huge building, known locally as the 'Monster Doss House'. Its looming bulk with its round turrets and soaring, dark brick walls, punctured by numerous tiny windows dominates this stretch of the walk. It opened in the late 19th Century as a hostel for the homeless, and now stands derelict, its future uncertain. Keep walking ahead, passing several streets that retain the atmosphere of the Victorian East End. Go left into New Road and continue to its junction with Whitechapel Road, noting Mount Terrace on the right, which also has a 19th-century look.

The helpless women at the Whitechapel Workhouse

Cross over Whitechapel Road at the traffic lights, and keep going straight along the continuation of New Road. Nothing now remains of either the Whitechapel Workhouse, or Thomas Street in which it stood. It used to be further along on the right and it was here that, one cold night in 1855, Dickens chanced upon a forlorn group of women, 'five bundles of rags', who had been refused entrance to the workhouse. He didn't believe one of them when she told him that she hadn't eaten for a day. 'Why look at me!' she cried, then 'bared her neck, and I covered it up again'. Dickens gave her a shilling for supper and lodgings elsewhere. 'She never thanked me,' he later recalled, 'never looked at me – melted away into the miserable night, in the strangest manner I ever saw.'

The Elephant Man

Go first right into Durward Street. The large building that dominates the far end was a 19th-century school that has now been converted into flats. It was a little beyond the left side of this building that the first Jack the Ripper murder, that of

Mary Nichols, occurred in the early hours of 31st August, 1888. Pass to the right of the building, turn right over the railway bridge and go through the passageway that brings you out onto Whitechapel Road. Turn right and on arriving at the crossing, pause outside No 259. It was in the shop that occupied this building in November 1884 that Joseph Merrick (1862–92), the so-called 'Elephant Man' was displayed in a freak show. A placard announced him as the 'Deadly Fruit of Original Sin'. **Dr Frederick Treves** (1853–1923), a surgeon at the London Hospital which is opposite, was so appalled by the cruelty shown Merrick, that he befriended him and, in 1886, had him moved into the hospital, where he lived in isolated rooms for four years until his death. His skeleton is now preserved in the hospital's museum, although this is not open to the public.

Dr Barnado
Backtrack along Whitechapel Road. The street market held here on most days began in the 1850s when the road was widened. In those days the traders were mostly Irish who had fled the 1845–48 potato famine. By the end of the 19th-century the majority of stall holders were Jewish. Today, they are mostly Asian. The London Hospital on the opposite side of the road was founded in 1740. In 1866 Thomas John Barnado (1845–1905) arrived here to study medicine with the intention of becoming a medical missionary. However, he was appalled by the number of homeless children on the streets of Stepney, and began teaching part-time in one of the local 'ragged schools', where he learnt a great deal about the plight of these youngsters. In 1868, he founded his East End Juvenile Mission and two years later established a hostel. The notice above the hostel's door read 'No destitute boy or girl ever refused admission'. Thus began the 'Dr Barnado's Homes', which still provide both residential and non-residential care for thousands of children in several parts of the world.

A home fit for a decayed mariner
Continue over Cambridge Heath Road at the traffic lights, and keep going ahead into Mile End Road, noting the bust of William Booth (1829–1912) the founder of the Salvation Army, who commenced his work hereabouts in July 1865. Keep going along Mile End Road, and a little further along on the left, are the Trinity Almshouses. Built in 1695 for '28 decay'd Masters & Commanders of Ships or ye Widows of such', these are thought to be the *Titbull's Almshouses* 'in the east of London... in a poor, busy and thronged neighbourhood... ' into which, according to Dickens in *The Uncommercial Traveller*, you 'drop... by three stone steps... '

Retrace your footsteps along Whitechapel Road to Whitechapel Underground Station and the end of this stroll through London's East End.

DOCKLANDS

Great changes have taken place in Docklands since Dickens's day, and a whole new city has been created where once ships from all over the world moored along the vast cliff-like walls of the docks. In *The Uncommercial Traveller* Dickens wrote that this part of London was generally known as 'Down by the Docks', and described it as being 'home to a good many people – to too many, if I may judge from the overflow of local population in the streets – but my nose insinuates that the number to who this is Sweet Home might easily be counted.' Now, the massive warehouses, where cargoes from all over the world were once stored, have been converted into luxury apartments and the pubs, once some of the most violent in London, have been spruced up to cater for their new well-heeled clientele. But scratch the surface and remnants of old Docklands are still there.

Start:	Shadwell Station (East London Underground line and Docklands Light Railway).
Finish:	Westferry (Docklands Light Railway).
Length:	2 miles (3.2 km).
Duration:	1³/₄ hours.
Best of times:	Daytime and summer evenings. I would not suggest walking the first section from Shadwell to Wapping in the evening.
Worst of times:	Winter evenings.
Refreshments:	Prospect of Whitby PH and The Grapes PH.

St George's Church

Exit Shadwell Station. Turn right onto Cable Street and just past the ornate library building dated 1860, go left through the gates. Keep walking ahead and proceed clockwise round the clearly visible St George's Church. **Nicholas Hawksmoor** designed this massive edifice with its impressive 160-foot (48.8-metre) tower between 1714 and 1726. Sadly it sustained terrible bomb damage in World War II and only its outer walls survive as testimony to its former grandeur. In the 1850s the church's rector and curate caused controversy by conducting their services according to 'Romish' practices. Dickens condemned this as 'miserable trifling... fancy-dressing and pantomime posturing'. The locals were even more incensed and brought barking dogs to church, whilst the men refused to remove their hats and smoked their pipes throughout the services! Having arrived at the west door of the church, you find a modern interior crouching within the older walls. With your back to this, exit through the gates opposite, turn left onto Cannon Street Road and left along The Highway.

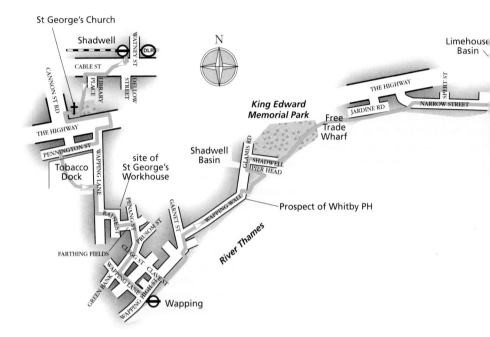

Dickens visits an opium den

In Dickens's day this was known as Ratcliff Highway and it was renowned for its crime and prostitution. Nowadays, it is little more than a busy and ugly thoroughfare. It was to the long-vanished court just beyond St George's Church that, shortly before his death, Dickens paid a visit to an opium den. Later, he sent John Jasper to the same neighbourhood in *The Mystery of Edwin Drood*. 'Eastward and still

Left: The opium den mentioned in Dickens's last unfinished novel The Mystery of Edwin Drood*.*

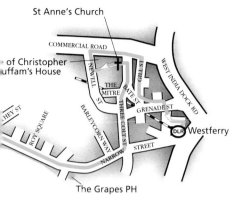

eastward through the stale streets... until he reaches his destination, a miserable court, specially miserable among many such.' His destination was the opium den where 'in the meanest and closest of small rooms' he lay upon a squalid broken-down bed and experienced opium-tainted visions.

Tobacco Dock

Keep ahead, and go over the pedestrian crossing. Bear right then first left into Wapping Lane, and right onto Pennington Street. A little way along go left to enter the interior of Tobacco Dock. This vast cavernous area was built between 1811 and 1813 and was used for the storage of skins, tobacco, tea and spices. When the docks closed, it was converted into a shopping centre, but this failed to attract the public in sufficient numbers and now it is an empty and haunting place where your footsteps echo in the crypt-like interior.

As you enter, there are two interesting statues of a little boy looking up at a huge tiger. These commemorate the days when the area was a landing stage, not just for exotic cargoes, but also for all manner of exotic beasts. These statues depict an incident in the early 19th Century when a full-grown Bengal Tiger, which had just been delivered to the nearby Jamrach's Emporium on Ratcliff Highway, escaped from its crate. It trotted down the road, scattering people as it went. An eight-year-old boy, who had never seen such a big cat, attempted to pat it on the nose, but the tiger seized the child between its jaws and trotted off with him. Mr Jamrach ran after them, forced his bare hands into the tiger's throat and managed to release the boy unscathed.

Mr Baker's Trap

Go down the steps and walk through the eerily gloomy brick arches of Tobacco Dock's lower level. Pause to admire the 19th-century ship figureheads displayed on the wall at the far end. Just past them, exit between the replicas of the two sailing ships that tower over you. Go up the steps, turn left and note the solid dock walls away to your right, which give some impression of the size of the shipping once accommodated here. Go up the next steps, turn right onto Wapping Lane and pass over the bridge. It was hereabouts that Dickens got lost while en route to Wapping Workhouse in *The Uncommercial Traveller* and arrived at 'a swing-bridge looking down at some dark locks in some dirty water'.

Enquiring of one of the locals what the place was called, he was told 'Mr Baker's Trap'. Mr Baker was the local coroner and this was a favoured spot for suicides.

A Charity School

Keep ahead, passing the old dock wall on your right. Go left into Raine Street and turn right after the former charity school, dated 1719. Be sure to look up at the first-floor niches from which the statues of a boy and girl resplendent in their smart uniforms look down. Note also the legend above the door, 'Come in and learn your duty to God and man'.

St George's Workhouse

Just before the Church of St Peter's, built in 1866, turn left into Farthing Fields, where the St George's-in-the-East workhouse used to stand. Dickens wrote in *The Uncommercial Traveller* that having knocked at its gate he 'found it to be an establishment highly creditable to those parts, and thoroughly well administered by a most intelligent master'. A few walls of the workhouse still survive behind the buildings to your left.

A Riverside Stroll

Go right along Penang Street, right into Prusom Street and left onto Wapping Lane. The council blocks give way to old docklands warehouses now converted into luxury apartments. Keep going ahead between the walls that cast the pavement into perpetual twilight, and turn left along Wapping High Street. Having passed Wapping Station and on arriving at the modern block of flats on the right, follow the signs for the Thames Path. Go up the ramp, push open the red gate and walk along the riverside. The massive tower of Canary Wharf looms ahead. A little way along, a gate bars your way, but just push the button on the wall to open it. A little further along pass through the large gate, where to your right steps lead down onto the shoreline, so if it's low tide you might like to take a riverbank stroll.

The Prospect of Whitby

Turn right onto Wapping High Street, go first right along Wapping Wall and keep ahead to arrive on the right at The Prospect of Whitby, the oldest riverside inn in London. Built in 1520, it was originally known as the Devil's Tavern, but its name was changed in 1777 after the collier the *Prospect*, from Whitby, North Yorkshire, which regularly moored alongside it. The pub doesn't

Opposite: The riverside pub The Grapes still overlooks the Thames just as it did when Dickens used it as the basis for The Six Jolly Fellowship Porters in Our Mutual Friend.

look that impressive from the outside, but once over the threshold you are pitched into a time warp that has changed little since the days when Dickens, amongst others, used to drop in for a tipple. Old prints and photos of the river adorn its walls. The flagstone floor and pewter-topped bar, perched on old beer barrels, are truly antiquated and have witnessed both the low and high life of London's docklands.

The Mormon Emigrants

Exit the pub. Turn right, and go almost immediately right onto the paved walkway to follow the Thames Path. Where the semi-circle of the Shadwell Pier Head juts out into the river, go left into Shadwell Basin. For an essay in *The Uncommercial Traveller* entitled 'Bound For the Great Salt Lake' Dickens visited the *Amazon*, an emigrant ship about to set sail for Utah with a large number of Mormons on board. He was most impressed to find everything in order for the long voyage. 'Two great gangways made of spars and planks connect her with the wharf' he wrote, 'and up and down these gangways, perpetually crowding to and fro and in and out, like ants, are the Emigrants...'

Limehouse Basin

Continue ahead, turning left along Glamis Road. Go over the red bridge and turn right again following the signs for the Thames Path. This dark, dismal pathway leads to the King Edward Memorial Park, and passes by the redbrick ventilation shaft from the Rotherhithe Tunnel, which runs under the river to your right. Go through the park and keep going ahead along the Thames Path. At the end of the path, go down the ramp, turn left and go straight ahead along Narrow Street. Continue over Limehouse Basin, which opened in 1820 as the Regent's Canal Dock and was London's main gateway to England's canal network. The huge lock gates can be seen to your left. In *Our Mutual Friend* Rogue Riderhood 'dwelt deep in Limehouse Hole, among the riggers, and the mast, oar and block makers...'.

Continue going straight ahead. As the modern apartments submit to a delightful terrace of 18th-century buildings on the right, you will find The Grapes pub. This is a genuine Dickensian survivor. The Grapes (known to Dickens as The Bunch of Grapes) looks out onto a river that was once the main highway into the capital, in an era when tea-clippers and schooners from the ends of the Earth turned the Thames into a thick forest of masts. In *Our Mutual Friend*, Dickens renamed the pub The Six Jolly Fellowship Porters, and his description of it as 'a tavern of dropsical appearance... long settled down into a state of hale infirmity...' with 'corpulent windows in diminishing piles' still holds true when viewed from the river. Its bar is cosy and intimate; Dickensian prints adorn the walls and an open fire glows in the back bar. Gazing from the back veranda, you can see how accurate Dickens's eye for detail was when he wrote: 'But it had outlasted and clearly would yet outlast many a better trimmed building, many a sprucer public house, indeed the whole house impended over the water, but seemed to have got into the condition of a faint-hearted diver who has paused so long on the brink that he will never go in at all.' The landlady of The Six Jolly Fellowship Porters, Miss Abbey Potterson, was actually based on Mary Ferguson, who in Dickens's day kept the Barley Mow pub (now demolished) that used to stand opposite The Grapes.

Exit the pub, and turn right along Narrow Street. Go left into Three Colt Street and pass through the gates of St Anne's Church to proceed anticlockwise around the church. It was in this Nicholas Hawksmoor-designed

Above: *The London docks crowded with tea-clippers and schooners.*

church that Miss Abbey Potterson 'had been christened... some sixty odd years before'. Its clock is the highest church clock in London. As you exit through the gates on the opposite side of the church, note the strange pyramid monument, originally meant to surmount the church itself. Go out through the gates, walk along the short cobblestone street and keep ahead into Newell Street. During Dickens's childhood this was known as Church Row and it was at No 5 that Christopher Huffam, Charles's godfather, lived. Huffam was a sail-maker and ship's chandler, and John Dickens often brought Charles on visits here. Many was the time that the young boy would stand upon his godfather's kitchen table and be urged to sing to an audience of admiring neighbours. On one occasion, according to Dickens himself, one witness declared the boy to be a 'prodigy.' Everything that Dickens saw hereabouts stayed with him, and his memories of the neighbourhood were such that he nearly always wrote of the docklands with affection.

An idea of the appearance of 19th-century Church Row can be gleaned from the line of houses situated to the left. However, your way lies to the right along Newell Street, and right onto Commercial Road, to go second right into Gill Street. Just before the railway bridge, go left along the pathway, left into Grenade Street, and first right, passing through the railway arch. Go left along Trinidad Street and keep going ahead to arrive at Westferry Station.

BLACKHEATH TO GREENWICH

Situated on the Old London to Dover Road, Blackheath still has a desolate feel about it. Dickens knew it well as it was on the route to Kent and he would think nothing of walking from his home in the centre of the capital to Gad's Hill in Kent. His parents lived hereabouts for a time, and it was over its bleak expanse that the Dover Coach rattled in the evocative second chapter of *A Tale of Two Cities*. Greenwich was always a favoured venue for him to visit and he wrote about the notorious Greenwich Fair in *Sketches by Boz*. He was fond of dining at the Ship Hotel, now gone, and the Trafalgar Tavern, which you can visit today. This walk might not be packed with Dickensian sites, but it offers a bracing stroll away from the congestion of London.

Start:	Blackheath Station (Overground trains from Cannon Street, Charing Cross and London Bridge).
Finish:	The *Cutty Sark* and the Maritime Greenwich Station (Docklands Light Railway).
Length:	2³/₄ miles (4.4km).
Duration:	2¹/₄ hours.
Best of times:	Daytime when Greenwich Park and the Maritime Greenwich attractions are open.
Worst of times:	Evenings.
Refreshments:	The Trafalgar Tavern. There is a café in Greenwich Park opposite the Old Royal Observatory. Goddard's Pie House, which has been serving up Pie and Mash since 1890.

Nathaniel Hawthorne

Come out of Blackheath Station, go over the crossing and bear right along Blackheath Village. Keep ahead onto Lee Road and just after Blackheath Halls go left into Blackheath Park. Keep going as far as St Michael's Church, after which, turn left into Pond Street. Pause a little way along on the right outside No 4, where the American writer Nathaniel Hawthorne (1804–64) stayed in 1856, six

Opposite: *St Alphege Church, Greenwich, where Bella Wilfer married John Rokesmith in* Our Mutual Friend.

years after his most famous book, *The Scarlet Letter* (1850), was published. Dickens was not overly impressed with Hawthorne's tale of New England guilt and sin and considered that the psychological aspects of the story were 'not truly done'. Dickens's opinion aside, the book met with critical acclaim and Hawthorne followed it in rapid succession with *The House of the Seven Gables* (1851) and *The Blithedale Romance* (1852). In 1853 he was appointed US Consul in Liverpool, spent the next four years in Britain, and in 1856 stayed for several months at this villa-style house that would not seem out of place in New England. Commenting on Dickens's reputation he wrote that he was 'evidently not liked nor thought well of by his literary brethren – at least the most eminent of them, whose reputation might interfere with his. Thackeray is much more to their tastes.'

Birthplace of Dr John Simon
Continue to the end of Pond Road. Turn right along South Row, pass Cator Manor on the right noting its splendid chimneys and go next right into The Paragon, dating from 1794 and restored between 1947 and 1957 following bomb damage in World War II. Dr John Simon (1816–1904), the great public health reformer, was born at No 10. In 1848 he was appointed the first Medical Officer for Health in London and for the rest of his life dedicated himself to researching and improving the public health of the metropolis. He was responsible for many of the sanitary reforms that, in the latter half of the 19th Century, helped make London an altogether more pleasant and disease free city.

Salem House *and* David Copperfield
Continue along The Paragon's graceful crescent. Having arrived at the end, go over South Row and strike diagonally left across Blackheath, heading towards the modern silver tower of Canary Wharf, which is clearly visible in the distance. Anyone of the graceful houses that surround the heath could be taken as the origin of Salem House, the school in *David Copperfield* where David met Steerforth and was forced by the ferocious Mr Creakle to wear a sign on his back marked, 'Take care of him – he bites'. The school and its sadistic headmaster were based on **William Jones** and his Wellington House Academy, which Dickens himself had attended. Dickens simply changed its name and moved its location to 'down by Blackheath'. During his long, lonely trek to Dover to seek out his aunt, Betsey Trotwood, David spends the night by a haystack in this vicinity.

The wild and dangerous heath
Continue diagonally left over Blackheath. In the 18th Century this was a wild and remote place and only the extremely brave or extremely foolhardy would dare cross its bleak expanse. Shooters Hill Road, which you eventually cross by the pelican crossing, was once a notorious haunt of highwaymen. It leads onto

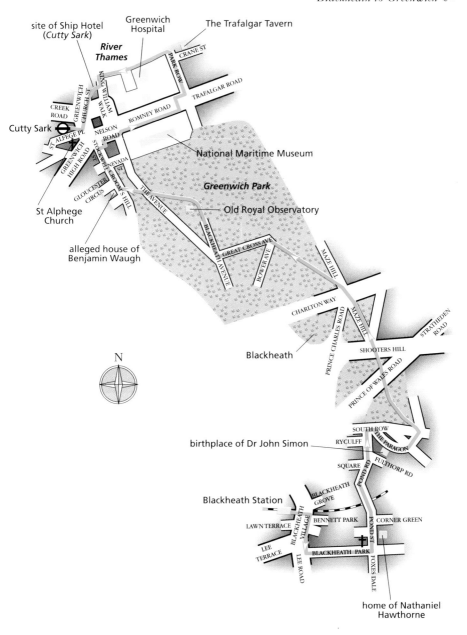

site of Ship Hotel
(*Cutty Sark*)

Greenwich
Hospital

The Trafalgar Tavern

*River
Thames*

CRANE ST

PARK ROW

KING WILLIAM WALK

GREENWICH CHURCH ST

TRAFALGAR ROAD

CREEK
ROAD

ROMNEY ROAD

Cutty Sark

ST ALFEGE PL

NELSON
ROAD

GREENWICH HIGH ROAD

STOCKWELL ST

NEVADA ST

National Maritime Museum

GLOUCESTER CIRCUS

CROOM'S HILL

Greenwich Park

St Alphege
Church

THE AVENUE

Old Royal Observatory

alleged house of
Benjamin Waugh

BLACKHEATH AVENUE

GREAT CROSS AVE

BOWER AVE

MAZE HILL

CHARLTON WAY

PRINCE CHARLES ROAD

MAZE HILL

STRATHEDEN ROAD

N

Blackheath

SHOOTERS HILL

PRINCE OF WALES ROAD

SOUTH ROW

THE PARAGON

birthplace of Dr John Simon

RYCULFF

SQUARE

POND RD

FULTHORP RD

Blackheath Station

BLACKHEATH GROVE

BLACKHEATH VILLAGE

BENNETT PARK

CORNER GREEN

LAWN TERRACE

POND ST

LEE
TERRACE

LEE ROAD

BLACKHEATH PARK

FOXES DALE

home of Nathaniel
Hawthorne

Shooters Hill up the muddy, mist-draped slopes of which in chapter two of *A Tale of Two Cities*, the Dover Coach was struggling one Friday night late in November 1775, when Jerry Cruncher – whom the guard threatens to shoot

183

thinking him a highwayman – overtakes to deliver a message to Mr Jarvis Lorry, who is heading for Paris in an attempt to find Dr Mannette.

A splendid view
Keep going towards the tower of Canary Wharf. On arrival at the somewhat dilapidated covered drinking fountain, cross the convergence of busy main roads and keep ahead onto Maze Hill. Walk along its left side and, on arrival at the railing, go left through the gate into Greenwich Park. Go straight ahead, keeping ahead when the railings of the Flower Garden end on your left side. On arrival at the drinking fountain, turn right onto Blackheath Avenue and walk to the end, where a truly stunning vista unfolds before you. The elegant white building in the foreground is The Queen's House, designed by Inigo Jones (1573–1652) for Charles I's wife, Henrietta Maria, and completed in 1635. Beyond that are the graceful domed towers of Sir Christopher Wren's early 18th-century Greenwich Hospital behind which is the Thames and the looming modernity of Docklands. To the left stretches the London skyline with St Paul's Cathedral clearly visible on the horizon.

A periodical breaking out at Greenwich Fair
Greenwich Fair was held on the slopes beneath you in the late- 18th and 19th centuries. When the railway came to Greenwich in 1836, the fair, which until then had been a local celebration, became a major event for the entire capital and thousands of Londoners flocked here by train and riverboat. In *Sketches By Boz* Dickens described it as, 'a periodical breaking out... a sort of spring-rash: a three days' fever, which cools the blood for six months afterwards, and at the expiration of which, London is restored to its old habits of plodding industry, as suddenly and completely as if nothing had ever happened to disturb them'. He went on to mention how the 'principle amusement is to drag young ladies up the steep hill which leads to the observatory, and then drag them down again, at the very top of their speed, greatly to the derangement of their curls and bonnet-caps and much to the edification of lookers-on from below'. However, the Fair's reputation for disorderly behaviour brought complaints from the locals and it was closed down in 1857.

The founder of the NSPCC
To your left are the buildings of The Old Royal Observatory, erected for the first Astronomer Royal, John Flamsteed (1646–1719) in 1675. With the observatory to your left, begin descending the hill via the flight of steps that lead onto the steep pathway, and where it arches around the benches, head towards the distant redbrick tower with its white clock. Go over the road and keep ahead to exit the park through the gate onto Croom's Hill. Go over the crossing, noting No 26 to

your left on the opposite side of Gloucester Circus. It has a plaque to Benjamin Waugh (1839–1908), who in 1884 founded the Society for the Prevention of Cruelty to Children (NSPCC). The plaque should actually be on No 62, further along, the mistaken location being caused by the renumbering of the houses in 1878.

Where Bella Wilfer married John Rokesmith
Bear right down Croom's Hill and keep ahead over Burney Street into Stockwell Street. Go over the crossing and bear left. The Church of St Alfege on the opposite side of the road was designed by **Nicholas Hawksmoor** and completed in 1714. It was here in *Our Mutual Friend* that Bella Wilfer married John Rokesmith: 'The church porch having swallowed up Bella Wilfer for ever and ever, had it not in its power to relinquish that young woman but slid into the happy sunlight Mrs John Rokesmith instead.'

The Trafalgar Tavern
Turn right into Nelson Road, keep ahead over King William Walk and continue along Romney Road. You may wish to pay a visit to The National Maritime Museum and the Queen's House, the entrance to which you pass on the right. Otherwise cross to the left side of the road, go first left into Park Row and at the end on the right is the Trafalgar Tavern. Built in 1837, this hostelry was a favoured haunt of Dickens, who came here to enjoy its celebrated whitebait dinners. Today, you can still enjoy these tasty little fish, although they no longer come fresh from the Thames outside! The restaurant at the back of the ground-floor bar has portraits on its walls of notable former diners, including Dickens and his wife, Catherine, **Mark Lemon**, **William Thackeray**, **Wilkie Collins**, **Thomas Hood**, **John Forster** and **George Cruikshank**.

The wedding dinner
Exit the Trafalgar and turn right. Go over the steps and follow the riverside, passing the buildings of the Royal Naval College, now occupied by the University of Greenwich. On arrival at Greenwich Pier, bear left and pass to the right of the *Cutty Sark*, the last and most famous of the great tea clippers built in 1869 and now a museum. It stands on the site of the Ship Hotel, one of Dickens's favourite Greenwich hostelries, and where the marriage dinner of John and Bella was held in *Our Mutual Friend*: 'What a dinner! Specimens of all the fishes that swim in the sea, surely had swum their way to it.' The Ship Hotel was destroyed by bombing in 1941.

You may wish to board a boat at Greenwich Pier and take a boat back to Central London. Otherwise keep ahead through Cutty Sark Gardens, along Greenwich Church Street, and just after Ottakar's bookstore, turn right into the shopping lane. Cutty Sark Station is on the right.

ROCHESTER

Rochester was Dickens's favourite city and, 'as a small queer boy', he was fond of exploring its 'old corners'. Rochester features in several of his novels. The Pickwickians come here in the early chapters of *Pickwick Papers*. Although not named, it is obviously the city featured in *Great Expectations,* and is Dullborough Town in an essay in *The Uncommercial Traveller*. In the unfinished *The Mystery of Edwin Drood* it becomes Cloisterham, and it is perhaps fitting that the last words Dickens ever wrote were about the city for which he felt genuine affection, and where he wished to be buried.

For three days every June, Rochester hosts the Dickens festival, a colourful extravaganza during which the city takes on the character of the Victorian age, as people dress in period costume and many of Dickens's most colourful characters walk the streets. A similar celebration takes place in December, when the cast of characters is swollen by bell ringers and carol singers, and thanks to the wonders of modern technology, snow is guaranteed!

Start and Finish:	Rochester Railway Station.
Length:	2 miles (3.2km).
Duration:	2½ hours.
Best of times:	Daytime when the castle, cathedral and Dickens Centre are open.
Worst of times:	Evenings.
Refreshments:	The High Street has many cafés with names like A Taste of Two Cities and Peggotty's Tea Rooms. Also several pubs are passed en route.

The purest jackass in Rochester?

Leave Rochester Station. Go right along High Street, cross over the pedestrian crossing and bear right. At the next lights go over the busy roads into the continuation of High Street, heading towards the clearly visible spire of Rochester Cathedral. Keep to the left side, and pause outside the black and white timbered building, just before Eastgate Terrace. A plaque reveals it to be the house of Mr Sapsea, auctioneer and Mayor of Cloisterham in *The Mystery of Edwin Drood*. There was a late 19th-century tradition that Mr Sapsea, 'the purest jackass in Cloisterham', as Dickens described him, was an amalgam of two local townsmen: a councilman who lived in this building, and a former mayor of Rochester. The house was also featured in *Great Expectations* as the home and shop of Uncle Pumblechook.

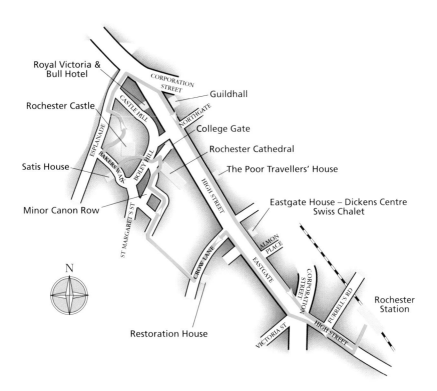

Dickens's Swiss Chalet

Go right through the gates on the opposite side of High Street, passing on the left the 16th-century Eastgate House. Go left through the iron gates to find the brown and lime Swiss Chalet, which formerly stood across the road from Dickens's house at **Gad's Hill**. The chalet was a gift from his friend, **Charles Fechter** (1824–79) in 1864, and Dickens used it as a summer study for the rest of his life. Indeed, it was in the upper room of the chalet that he wrote his last words on the afternoon of 8th June, 1870.

The Charles Dickens Centre

Backtrack to the entrance of Eastgate House. In Dickens's day this was a girls' school, and he featured the building in *The Mystery of Edwin Drood* as The Nun's House, a Seminary for young ladies run by the eminently respectable Miss Twinkleton. Dickens's description of it as 'a venerable brick edifice... The house-front... so old and worn... ' still holds true today. It was at this seminary that Rosa Bud, Edwin Drood's fiancée, was a pupil. Dickens had also used the house in *Pickwick Papers* as Westgate House girl's boarding school, albeit he transported it lock, stock and barrel to Bury St Edmunds! The Charles Dickens Centre now occupies the property, wherein are exhibited many relics of his life and times. Imaginative recreations together with audio-visual displays, bring both Dickensian London and England vividly to life. Allow yourself a good 40 minutes to enjoy what is an essential part of the walk.

The home of Miss Havisham

Return to High Street, go right then next left into Crow Lane and walk up the hill. Three quarters of the way along on the left is the dark redbrick Restoration House, so called because Charles II stayed here on his return to England in 1660. In *Great Expectations* this was Satis House, 'with its seared brick walls, blocked windows and strong ivy, clasping even the stacks of the old chimney's...' Here lived the embittered, jilted bride Miss Havisham, and here Pip met with the cold and contemptuous Estella, with whom he fell desperately in love.

On the afternoon of Monday 6th June, 1870, three days before he died, Dickens was seen leaning against the wooden railing across the street from Restoration House, studying it intently as if committing every brick to memory. There was comment at the time that 'there would be some notice of this building' in *The Mystery of Edwin Drood*.

Minor Canon Row

Go up the steps opposite, and keep going ahead along the asphalt path into The Vines, which was once the vineyard of the monks of St Andrew's Priory. Take the right path, and continue through the gap in the wall, to turn right and follow the road left into Minor Canon Row, a shabby, almost neglected terrace, built in 1723 for the lesser clergy of Rochester Cathedral. A 'wonderfully quaint row of red-brick tenements...' was how Dickens described them in 'The Seven Poor Travellers'; 'they had odd little porches over the doors, like sounding-boards over old pulpits'. In *The Mystery of Edwin Drood* this was Minor Canon Corner, 'a quiet place in the shadow of the cathedral, which the cawing of the rooks, the echoing footsteps of rare passers, the sound of the Cathedral bell, or the roll of the Cathedral organ, seemed to render more quiet than absolute silence...'

A fine old sarcophagus

Continue as the road swings right passing on the left the 15th-century Prior's Gate. Follow it left, and a little way along, go through the iron gate on the right,

Opposite: The redbrick Restoration house was re-named Satis House in Great Expectations. *It was here that the jilted bride Miss Haversham lived as a recluse and strove to take her revenge on mankind through the cold-hearted Estella.*

down the steps and into Rochester Cathedral. In *Pickwick Papers* Alfred Jingle described the cathedral as having an 'earthy smell' and being a 'Sarcophagus – fine place – old legends too – strange stories: capital...' Dickens returned to the cathedral in *The Mystery of Edwin Drood*, imbuing it with a haunting atmosphere in some of the most poetic prose he ever wrote.

'"Dear Me," said Mr Grewgious, peeping in, "it's like looking down the throat of Old Time". Old Time heaved a mouldy sigh from tomb and arch and vault; and gloomy shadows began to deepen in corners; and damps began to rise from green patches of stone; and jewels, cast upon the pavement of the nave from stained glass by the declining sun, began to perish... all became grey, murky and sepulchral, and the cracked monotonous mutter went on like a dying voice, until the organ and the choir burst forth, and drowned it in a sea of music.'

The Cathedral today is a light and airy place, evidently much changed since Dickens wrote those words. However, the crypt – the steps to which are situated almost immediately on the right as you enter – still has a musty, earthy smell, and as you descend into it, it is, indeed, 'like looking down the throat of Old Time'. Exit the crypt, turn left and ascend the steps. Pass straight ahead through the doorway and pause to the left of the ornate Chapter House doorway, where there is a brass memorial plaque to Charles Dickens.

Richard Watts and Satis House

Go left through the gates to cross in front of the high altar. Keep going ahead through the choir stalls, and pass beneath the organ. Go down the steps, bearing left at the lower altar and cross to the side alcove, where above the reclining figure with his hands clasped, is the wall memorial to Richard Watts (1529–79), by whose charitable bequest the Poor Travellers' House on High Street was founded. On 11th May, 1854, Dickens was looking around the cathedral when he came upon this memorial. Fascinated by this charity, he asked a verger for directions to the house, and 'The way being very short...' set out to visit it.

Exit the cathedral through the door at the end of the right aisle, where straight away the castle looms ahead of you. Turn left, follow the cobbles as they swing right, and cross over the road. Pause by the wall on the other side, to look down upon the gravestones in the 'little graveyard under the castle wall', where Dickens expressed a wish to be buried.

Go down the slope to cross the moat diagonally left and pass through the arch at the top of the steps in the far-left corner. Keep ahead and continue through the gates surmounted by the stone lion heads then pause outside the cream building in the corner. This is Satis House, formerly the residence of Richard Watts of Poor Travellers fame. In 1573, whilst Queen Elizabeth I was being entertained here, she summed up his hospitality by uttering a single Latin word

– *Satis* (enough) – hence the property's name. Dickens used the name, though not the actual building, for Miss Havisham's house in *Great Expectations.*

With your back to Satis House, go down the pathway, pass by the two gateposts, and cross the road. Bear left down the hill and a little way along, on the right, go through the gate to enter the grounds of Rochester Castle, the entrance to which is clearly visible on the right.

Rochester Castle and a Dickensian view

Built in 1128 Rochester Castle is a magnificent, ruined fortress, whose lofty heights afford stunning views of the town below. As a child, Dickens had often pottered about these ruins, and they feature in the pages of several of his novels. Alfred Jingle in *Pickwick Papers* calls it a 'fine place... glorious pile – frowning walls, tottering arches – dark nooks – crumbling staircases'. Indeed, it is from the timeworn ramparts reached via its crumbling stairs, that you can best appreciate the final lines that Dickens wrote about Rochester on the day before he died. 'A brilliant morning shines on the old city. Its antiquities and ruins are surpassingly beautiful, with a lusty ivy gleaming in the sun, and the rich trees waving in the balmy air. Changes of glorious light from moving boughs, songs of birds, scents from gardens, woods and fields... penetrate into the cathedral, subdue its earthly odour and preach the Resurrection and the Life. The cold stone tombs of centuries ago grow warm; and flecks of brightness dart into the sternest marble corners of the building, fluttering there like wings.'

The Guildhall

Exit the castle, go down the wooden steps, bear right and keep going ahead on the broad path to pass the large cannon. Descend the steps, and turn right onto the Esplanade. The balustrade that borders the river came from the medieval Bridge taken down in 1857, and which Dickens mentioned in *Pickwick Papers.* Go right by the Crown Pub onto the High Street to reach, on the left, the light brown building, which is a wonderful museum furnished in the fashion of the mid 1870s. Next door is Rochester's Guildhall, that 'queer place... with higher pews in it than in a church', where Pip came to be articled as Jo Gargery's apprentice in *Great Expectations.* The museum that occupies this building contains a recreation of one the great Prison Hulks, the ships that were once moored in the Thames estuary, and from one of which Abel Magwitch escaped in the same novel.

Where Princess Victoria stayed

On the opposite side of High Street is the Royal Victoria and Bull Hotel, an 18th-century coaching inn, where Princess – later Queen – Victoria stayed in 1836. In those days it was known simply as the Bull Inn, and Dickens mentions it in several novels notably in *Pickwick Papers* and *Great Expectations.*

The moon-faced clock

Continue along the High Street, passing beneath the huge clock that juts out from the wall of the Old Corn Exchange on the left. In *The Uncommercial Traveller,* Dickens wrote how he had once supposed this to be 'the finest clock in the world; whereas it now turned out to be as inexpressive, moon-faced, and weak a clock as ever I saw'.

Was Edwin Drood murdered?

Keep to the right side of High Street and, having crossed Boley Hill, pause alongside the 15th-century Chertseys, also known as College Gate. This was the home of Edwin Drood's wicked uncle, John Jasper; the man who may, or may not, have murdered his nephew, so jealous was he of Edwin's betrothal to Rosa Bud. Perhaps Edwin, whose disappearance is the mystery of the title, was murdered here and his body hidden in a grave in the crypt of the Cathedral, a little beyond the gatehouse? Sadly we will never know what Dickens intended for his vanished protagonist, for his untimely death, when the novel was but a quarter finished, has left one of the greatest 'whodunits' of English literature.

Continue along High Street. A plaque on the next building on the right states that this was the home of Mr Tope, the chief verger at Cloisterham Cathedral in *The Mystery of Edwin Drood.* The last words that Dickens wrote were concerning a 'very neat, clean breakfast' that Mrs Tope laid out for their lodger.

Was Dickens a rogue?

Keep going along the High Street until, just after the Visitor Centre on the left, you arrive at The Poor Travellers' House. Its name derives from a bequest left by Richard Watts for 'Six Poor Travellers, who not being ROGUES or PROCTORS' were to be provided with 'one Night Lodging, Entertainment, and Fourpence'. When Dickens visited the house in 1854, he stood in the street outside pondering that since 'I know I am not a Proctor, I wonder whether I am a Rogue!' Looking up, he noticed 'a decent body, of a wholesome matronly appearance...' watching him from one of the open lattice windows. This 'matronly presence' showed him around the property, and his visit subsequently became the subject of his Christmas story 'The Seven Poor Travellers', which appeared in *Household Words* that year. The house is now a delightful museum, which details the history of this property, and the rooms in which the poor travellers ate and slept until the house was closed on 20th July, 1940 can be visited.

Go left out of the house and continue to the end of the High Street where, having crossed the traffic lights, follow its continuation to arrive back at Rochester Railway Station and the end of this walk.

A COUNTRY RAMBLE

This bracing walk will take you through some of the beautiful Kent countryside that Dickens both knew and loved. He discovered the area when, as a small boy, his father John would take him on long hikes from their home in Chatham. This was the happiest and most settled period of his childhood. As an adult, he returned to the area many times, both in his life and fiction, and it was here that, having purchased a house that his father had pointed out to him on their country rambles, he spent most of the final years of his life.

Start:	Sole Street Railway Station (trains from London Victoria).
Finish:	Higham Station (returning to Charing Cross and London Bridge).
Length:	7 miles (11.3km).
Duration:	4–5 hours.
Best of times:	Anytime. Although on the first Sunday of the month Gad's Hill School is open to visitors.
Worst of times:	None.
Refreshments:	Leather Bottle Inn, Cobham; Rose and Crown PH, Shorne; Sir John Falstaff Inn, Gad's Hill.

Go left out of the station, left again onto the main road and continue walking ahead for some distance turning right along Gold Street. This narrow, twisting lane has several blind bends, so you need to be extremely careful. When you arrive at 'The Whitehouse', go left through the gate opposite and veer right along the grass track. Continue through the iron gate and keep ahead as the footpath meanders through a delightful orchard. After the first section, follow the path left and then bear diagonally right, heading towards the two electricity pylons in the distance that appear to be side by side.

The pylons are the only modern blight upon a landscape that has, apparently, changed little in over a hundred years. The way is lined by fruit trees that are heavy with apples and pears in season. Follow the track over the intersecting main path and bear right. Keep ahead as the clearly defined path passes between the two pylons, and head for the clump of trees in the distance. When you arrive at them go through the iron gate into Cobham Churchyard. Pass the bench, turn left up the asphalt walkway, and just before arriving at the church, go right then right again through the tiny doorway into the New College of Cobham.

The New College of Cobham

Hidden from the outside world by the bulk of Cobham Church, this delightful and secret place originally dates from 1362, when Sir John de Cobham founded and endowed a college for priests here. It was dissolved between 1539 and 1540 and, having lain derelict for almost 60 years, the buildings were converted into almshouses in 1598 and have remained in use ever since. Be sure to step through the doorway in the far-left corner to admire the old hall. Exit the New College, and walk round to the main entrance of Cobham Church.

Having visited the church of St Mary Magdelene, descend the path through the lichen-encrusted tombstones, amongst which Mr Pickwick and Mr Tupman could be seen pacing to and fro as the former tried to reverse the latter's resolution to renounce life (see below). Cross over the road and a true Dickensian landmark awaits you.

The Leather Bottle Inn

Built in 1629, this attractive half-timbered inn became known as Ye Olde Leather Bottle in about 1720 when a leather bottle containing gold sovereigns was found on the premises. This was one of Dickens's favourite hostelries and in later years, when he lived at nearby Gad's Hill, he delighted in showing the 'clean and commodious village alehouse' to American visitors. Today, the place is a veritable shrine to his memory. Its walls are adorned with close on 1,400 Dickensian prints, drawings and photographs – some of Dickens himself, the majority depicting his characters and scenes from his novels. In the hotel reception sits the chair that Dickens reputedly occupied whenever he visited.

In *Pickwick Papers,* following his jilting by Rachel Wardle, Mr Tupman becomes depressed and, having left a note telling Mr Pickwick that 'Life... has become insupportable to me...', disappears. Convinced he is about to commit suicide, the Pickwickians pursue him to the Leather Bottle. You can still walk down the same passage into the 'long, low-roofed room' where at the upper end was a table 'well covered with a roast fowl, bacon, ale, and etceteras: and at the table sat Mr Tupman, looking as unlike a man who had taken leave of the world, as possible'.

A Victorian murder

Leave the Leather Bottle Inn. Turn left along The Street, passing The Ship Inn, from where in the fading light of day on Monday, 28th August, 1843, Robert Dadd, and his artist son, Richard, set out to enjoy a circuitous walk around Cobham Park, for which you are now heading. Doctors had recently diagnosed

Opposite: Cobham's Leather Bottle Inn was one of Dickens's favourite hostelries and now possesses a remarkable collection of Dickensian memorabilia. This chair is said to have been the one he used whenever he dropped by for a tipple.

Richard as mentally unstable and, as a result, his father was keeping a constant, concerned parental watch on him. But as they left The Ship that night, Dadd the elder had no inkling that, in his son's troubled mind, he had become 'The man who calls himself my father', nor that the Egyptian god Osiris had ordered Richard to kill the impostor.

As the two men headed back to the village across Cobham Park, Robert Dadd turned towards a tree to relieve himself. Suddenly, his son launched at him and stabbed him to death. Fleeing the scene, Richard hurried over a stile, leaving bloody handprints on its top rung, and fled into the night. With him went his prospects as one of the most promising young artists of his generation. Brought to justice, he was declared insane and spent the remainder of his life in the new asylum for criminal lunatics at Broadmoor. Dickens often showed visitors the stile near which the murder had taken place, and as one guest remembered, would delight in acting 'the whole scene with his usual dramatic force...'

Continue to the war memorial – it was off Halfpence Lane to your left that the murder took place – and carry on into the unpaved Lodge Lane. On arrival at the little yellow cottage, go through the gate and keep ahead. Passing through a tunnel of trees, go left through the iron gate, over the little bridge and, just past the alarming sign that warns you to 'beware of flying golf balls', take the left path and keep straight.

Cobham Hall

You are now walking one of Dickens's favourite routes. To your right is the wood through which Mr Pickwick and his companions made their way to Cobham: 'A delightful walk it was... their way lay through a deep and shady wood cooled by the lightly wind which gently rustled the thick foliage... They emerged upon an open park, with an ancient hall, displaying the quaint and picturesque architecture of Elizabeth's time...' The hall in question was Cobham Hall, the turrets and chimneys of which peek over the tops of the trees to your left. When Dickens was a young boy, one of their family's servants, Mary Weller, would often terrify him with ghost stories about the old hall.

After the footpath bends left, turn right, go through the clump of trees, over the gravel path and ahead onto the grass track. Pass to the left of an industrial premises, descend through the woodlands, continue along the gravel path, through the gate and turn left onto the road. Pass under the rail bridge, over the road bridge, and follow the pavement right down the hill to go left along the narrow pathway to the left of the grey steel fence.

Having clambered over the stile, keep ahead up the gentle slope. Follow the nettle and holly fringed track through dark tunnels of trees, to emerge onto a neatly manicured lawn which you cross. Go over the stile and keep ahead along a road lined with modern housing. Turn left along the main road, and

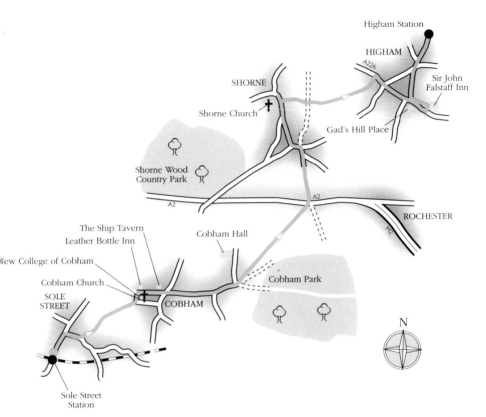

take the first right into Tanyard Cottages. Continue onto Tanyard Hill, at the foot of which, cross to the left side. Follow the road as it swings left onto The Street and enters the old village of Shorne. Go past the picturesque, timber-framed dwellings, passing the pretty Rose and Crown pub. Ascend Butchers Hill and bear left into the churchyard.

St Peter and St Paul, Shorne

This charming Saxon Church is ringed by one of the most tranquil churchyards imaginable. Huge elms tower over you, whilst apple trees dot its picturesque slopes. Dickens was particularly attracted to this spot and describes it in *Pickwick Papers* as 'one of the most peaceful and secluded churchyards in Kent, where wild flowers mingle with the grass, and the soft landscape around forms the fairest spot in the garden of England'. It was one of the places where he wished to be buried, and was the one that his family favoured, in the immediate aftermath of his death. But in the unholy clamour to claim his remains, it was deemed that only Westminster Abbey could provide a suitable resting-place. Thus this idyllic retreat must remain content with the knowledge that, but for the meddling of the powers that were, it could easily have become a place of literary pilgrimage.

Backtrack past the Rose and Crown, go left into Swillers Lane, keep ahead onto the rough path, at the end of which swerve right over the brook and keep ahead. Bear left at the iron gate, and in the next corner of the field, go up the hill to the right of the fence and take the right track that ascends into the woods. Follow it as it turns sharp left and twists through thick woodland. After a steep descent, take the right fork, which is virtually straight ahead, and a little further along, turn onto the first obvious path on the right. Follow it as it bears sharp left and descends through a dense thicket of trees. Bear right along a far more pronounced path that exits the wood where you turn right along the busy A226. Cross Pear Tree Lane, continue over Crutches Lane and on the opposite side pause outside the drive of Gad's Hill School.

Dickens's little Kentish freehold

As a child 'not half as old as nine', Dickens often came this way on long hikes with his father. He later recalled how they would often pause to look at this house and his father 'seeing me so fond of it,... often said to me "If you were to be very persevering and were to work hard, you might some day come to live in it". The house came to haunt Dickens's imagination and he returned to gaze upon it many times throughout his childhood and adulthood. Its image flickered across the pages of *A Christmas Carol*, when Scrooge was taken back to his old school by the ghost of Christmas past. 'They left the high-road... and soon approached a mansion of dull red brick, with a little weathercock-surmounted cupola, on the roof, and a bell hanging in it...' This description is still recognizable today.

In 1855, whilst passing it with his *Household Words* colleague W.H. Wills, he told him of his long-standing fondness for the house. That night Wills dined with the novelist Mrs Lynn Linton and mentioned the area to her. She told him that she had grown up there at 'a house they call Gad's Hill Place'; that her recently deceased father had left it to her and that she was now looking to sell it. The next morning Wills excitedly told Dickens, 'It is written that you are to have that house... so you must buy it. Now or Never!' Finally, on Friday 14th March, 1856 after seemingly endless negotiations, Dickens paid £1,790 for the house of his dreams. He later referred to it as 'my little Kentish freehold looking on as pretty a view out of my study window as you will find in a long day's English ride'. In 1860, it became his primary home and remained so for the rest of his life.

Sir John Falstaff Inn

Cross the A226 via the central reservation a little way past Gad's Hill Place where on the opposite side is the Sir John Falstaff Inn. One of the many attractions that Gad's Hill held for Dickens was its location on the very hill where Shakespeare's Sir John Falstaff and his friends had once robbed travellers bound for Canterbury and London: 'Falstaff ran away from the identical spot of ground now covered by the room in which I write. A little rustic alehouse, called the Sir John Falstaff, is over the way, has been over the way ever since, in honour of the event.' Today, it remains a pleasant little haven, with Dickensian etchings upon its walls, although quite what Dickens would have made of its menu of ostrich and kangaroo steaks is open to debate!

The Wilderness and Dickens's Swiss Chalet
Exit the pub, turn right and pause at the green railings. The area beyond is known as The Wilderness and Dickens, having purchased this land along with Gad's Hill Place, had a tunnel driven beneath the road in 1859, the steps to which you are looking down upon. It was here that he erected the Swiss Chalet, which was sent to him by his friend, actor **Charles Fechter** in 1864, and which became his summer study.

The death of Dickens
On Wednesday, 8th June, 1870 Dickens spent the day working on *The Mystery of Edwin Drood* in the chalet. That evening, he returned to Gad's Hill Place through the tunnel, and at 6pm sat down to dinner with Georgina Hogarth. She was alarmed by a sudden change in his colour and expression and asked if he was ill. 'Yes, very ill; I have been very ill for the last hour', he replied. She wished to send for a doctor, but he insisted that they finish dinner and told her that afterwards he would go to London. But then he was overcome by some kind of fit against which he struggled, began talking very quickly and rose unsteadily to his feet. Georgina attempted to steady him and begged him to lie down. 'Yes,' he replied, 'on the ground.' So saying, he slid from her arms and fell unconscious to the floor. The servants lifted him onto a sofa, wrapped him in a rug and placed hot bricks at his feet. That night his daughters Mamie and Kate, and his son Charley arrived to be with him. He lingered throughout the next day, his breathing becoming more and more laboured. Ellen Ternan arrived to be with him in the afternoon. Just before 6pm his breathing grew softer and he sobbed. Fifteen minutes later, a tear rolled down his cheek and, with a shudder, Charles Dickens died.

Continue past the railings and turn right into Forge Lane. Here you can make a detour through the gates on the right to look down into the tunnel. Otherwise continue for a little over a mile until, on the right, you arrive at Higham Railway Station. This station was often used by Dickens on his journeys to and from London and it was from here that his body was transported for burial in Westminster Abbey. A melancholic end, perhaps, to a wander through a landscape that Dickens knew and loved.

FURTHER READING

Ackroyd, Peter, *Dickens*. Minerva, 1990

Allbut, Robert, *London and Country Rambles With Charles Dickens*. Shepherd and St John, 1886

Chancellor, E. Beresford, *The London of Charles Dickens*. Grant Richards Ltd., 1936

Chesterton, Gilbert Keith, *Charles Dickens*. Methuen, 1906

Dexter, Walter, *The London of Dickens*. Cecil Palmer, 1930

Dudgeon, Piers, *Dickens' London: An Imaginative Vision*. Headline, 1989

Fido, Martin, *Charles Dickens: An Authentic Account of His Life and Times*. Hamlyn, 1972

Fitzgerald, Percy, *Bozland: Dickens Places and People*. Downey and Co., 1895

Forster, John, *Life of Charles Dickens*. (3 vols), Chapman and Hall, 1874

Hardwick, Michael and Mollie, *The Charles Dickens Companion*. John Murray, 1969

Hardwick, Michael and Mollie, *Dickens's England: The Places in his life and works*. Book Club Associates, 1976

Hibbert, Christopher, *The Making of Charles Dickens*. Longmans, 1967

House, Humphrey, *The Dickens World*. Oxford University Press, 1979

Karl, Frederick, *George Eliot: A Biography*. Flamingo, 1996

Lynch, Tony, *Dickens's England: A Travellers Companion*. B.T. Batsford, 1986

Monsarrat, Ann, *An Uneasy Victorian: Thackeray the Man*. Nationwide Book Service, 1980

North, Monica, *Dickens Country*. Yorick, 2002

Pope-Hennessy, Una, *Charles Dickens: 1812-1870*. Chatto and Windus, 1945

Schlicke, Paul (Editor), *Oxford Reader's Companion to Dickens*. Oxford University Press, 2000

Tomalin, Claire, *The Invisible Woman: The Story of Nelly Ternan and Charles Dickens*. Penguin, 1991

Wilson, A.N., *The Victorians*. Hutchinson, 2002

Wilson, Angus, *The World of Charles Dickens*. Panther, 1983

USEFUL INFORMATION

INTRODUCTION

Charles Dickens' Birthplace Museum
393, Old Commercial Road,
Portsmouth, Hampshire P01
Tel: 0239 282 7261
www.charlesdickensbirthplace.
co.uk
Open: November–March: daily
10am–4pm; April–October:
daily 10am–5.30pm.
Admission charged.

TOWER HILL TO BARBICAN

Tower of London
Tower Hill, EC3N
Tel: 0870 751 5177
www.hrp.org.uk
Open: November–February:
Tuesday–Saturday 9am–5pm,
Sunday & Monday 10am–5pm;
March–October:
Monday– Saturday 9am–6pm,
Sunday 10am–6pm.
Admission charged.

St Olave's Church
Hart Street, EC3
Tel: 020 7488 4318
Open: Monday–Friday
9am–6pm.

St Peter's Church
Cornhill, EC3
Tel: 020 7283 2231
Open: by arrangement.

George and Vulture restaurant
3 Castle Court, EC3
Tel: 020 7626 9710
Open: Monday–Friday
12pm–2.30pm.

The Royal Exchange
Cornhill, EC3
Open: Monday–Friday
10am–8pm.

Guildhall Art Gallery
Guildhall Yard, EC2P

Tel: 020 7332 3700
www.guildhall-art-gallery.org.
uk
Open: Monday–Saturday
10am–5pm, Sunday
12pm–4pm.
Admission charged.

Guildhall
London, EC2P
Tel: 020 7606 3030, xtn 1463
Guildhall closes for city func-
tions. Call for opening times.
Admission free.

Museum of London
London Wall, EC2Y
Tel: 020 7600 3699
www.museum-london.org.uk
Open: Monday–Saturday
10am–5.50pm, Sunday
12pm–5.50pm.
Admission free.

CLERKENWELL TO CHANCERY LANE

The Charterhouse
Charterhouse Square, EC1
Tel: 020 7353 9503
Open: by guided tour only
April–July: Wednesday pm.
Admission charged.

St John's Gate Museum
St John's Lane, EC1M
Tel: 020 7324 4070
www.sja.org.uk
Open: Monday– Friday
10am–5pm, Saturday
10am–4pm. Tours: Tuesday,
Friday & Saturday 11am &
2.30pm.
Admission free. A £5.00 donation for tours is requested.

Jerusalem Tavern
55 Britton Street, EC1M
Tel: 020 7490 4281
Open: Monday–Friday
11.30am–11pm. Food served.

The One Tun PH
125/126 Saffron Hill, EC1

Tel: 020 7405 1521
Open: Monday–Friday
11.30am–11pm.

Ye Olde Mitre Tavern
1 Ely Place, EC1
Tel: 020 7405 4751
Open: Monday–Friday
11.30am–11pm.

St Andrew's Church
Holborn Viaduct, EC1
Tel: 020 7353 3544
Open: Monday–Friday
8.30am–6pm.

CHANCERY LANE AND HOLBORN

Staple Inn
London, WC1
Open: public access
Monday–Friday 8.30am–6pm.

Lincoln's Inn
London, WC2
Open: public access
Monday–Friday 9.30am–6pm.

The Museums of the Royal College of Surgeons
35-43 Lincoln's Inn Fields,
WC2A
Tel: 020 7405 3474
www.rcseng.ac.uk/services/
museums
Open: Monday–Friday
10am–5pm.
Admission free.

Sir John Soane Museum
13 Lincoln's Inn Fields, WC2A
Tel: 020 7440 4263
www.soane.org
Open: Tuesday–Saturday
10am–5pm; first Tuesday of
every month 6pm–9pm.
Admission free. Tour £3.

Gray's Inn
London, WC1
Open: public access
Monday–Friday 8am–6pm.

The Dickens House Museum
See Bloomsbury

**KING'S CROSS TO
REGENT'S PARK**

St Pancras Old Church
Off Pancras Road, NW1
www.stpancrasoldchurch.org.
uk
Open: daily 10.30am–3pm.

London Zoo
Regent's Park, NW1
Tel: 020 7722 3333
www.londonzoo.org
Open: November–February:
daily 10am–4pm; March–
October: daily 10am–5.30pm.

**MARYLEBONE TO
MARBLE ARCH**

St Marylebone Parish
Church
Marylebone Road, NW1
Tel: 020 7935 7315
www.stmarylebone.org

The Wallace Collection
Hertford House, Manchester
Square, W1U
Tel: 020 7563 9500
www.wallace-collection.org.uk
Open: Monday–Saturday
10am–5pm, Sunday
12pm–5pm.
Admission free.

HAMPSTEAD

The Spaniards Inn
Spaniards Road, NW3
Open: daily 12pm–11pm.
Food served.

Kenwood House
Hampstead Lane, NW3
Tel: 020 8348 1286
Open: April–October:
10am–6pm; November–March:
10am–4pm.
Admission free.

HIGHGATE

The Gate House PH
1 North Road, N6
Tel: 020 8340 8054
Open: Monday–Saturday
10am–11pm, Sunday
12pm–10.30pm.
Food served.

St Michael's Church
South Grove, N6
Tel: 020 8340 7279
Open: Thursday–Tuesday
10am–12pm.

The Flask PH
77 Highgate West Hill, N6
Tel: 020 8348 7346
Open: Monday–Saturday
12pm–11pm, Sunday
12pm–10.30pm. Food served.

Highgate Cemetery
Swains Lane, London N6
www.highgate-cemetery.org
Tel: 020 8340 1834
Open: West Cemetery by
guided tour only, call for
details. East Cemetery: call
for details.
Admission charged.

**ISLINGTON AND
HIGHBURY**

Joseph Grimaldi Park
Rodney Street, N1
Islington Council:
020 7527 2000
Open: daily 8am–dusk.

BLOOMSBURY

St George's Church
1 Bloomsbury Way, WC1
www.stgeorgesbloomsbury.org.
uk
Open: Monday–Friday
11am–3.30pm.

Jarndyce Booksellers
46 Great Russell Street, WC1B
Tel: 020 7631 4220
www.Jarndyce.co.uk
Open: Monday–Friday
10.30am–5.30pm.

The British Museum
Great Russell Street, WC1
Tel: 020 7323 8838
www.thebritishmuseum.ac.uk
Open: daily 10am–5.30pm.
Admission free.

The Dickens House Museum
48 Doughty Street, WC1N
Tel: 020 7405 2127
www.dickensmuseum.com
Open: Monday–Saturday
10am–4.30pm, Sunday
11am–4.30pm.
Admission charged.

FITZROVIA

Fitzroy Tavern
16 Charlotte Street, W1T
Tel: 020 7580 3714
Open: Monday–Saturday
12pm–11pm, Sunday
12pm–10.30pm. Food served.

SOHO

The House of St Barnabas-
in-Soho
1 Greek Street, W1D
Tel: 020 7437 1894
Open: by tour only on
Wednesdays at 2.30pm.
Admission free.

**SLOANE SQUARE TO
SOUTH KENSINGTON**

The Cross Keys
1 Lawrence Street, SW3
Tel: 020 7349 9111
Open: Monday–Saturday
12pm–11pm; Sunday 10.30pm.
Food served.

Thomas Carlyle's House
24 Cheyne Row, SW3
Tel: 020 7352 7087
Open: April–October:
Wednesday–Friday 2pm–5pm,
Saturday & Sunday 11am–5pm.
Admission charged. Free for
National Trust members.

St Luke's Church
Sydney Street, SW3
Tel: 020 7351 7365

**SOUTH KENSINGTON TO
HIGH STREET
KENSINGTON**

The Victoria & Albert
Museum
Cromwell Road, SW7
Tel: 020 7942 2000
www.vam.ac.uk
Open: Thursday–Tuesday
10am–5.45pm, Wednesday
10am–10pm.
Admission free.

HOLLAND PARK

Leighton House Museum
12 Holland Park Road, W14
Tel: 020 7602 3316
www.rbkc.gov.uk/Leighton
HouseMuseum

Open: Wednesday–Monday
11am–5.30pm.
Admission free.

Linley Sambourne's House
18 Stafford Terrace, W8
Tel: 020 7602 3316 xtn 305
www.rbkc.gov.uk/linley
sambournehouse
Open: by guided tour only, call
for details.
Tours charged, booking
required.

**KENSAL GREEN
CEMETERY**

All Souls Cemetery
Harrow Road, W10
Tel: 020 8969 0152
www.kensalgreen.co.uk
Open: daily 10am–4pm.

**GREEN PARK TO
WESTMINSTER**

Burlington Arcade
Piccadilly, SW1
Open: Monday–Saturday
9am–6pm.

The Red Lion PH
48 Parliament Street, SW1A
Tel: 020 7930 5826
Open: Monday–Saturday
12pm–11pm, Sunday
12pm–10.30pm. Food served.

The Houses of Parliament
Westminster, SW1A
Tel: 020 7219 4272
www.parliament.uk
Open: August & September
for tours.

Westminster Abbey
Westminster, SW1P
Tel: 020 7654 4900
www.westminster-abbey.org
Open: Monday–Friday
9.30am–3.45pm, Saturday
9.30am–1.45pm, Sunday open
for worship only.
Admission charged.

**WESTMINSTER TO
HOLBORN**

Rules restaurant
35 Maiden Lane, WC2
Tel: 020 7836 5314
www.rules.co.uk
Open: daily 12pm–12am.

The Royal Opera House
Bow Street, WC2E
Tel: 020 7304 4000
www.royaloperahouse.org
Tours: Monday–Friday
10.30am, 12.30pm & 2.30pm.
Tours charged.

**The Theatre Royal, Drury
Lane**
Catherine Street, WC2B
Tel: 0870 890 1109
Tours: Wednesday & Saturday
10.15am & 12pm. Monday,
Tuesday, Thursday, Friday &
Sunday 2.15pm & 4.45pm.
Tours charged.

**TEMPLE AND FLEET
STREET**

St Bride's Church
Fleet Street, EC4
Tel: 020 7427 0133
Open: Monday–Friday 8am–
5pm, Saturday 10am–3pm.

Ye Olde Cheshire Cheese
Wine Office Court, EC4
Tel: 020 7353 6170
Open: Monday–Saturday
11.30am–11pm, Sunday
12pm–3pm. Food served.

Dr Johnson House
17 Gough Square, EC4
Tel: 020 7353 3745
Open: Monday–Saturday
11am–5pm.
Admission charged.

The Temple
Temple, EC4Y
Open: Monday–Friday
10am–6pm. All other times
access is via Tudor Street.

Temple Church
c/o The Masters House,
Temple, EC4Y
Tel: 020 7353 8559
Open: Wednesday–Friday
10am–4pm.

Prince Henry's Room
17 Fleet Street, EC4
Tel: 020 7936 2710
Open: Monday–Friday
11am–2pm.
Admission free.

Somerset House
Strand, WC2

Tel: 020 7845 4600
www.somerset-house.org.uk
Open: daily 10am–6pm.

**MANSION HOUSE TO
SMITHFIELD**

Shakespeare's Globe
New Globe Walk, SE1
Tel: 020 7902 1500
www.shakespearesglobe.org
Open: May–September: daily
9am–12pm; October–April:
daily 10am–5pm.
Admission charged.

Tate Modern
Bankside Power Station,
Sumner Street, SE1
Tel: 020 7401 7271
www.tate.org.uk
Open: Sunday–Thursday
10am–6pm, Friday–Saturday
10am–10pm.
Admission free.

St Paul's Cathedral
St Paul's Churchyard, EC4
Tel: 020 7246-8319
www.stpauls.co.uk
Open: Monday–Saturday
8.30am–4pm, Sunday: services
only.
Admission charged.

**St Bartholomew's Hospital
Archives and Museum**
North Wing, West Smithfield
EC1A
Tel: 020 7601 8152
Open: Tuesday–Friday
10am–4pm.
Admission free.

SOUTHWARK

The Monument
Fish Street Hill, EC3
Tel: 020 7626 2717
Open: daily 9.30am–5pm.
Admission charged.

St Magnus The Martyr
Lower Thames Street, EC3
Tel: 020 7626 4481
Open: Monday–Friday
10am–3.30pm; second
Tuesday of every month
1.05–1.45pm.
Admission free.

Southwark Cathedral
Montague Close, SE1

Tel: 020 7367 6700
Open: daily 8am–6pm,
Sundays 9am–7pm.

The Old Operating Theatre Museum
9a St Thomas Street, SE1
Tel: 020 7955 4791
www.thegarret.org.uk
Open: daily 10.30am–5pm.
Admission charged.

The George Inn
Borough High Street, SE1
Tel: 020 7407 2056
Open: Monday–Saturday
11am–11pm, Sunday
12pm–10.30pm. Food served.

St George The Martyr
Borough High Street, SE1
www.stgeorgethemartyr.fsnet.
co.uk
Call for times.

THE EAST END

Bevis Marks Synagogue
Bevis Marks, EC3
Tel: 020 7626 1274
Open: call for details.

Spitalfields Centre
19 Princelet Street, E1
Tel: 020 7247 5352
www.19Princeletstreet.org.uk
Open: call for details.

Whitechapel Bell Foundry
32/34 Whitechapel Road, E1
Tel: 020 7247 2599
www.whitechapelbell-
foundry.co.uk
Open: Monday–Friday
8am–4.15pm. Tours: Saturday
10am & 2pm.
Tours charged, booking
required.

DOCKLANDS

The Prospect of Whitby PH
57 Wapping Wall, E1W
Tel: 020 7481 1095
Open: Monday–Friday
11.30am–3pm &
5.30pm–11pm, Saturday
11.30am–11pm, Sunday
12pm–10.30pm. Food served.

The Grapes PH
76 Narrow Street, E14
Tel: 020 7987 4396

Open: Monday–Friday
12pm–3pm & 5.30pm–11pm,
Saturday 7pm–11pm, Sunday
12pm–3pm & 7pm–10.30pm.
Food served.

BLACKHEATH TO GREENWICH

The Old Royal Observatory
Greenwich Royal Park, SE10
Tel: 020 8858 4422
Open: daily 10am–5pm (6pm
in summer).
Admission free.

The National Maritime Museum and Queens House
Romney Road, SE10
Tel: 020 8312 6565
www.nmm.ac.uk
Open: daily 10am–5pm.
Admission free.

The Trafalgar Tavern
Park Row, SE10
Tel: 020 8305 4701
Open: Monday–Saturday
12am–11pm, Sundays
12am–10.30pm. Food served.

The Cutty Sark
King William Walk, SE10
Tel: 020 8858 3445
www.cuttysark.org.uk
Open: daily 10am–4.30pm.
Admission charged.

ROCHESTER
National Rail Enquiries:
0845 7484950

The Charles Dickens Centre
Eastgate House, High Street,
Kent
Tel: 01634 844176
Open: April–September: daily
10am–5pm; October–March:
daily 10am–3.15pm.
Admission charged.

Restoration House
17-19 Crow Lane, Kent, ME1
Tel: 01634 848520
www.restorationhouse.co.uk
Open: June–September:
Thursday & Friday 10am–5pm.
Admission charged.

Rochester Cathedral
The Keep, Kent, ME1
Tel: 01634 401301
Open: daily 10am–4pm

(depending on Services).
Admission free, but a £3.00
donation is requested.

Rochester Castle
Tel: 01634 402276
Open: April–September: daily
10am–6pm; October–March:
daily 10–4pm.
Admission charged.

The Guildhall Museum
High Street, Rochester, Kent
Tel: 01634 848717
Open: daily 10am–4pm.
Admission free.

Watts Charity, The Seven Poor Travellers' House
97 High Street, Kent
Tel: 01634 845609
Open: March–October: daily
2pm–5pm.
Admission free.

A COUNTRY RAMBLE
National Rail Enquiries:
0845 7484950

The New College of Cobham
Cobhambury Road, Cobham,
Nr Gravesend, Kent, DA12
Tel: 01474812 503
Open: April–September: daily
10am–7pm; October–March:
daily 10am–4pm.

The Leather Bottle Inn
54-56 The Street, Cobham,
Kent
Tel: 01474 814327
Open: Monday–Friday
12pm–11pm, Sunday 12pm–
10.30pm. Food served.
Accommodation available.

Gads Hill School
Higham, Kent, ME3
Tel: 01474 822366
Open: first Sunday of every
month 2pm–5pm.
Admission charged.

Sir John Falstaff
Higham, Kent
Tel: 01634 717104
Open: Monday–Saturday
11am–11pm, Sundays 12pm–
10.30pm. Food served.

INDEX

ACKNOWLEDGEMENTS

So many people helped with the research and the writing of this book. The staff at the excellent Guildhall Library in London were, as always, a mine of information, as were Andrew Xavier and his staff at The Dickens House Museum. The people at the Tourist Information Centre in Rochester, Rochester Cathedral and Gad's Hill School were always willing to answer my questions. Staff and attendants at the many small museums and attractions I visited were always ready with an interesting fact or a bit of gossip. Brian Lake and Janet Nassau at Jarndyce Antiquarian Booksellers were ever willing to help me find obscure bits of information and advise on source material. To all of you and those I haven't mentioned I offer my sincere thanks. At New Holland, I'd like to thank Jo Hemmings, Camilla MacWhannell and Gulen Shevki. Also Caroline Jones (no relation) for her photography.

On a personal level I'd like to say a huge thank you to my sister Geraldine Hennigan and my wife Joanne for, as ever, being willing to listen and offer helpful suggestions. Christopher Unwin for testing some of the routes for me. Finally, I'd like to say a big thank you to my sons Thomas and William who, unhindered by being just five and three, were ever willing to proffer critical appraisals!